International Political Economy Series

Series Editor: **Timothy M. Shaw**, Visiting Professor, University of Massachusetts Boston, USA and Emeritus Professor, University of London, UK

Titles include:

Don Marshall
CARIBBEAN POLITICAL ECONOMY AT THE CROSSROADS
NAFTA and Regional Developmentalism

Juan Antonio Morales and Gary McMahon (editors)
ECONOMIC POLICY AND THE TRANSITION TO DEMOCRACY
The Latin American Experience

Manuela Nilsson and Jan Gustafsson (editors)
LATIN AMERICAN RESPONSES TO GLOBALIZATION IN THE 21st CENTURY

Leo Panitch and Martijn Konings (editors)
AMERICAN EMPIRE AND THE POLITICAL ECONOMY OF GLOBAL FINANCE

Eul-Soo Pang
THE INTERNATIONAL POLITICAL ECONOMY OF TRANSFORMATION IN
ARGENTINA, BRAZIL, AND CHILE SINCE 1960

Julia Sagebien and Nicole Marie Lindsay (editors)
GOVERNANCE ECOSYSTEMS
CSR in the Latin American Mining Sector

Henry Veltmeyer, James Petras and Steve Vieux
NEOLIBERALISM AND CLASS CONFLICT IN LATIN AMERICA
A Comparative Perspective on the Political Economy of Structural Adjustment

Henry Veltmeyer, James Petras
THE DYNAMICS OF SOCIAL CHANGE IN LATIN AMERICA

Chris Wylde
LATIN AMERICA AFTER NEOLIBERALISM
Developmental Regimes in Post-Crisis States

International Political Economy Series
Series Standing Order ISBN 978–0–333–71708–0 hardcover
Series Standing Order ISBN 978–0–333–71110–1 paperback
(outside North America only)

You can receive future titles in this series as they are published by placing a standing order.
Please contact your bookseller or, in case of difficulty, write to us at the address below with
your name and address, the title of the series and the ISBN quoted above.

Customer Services Department, Macmillan Distribution Ltd, Houndmills, Basingstoke,
Hampshire RG21 6XS, England

Employment and Development under Globalization

State and Economy in Brazil

Samuel Cohn
Professor of Sociology, Texas A and M University, USA

First published 2012 by
PALGRAVE MACMILLAN

Palgrave Macmillan in the UK is an imprint of Macmillan Publishers Limited, registered in England, company number 785998, of Houndmills, Basingstoke, Hampshire RG21 6XS.

Palgrave Macmillan in the US is a division of St Martin's Press LLC, 175 Fifth Avenue, New York, NY 10010.

Palgrave Macmillan is the global academic imprint of the above companies and has companies and representatives throughout the world.

Palgrave® and Macmillan® are registered trademarks in the United States, the United Kingdom, Europe and other countries.

ISBN 978–1–137–00140–5

This book is printed on paper suitable for recycling and made from fully managed and sustained forest sources. Logging, pulping and manufacturing processes are expected to conform to the environmental regulations of the country of origin.

A catalogue record for this book is available from the British Library.

Library of Congress Cataloging-in-Publication Data
Cohn, Samuel, 1954–
  Employment and development under globalization : state and economy in
  Brazil / Samuel Cohn.
    pages cm. – (International political economy series)
  Includes bibliographical references.
  ISBN 978–1–137–00140–5
    1. Labor market–Brazil. 2. Brazil–Economic policy.
3. Globalization–Brazil. I. Title.

HD5754.C64 2012
331.10981–dc23   2012016706

10   9   8   7   6   5   4   3   2   1
21 20 19 18 17 16 15 14 13 12

Printed and bound in Great Britain by
CPI Antony Rowe, Chippenham and Eastbourne

To Daisaku Ikeda,
Scholar and Teacher –
Master Methodologist of Positive Social Change

Contents

List of Tables and Figures

Tables

Figures

Acknowledgments

This book owes an enormous debt to a huge number of people who made a gigantic difference.

The financial support for this work came from the National Science Foundation, the Institute for International Education, Texas A and M University and the Universidade Federal Fluminense. The National Science Foundation provided two separate $70,000 grants to do the fieldwork associated with this study. The Institute for International Education and the Universidade Federal Flumense collaborated to support a Fulbright Grant in Niteroi in 2002. This became the base for the fieldwork in Aracaju, and Cuiabá as well as much of the work with census materials in Rio. Texas A and M provided sabbatical support as well as multiple small grants to support shorter trips and undergraduate labor.

Three individuals were absolutely essential to making this project feasible.

Fernando Sá of the History Department of the Universidade Federal de Sergipe made the entire barber component of this project possible. He introduced me to the barbers of Aracaju; he trained me in the use of Sergipano archives; he patiently explained the aspects of Sergipana history that were fundamental to my understanding the labor markets of the time; he set up the collaboration with SENAC-Sergipe that led to the critical wave of interviews on the survival strategies of beauticians, and he vastly increased my knowledge of social movements, progressive social change in Brazil and the history of Brazilian popular culture. He has made substantial efforts to document and archive the oral histories of the Sergipe barbers – to provide a lasting resource for future generations of social historians. My debt of gratitude to Fernando Sá is overwhelming.

Jenny Barbosa of the Universidade Federal de Sergipe business school was instrumental to the analysis of hotels and restaurants. An expert on tourism in the Brazilian northeast, her insights on Nordestino business conditions and the struggles of the Northeast to become established as a center of tourism are fundamental to my thinking today. She generously made the facilities of the Business School available to me in my research – and the facilities of her home. She provided multiple opportunities to speak publicly in academic settings. She herself gave some months of her time to collaborating on cognate research on tourism development in Espirito Santo and Alagoas. She introduced me to a vast number of people, many of whom provided me with crucial interviews. However, her primary contribution was intellectual. In the early stages of the project, few people did more to educate me on the dynamics of hotels and restaurants – causing me to abandon a vast number of ill-informed ideas.

Marcilio Brito, Professor of Tourism at Pio X, with a long record of public service in tourism policy and development, was equally fundamental. He traveled with me to Recife and to Brasilia to obtain critical data. Several fundamental statistical analyses would have been impossible without the datasets he was miraculously able to obtain. He put me up in his home. He too was a critical part of the early education process, particularly on the history of state policy concerning tourism. He did cognate research on Pernambuco and Rio Grande do Norte which changed much of my thinking on the state and development – including digging up uncomfortable historical facts which did not fit my pat models. He is also an accomplished poet and a sophisticated man of the arts. My appreciation of Brazilian literature, music and gastronomy would not be the same without him.

Silvia Matos and Eduardo Teles (the Brazilian undergraduate, not the similarly named Princeton professor who also, incidentally, contributed significantly to the project – see below) were my research assistants in Sergipe. Both of them accompanied me on interviews, translated my awkward questions into more suave and acceptable Portuguese versions, and explained to me the subtleties of what my informants were telling me. Either of these undergraduates would have been superstars in an American research setting.

Rivanda Teixeira of the UFS business school was responsible for serving as my initial contact in Sergipe. She welcomed my cold-call emails and set up the original meetings that met research feasible in Aracaju. Ricardo Lacerda of the UFS economics department provided endless scholarly material on the Sergipana economy. I only had one interview with Vera França, the UFS geographer. Her work, however, is first rate and profoundly informed most of my views on Aracaju and on economic geography. Carlos Eduardo Traversa of SENAC-Sergipe was extraordinarily kind in providing the data on barber/beautician vocational trainees that provided the basis for much of the analysis on job training.

Ruth Dweck of the Economics Department of the Universidade Federal Fluminense was critical in arranging for my stay in Rio de Janeiro. Her work on the economics of the beauty business identified many of the critical issues that motivated my subsequent researches on this issue. Ruth was a member of a key 1990s team from MITI that put Brazil in the forefront of the study of employment in services. The other members of that team, notably Alberto DiSabbato, Hildete Pereira de Melo and particularly Frederico Rocha, spent substantial time with me educating me on the dynamics of the service sector.

In Rio de Janeiro I also received critical support from the technical personnel at IBGE, the Brazilian Census agency. Roberto da Cruz Saldanha spent a great deal of time teaching me about the methodology of census collection on the service sector. Vania Prata was critical for arranging access to a key statistical dataset that provided the methodological insights that structured the rest of the econometric analysis.

In Cuiabá I received wonderful support from the economists and sociologists at the Universidade Federal de Mato Grosso. Wilson Oliveira was my primary contact at the university and an extraordinarily perceptive observer of the social dynamics of the Center-West. Carlos and Sueli Castro did everything to open up the resources of both their departments and made many critical introductions. Joaõ Carlos Barrozo is a remarkable expert on rural uprisings in Mato Grosso. His discussions of land tenure dynamics in Mato Grosso proved to be more relevant to the study of hotels and restaurants than I ever would have imagined.

The work on PRODETUR and airports was highly dependent on support from the staff at ETENE at the Banco do Nordeste in Fortaleza. Biágio de Oliveira Mendes Júnior was very generous in providing the full assistance of the research wing of the BNB. He not only arranged for interviews with both past and present staff, and provided a full range of access to documentary materials, but provided a significant amount of insight concerning the dynamics of development banking in the Northeast. Laura Friere and Joao Augustinho Teles were particularly informative and insightful about the dynamics of development projects at the bank.

In the United States, Edward Telles, (this time the Princeton professor), provided not only encouragement but practically a seminar's worth of information on the methodology of labor market analysis in Brazil. Gaye Seidman provided significant early insight and encouragement, although I think she would have wanted to see a quicker and more conflict-based manuscript. Bryan Roberts provided critical encouragement and advice, particularly at one very dark moment for the project. Zulema Valdez, Andrew Walder and Fred Block all read earlier versions of parts of the manuscript and told me true things I did not want to hear. Kirk Bowman of the political science department of Georgia Tech trained me in the basic history of international development banking and its engagement with tourism. Hank Johnston and Ben Aguirre gave me basic and much needed training in how to do an interview (and even with their excellent advice, my undergraduate Brazilian assistants still had to correct my lack of good social skills in speaking to informants.)

I was helped by a large population of capable and talented undergraduate research assistants at Texas A and M. Matt Bradshaw, Elizabeth Rainwater, Jessica Schuett and David Watkins provided analyses of such quality that they merited co-authorship on the sections of the project they worked on. Kristin Miller provided key set-ups for the final year of analysis. Ariel Chisholm, Abbey Turner and Jennifer Borkowski were very important in the early and middle stages of the project.

I am particularly grateful to Nair Edwards, who taught me Portuguese. She also taught me the basics of Brazilian living and those aspects of the history of Mato Grosso do Sul that you cannot find in the history books. She continues to be one of the wisest women I have ever met.

Andrea Simao of CEDEPLAR and Ana Fereira of Campinas provided both hospitality and advice in the early stages of the project. Salvador Sandoval provided many conversations on Brazilian class conflict and Brazilian university dynamics that turned out to be relevant more often than I would have imagined.

The barbers and beauticians of Sergipe gave generously of their time to tell me their life stories and of the challenges they faced to their security and to their economic survival. Beatrice Caetana of EMBRATUR, Luiz Carlos da Silva Lima of Goiana, Ella Lazare, and Dilma of the Pousada dos Caminhos gave me eye-opening interviews that led me to change my thinking significantly on several issues.

Mike Curtis and Liz Gant Britton of the Soka Gakkai provided profound encouragement when the book ran into intractable obstacles in the writing stages.

And last, but certainly the most important of them all, is my wife Lynn Wallisch. She and my son followed me through Brazil on many occasions, and dealt with an absentee stressed husband for much of the time it took to bring this book to fruition. Her spiritual guidance, endless patience, and common-sense guidance for my methodological and fieldwork woes made her contribution to this work far greater than can be expressed here.

1
Rethinking the State and Development: The Importance of Palliative Development

Globalization has changed the models of development that are open to most states both in the industrialized and less industrialized world. The debt crisis of the last 30 years has challenged import substitution models that combined multinational penetration with substantial state investment in heavy industry. It was expected that globalization would produce either a triumph of effusive growth free market neoliberal reform (by writers on the right) – or a complete collapse of all forms of state-led growth (by writers on the left). The expectations of the Washington Consensus were dashed by the slow growth of employment in neoliberal reformers, and the experience of Asia post 1997 – where those nations who defied the IMF prospered, while those who followed the IMF stagnated. The expectations of the left that the role of the government and the nation-state in development would be eliminated were dashed by robust development and improvements of standards of living in China and elsewhere in East Asia despite extensive participation in the globalization process. The effects of globalization have been anything but uniform – and anything but predictable.

What is clear, however, is that globalization has changed the role of the state in economic development – and the creation of employment. It is widely acknowledged that any theory of the role of the state under globalization now has to take the East Asian experience into account. The present work argues that there are further surprises in other nations as well. Contrary to expectations, a wide variety of states have maintained the capacity to increase employment and reduce poverty – even in the face of the well-known obstacles of fiscal crisis, vulnerability to international bond markets, increased international competition both from hi-tech producers in the developed world, and other low cost producers in the global south, and capital repatriation due to increased

1

multinational penetration. The issue is not so much that states challenged multinational corporations and international bond markets and won (although there are settings where this occurred.) The issue is more that both in East Asia and in the examples described in this work – states found alternative policies that were not materially affected by these dynamics. An excessive focus on "globalization" misses the simpler less dramatic processes that occur within Third World nation-states themselves – that are beyond the capacity or the interest of multinational actors to control. These policies that are often indifferent to the dynamics discussed in traditional globalization accounts have significant effects on employment and development.

This book is about the economic policies available to Third World governments that actually raise employment. The emphasis is on simple, basic, unglamorous programs that have observable effects on reducing poverty.

Even though this book is about Brazil, it is very different from traditional discussions of BRIC economies. The BRIC nations have attracted interest because of their spectacular rates of economic growth. Most of the literature on the state and development is interested in *transformative development*. Readers want to know about dramatic successes: rapid changes from poor to rich or in some cases, movement from the periphery to the core. It is reasonable to ask what allows countries to make such extraordinary transitions: The English Industrial Revolution, Japan's rise to core status, the rapid industrialization of South Korea, Taiwan and Singapore, or more recently, China's rise to become a important world economic power.

This book in contrast is about *palliative development*. How do states reduce poverty in the Third World and raise overall standards of living? Palliative development, more so than transformative development, is concerned about the economic benefits of growth being widespread. It is opposed to disarticulation. It is opposed to the benefits of development being limited to a select few. It is opposed to labor repressive regimes that gain advantage in world markets by the suppression of income and standards of living. It is about development that immediately reduces poverty by raising the employment and income of the lower classes.

Palliative development is important – because not all Third World governments have the capacity to become developmentalist states. The general response of the literature on the state and development has been to offer few policy options to governments that do not meet the rigorous historical preconditions that have allowed for rapid economic growth in East Asia. The great East Asian developmentalist states were blessed by favorable colonial administrative legacies, geopolitical position that caused America to be relatively tolerant of endogenous development, weakened agrarian classes, and in some cases, high levels of literacy. (Cumings 1984, Lange and Rueschemeyer 2005, Kohli 2004, Amsden 2007) Even modest deviations from this formula produce dramatically worse results, as Chibber (2006) has so carefully demonstrated for India.

But what are governments that live in the rest of the world supposed to do? Are they just supposed to roll over and die? Is there nothing that a government minister can do to raise standards of living in Kenya? Is there anything an elected politician can do in Uruguay that would make good on his promises to help create jobs in his nation's slums?

Palliative development explicitly speaks to this question. It asks how Third World governments can raise employment and income in their countries now, to reduce overall levels of poverty. It does not assume a perfect institutional base for growth. Governments can be financially constrained in their options. The technical capacity of public organs may be weak. Corruption or clientilism may be present. The human capital stock of the population may be less than ideal. World economic conditions may be recessionary. In an imperfect world, with substantial obstacles for growth, what can poor countries – with limited resources and limited bureaucratic capacity – that can still make a difference in improving poor people's lives?

Palliative development does not focus on dramatic coups that produce world class industries out of nothing. It emphasizes the unglamorous business of routine government administration that – in its own invisible way – has an impact on human development. The focus here is on the smaller, normal, routine actions of states. These programs can contribute to national rates of economic growth, even if those accomplishments are much less heralded. Explaining economic growth by only looking at dramatically successful government interventions is much like explaining successful soccer by only looking at highlight films of goals being scored. A fully adequate view of what states do to produce economic development needs to consider the economic "defenders and midfielders", the everyday business of routine public programs that produce wealth for the economy and jobs for poverty populations. Defenders and midfielders make an important contribution – even if they do so while working in obscurity.

National economic development programs are bundles of policies, rather than a single policy. How likely is it that *everything* that Taiwan did contributed spectacularly to economic growth? How likely is it that there is *nothing* a Subsaharan African government has ever done that has improved on its rate of economic growth? If one insists that an industrial policy is only effective if it moves a country from the periphery to the core in 20 years, and one only looks at the most rapid developers hoping to find such a magic bullet, one will naturally be pessimistic about state policies in countries with slower rates of economic growth. However, it is bad macrosociology to conflate Mexico with Zaire just because neither one of them is Singapore. Small gains accumulate into real growth, and theorists of development need to include such smaller gains into their models. Practitioners need to spend more time figuring out just what policies actually do produce such small gains, so they can provide constructive advice to governments trying to create humanistic programs for growth.

Let us defer for a moment the theoretical question of how palliative development and its causes would cause one to reassess the pre-existing literature on development. Chapter 11 consists of an extensive engagement with a broad range of development sociologists and economists discussing what palliative development theory would look like and how it would support and not support previous well known models of the state and development. For now – what matters is how to study palliative development – because the methodologies of analysis suitable for transformative and palliative development are profoundly different. Palliative development requires looking at radically different nations and different industries than does the analysis of transformative development. Restructuring empirical case bases almost always leads to a restructuring of underlying theory.

Three keys to identifying palliative individual programs that effectively create employment

The strategy of studying palliative development is different than the strategy of studying transformative development. In the analysis of transformative development, one identifies a "miracle" economy, and tries to isolate the factors that distinguish this high performer from the less impressive performers in the rest of the world. Not surprisingly, there is a certain amount of overdetermination, since the super-performers tend to have many intrinsic advantages leading to substantial debate about which exact advantage produced the observed favorable outcomes. Did East Asian advantage stem from brilliant allocation of capital by highly competent state planners (Johnson 1982, Wade 1990), or from a simple increase in the gross level of savings (Krugman 1999), or from population control and a demographic dividend (Kinugasa and Mason 2007) or from high human capital, educational and scientific advantages (Szirmai 2005) or from the grudging beneficence of Japan and America in geopolitical matters. (Cumings 1984) Analysts of transformative development spend a lot of time parsing out such alternative explanations.

Students of palliative development have an easier approach because there are simply more cases to work with – allowing for the more natural use of large sample statistical models. However, in palliative development no more than any other form of inquiry, mindless compilation of numbers without an intellectual strategy is not likely to get one very far. There are three methodological strategies that increase the likelihood of correctly identifying what government programs contribute to palliative development by actually creating jobs

---

Three Keys to Understanding the Capacity of States to Create Employment Using Palliative Strategies

1. Compare Observed Employment With That That Would Have Been Expected Had There Been No Government Action.

2. Look at Industries With High Capacity to Absorb Surplus Labor.

3. Relax the Assumption That Less Developed Nations Are Different From More Developed Nations.

Finding effective government programs by seriously modeling "what-if" government programs had not existed. The reason that it is hard to know what government programs increase or do not increase employment is that changes in job levels vary for many reasons that are unrelated to government policy. Favorable macroeconomic conditions, the intrinsic prosperity of a region based on its pre-existing factor endowments, and the beneficial effects of past public policies all have an effect on present growth rates – net of anything the government may have done recently. One would not want to attribute the rise of Silicon Valley exclusively to the government programs of the State of California in the 1970s. At a minimum, the presence of Stanford University has something to do with the rise of computer employment in this region. Even if a government does nothing there will always be some jobs in some industries that are brought about by market factors.

The measure of success of government policy is the degree to which it can raise economic growth or employment above the level that would have been expected from non-political factors alone.

A government that can raise employment above what the market would have produced by itself has made a significant contribution to growth. A government whose policies produce employment exactly at market level has policies that are essentially irrelevant. Having government programs that can produce employment below market levels would be of great concern because these programs may be significantly harming the economy.

There is another way to state the previous conclusion – that uses statistical jargon to good effect:

Successful economic policies are those that positively correlate with the residuals from a market model of growth or employment.

"Residuals" is a term from regression analysis. In regression analysis, a statistical model is used to create theoretical predictions of the levels of a dependent variable. Since even the best models generally have some imperfections, these models will rarely predict the exact value of real world cases with 100 percent accuracy. The differences between the theoretical predictions and real world outcomes are known as "residuals". High residuals represent cases that have higher values – in this case higher economic growth or greater employment – than what would be expected from the model. Low residuals represent cases that have lower values – in this case lower economic growth or lower employment – than what would be expected from the model.

If one wished to identify settings that have relatively successful or unsuccessful policies – a reasonable exploratory analysis would be run a statistical model of market factors to find the levels of growth that would be explained by straightforward economic considerations – and then examine the residuals. The high cases are likely to be places that have the good policies and the low cases are likely to be the cases that have the bad policies. Admittedly, there may be some non-governmental sociological variable that explains the deviant cases. However, careful analysis of individual cases would suggest what political or social variables might be related to the residuals. A subsequent fuller model could then be run to test whether the policies suggested by the case analyses do or do not correlate with the observed residuals.

Analyses of this kind are rare. Economic sociologists, sociologists of economic development, underdevelopment theorists or developmental state theorists pay detailed attention to variations in state policy and social structure. However, they rarely construct null models and are relatively disinterested in analyzing market determinants of their dependent variables. As such, many of their findings are zero order findings that may or may not survive the inclusion of appropriate controls.

Development economists are much more comfortable constructing market-based models. A journal such as *World Development* will have many articles per issue that use sophisticated statistical controls to excellent effect. However, in some cases, the control variables are drawn from the traditions of the single intellectual discipline of the author and their analyses explore a relatively limited range of public policies. There is all too often only a limited interest in exploring a full range of governmental actions that could explain deviations from the market model.

What is needed is a convergence of the two approaches – a consideration of a broad range of policy factors that can explain variations in employment or growth – that take as a starting point considering the deviations from a careful constructed market-based model of what would have occurred in the absence of government intervention into the economy. Exhaustive political and social analysis combined with a clear vision of those changes that would have occurred through market forces alone allow for the identification of the maximum number of social policies that work without the artificial enhancement of favorable changes that would have occurred anyway.

Finding effective government programs by examining industries that have high potential for absorbing surplus labor. Typically, studies of economic development consider entire national economies, or concentrate on a "strategic" sector, generally a highly technological, capital intense sector. This is despite the fact, that many Third World countries suffer from severe "disarticulation", economic growth that fails to generate comparable increases in employment, and which thus has a more limited impact in reducing poverty or raising standards of living. (Stokes and Anderson 1990) Disarticulation generally is caused capital intensive strategies of economic development, in which increases in output are achieved with machinery rather than human inputs. (Furtado 1968)

The solution to disarticulation is promoting employment in labor intensive industries and services. Beauty shops, construction, retail sales, repair shops, restaurants, and ground transportation all hire enormous quantities of people. At the expense of being obvious, labor intensive sectors provide far more employment than do capital intensive ones.

Jobs in these industries require low levels of education – and as such are openly available to poor people who would be excluded from other forms of employment because of a lack of educational credentials. This last point is very important, because increasing educational attainment is a slow and expensive process which will require time to implement, while unemployment is an urgent issue that demands remediation in the short term. Creating employment for uneducated workers provides important immediate improvements in human welfare without having to wait for structural reform in the school system.

Labor intensive sectors often have a bad reputation because they do not produce significant technological change. However, exclusive focus on transformative sectors underestimates the effects of multiplier effects in producing growth. The impact transformative sectors have on employment as a whole depends in part in how much "multiplier effect" is generated by the rest of the economy. Once a strategic sector has increased its employment, the size of the multiplier effect will depend on the extent of the extent to which that industry makes upstream purchases within the local economy, the amount of salaries paid to workers, and the relation of the salaries paid to workers in the upstream and strategic sectors to employment in the sectors that provide consumer goods and services. This last consideration receives insufficient attention in the sociology of development. It is always latently assumed that all economies have the same capacity of providing employment in the consumer goods and services sectors given the same stimulus. The evidence presented in this book suggests that this assumption is untrue. Economies vary *substantially* in their capacity to provide multiplier employment in goods and services; government programs have very noticeable effects in increasing the amount of multiplier employment that any given economic stimulus provides. Looking at labor intensive sectors provides a fertile terrain for finding the government programs that make such a difference.

Finding effective government programs in less developed countries by examining local counterparts of government programs wealthy nations use to create employment. What works in wealthy nations often works in poorer nations as well. Development economists have no problem with this approach. Their analyses are drawn from general models that are meant to be used for all economies regardless of location.

Development sociologists are more skeptical of such a methodology. Modernization theory (Rostow 1960, McClelland 1966) gave "one-size-fits-all" formulations a bad name with its unrealistic emphasis on the power of the transmission of Western values, and its blindness to conflicts of interest between the global core and periphery. The most productive innovations in development sociology – underdevelopment theory (Frank 1967), world systems theory (Wallerstein 1974), strong state bargaining theory (Evans 1979) and developmental state theory

(Amsden 1985) – all work under a Gershenkronian (1962) perspective in which early and late developers need to use completely different strategies to generate growth. These models usually incorporate explicit claims that late developers grow by neutralizing anti-growth obstacles imposed on them by early developers.

But some sociological factors really do operate in a similar way in both core and periphery. Education is a powerful force for development in both settings, as is the implementation of fertility control. Looking at factors that promote development in rich nations can be a rough guide to what might work in poor nations, provided that critical reflection is used to consider the degree of transferability of specific programs.

There are many models that can be usefully applied, once parallels between developed and underdeveloped societies are drawn. This particular work will make great use of the neo-Marxist theory of James O'Connor (1973). James O'Connor has a relatively unusual model of capitalist development that integrates government policy, physical infrastructure development, human capital development, taxation, inflation and fiscal crisis. His arguments were developed within the context of the United States. However, any reader familiar with Latin America will recognize that a model of the state and economic development that emphasizes weak infrastructure, fiscal crisis, inflation, and constrained growth would be highly germane to most Latin American nations. The present work hopes to combine the three methodological approaches suggested above to generate new findings concerning the state and economic growth.

The present design

This book analyzes the determinants of employment in hotels, restaurants and barber and beauty shops in Brazil from 1940 to 2000.

Why Brazil? Obviously, Brazil is one of the largest developing nations in the world. The economic decisions of its government affect the well being of millions of people.

Brazil is also an innovative place. Innovative places are likely to generate innovative policies. It was one of the first countries to develop hard-bargaining tactics between the state and multinationals. (Evans 1979) It was one of the first countries to stimulate employment by building a new national capitol on its frontier. The city of Porto Alegre is famous throughout the world for its adoption of participatory budgeting. Brazil's less well known policies are also worthy of respect. Brazil has an extensive, long-standing and relatively effective system of vocational education. (This is a marked contrast with its more problematic elementary, secondary and university education). Brazil was an early adopter of small business promotion as a reaction to globalization and disarticulation. The small business agency, SEBRAE, has been rightly praised for its technocracy and competency. (Tendler 1998) It was an early adopter of tourism development as a strategy for promoting sustainable development. The Amazon, the Pantanal (one of the largest and most ecologically diverse wetlands in the world), and the Brazilian coast have all benefited from this commitment. Brazil is a leader in the promotion of the *Economia Solidária*, the Latin American movement to promote local economic development by encouraging residents to resist globalization by supporting each other's businesses. Many of the effective and important policies discussed in the book will be more routine than the "headline-grabbing" programs listed above. However, these show that Brazilian policymakers are nimble and creative. New ideas abound in Brasilia, in Brazilian state capitals and Brazilian city halls. Many of these ideas turn into programs, and these programs can be both innovative and effective.

From a technical standpoint, Brazil is an ideal case because of its high quality statistics and large size. Brazil has for a long time had one of the most professionally executed censuses in Latin America. The availability of excellent data running from 1940 to the present day allows for an analysis of the long-term implications of the policies under discussion. Other advantages of Brazil include its size, and urbanization. Any statistical study requires a large number of cases. Many of the industries that will be examined have an urban base. In 1980, there were over 100 cities of greater than 100,000 in Brazil providing an ideally large case base for the econometrics of the analysis. A third technical advantage is Brazil's broad regional disparities. Brazil is well known for having a prosperous South, with practically European standards of living, a strong industrial south east, an agrarian and newly wealthy center-west, an impoverished Northeast with levels of economic development that lag far beyond the rest of the country, and an Amazonian frontier. (Henshall and Momsen 1974) Such variability raises significant development strategy and social equity issues. However, it facilitates the development of a market-based control model, since there is substantial variability in the economic predictors that would be required for such a task.

Such variability also spills into social policy-making. Brazil is an important laboratory for economic and social experimentation. Brazil is relatively centralized from a legal standpoint – but is surprisingly decentralized at the level of policy implementation. Different states often have completely different political approaches to the challenge of stimulating economic growth. São Paulo, the wealthiest state, is justly renowned for a state university system of distinction – unparalleled anywhere else in Brazil. (Schwartzman 1992) Rio Grande do Sul, the most leftist state is known for its participatory budgeting. (Gret and Sintomer 2005) Ceará is famous for a technocratic state government which makes superior use of a wide variety of federal programs. (Tendler 1998) The additional variability that comes from the contributions of the state governments makes Brazil a rich field for exploring positive initiatives in economic policy.

Brazil as a case of transition from slow to rapid growth

The Brazilian case has obtained increased saliency in recent years because its economic growth rates have dramatically improved. Traditional accounts noted its impressive endowment of natural resources and its successful development of automobile and petrochemical complexes. However, these accomplishments were overshadowed by a) extreme disarticulation with capital intensive industry failing to provide the employment required to produce meaningful reductions in poverty b) macroeconomic mis-management leading to persistent inflation, monetary instability, and cripplingly high interest rates c) underinvestment in education and phys-ical infrastructure leaving Brazil poorly equipped to provide the man-power for modern high tech industry or the roads and ports necessary to support its commodity sector and d) an oppressive structure of tax and labor laws that produced significant impediments both to entrepreneur-ship and to the hiring of workers. (Abreu 1989, Baer 2004, Pastore 1998) Brazil was always viewed as a failure relative to East Asian alternatives. The standard joke on Brazilian economic development was "Brazil is the land of the future, and it will always be that way."

Now, Brazil is a member of BRIC – the Brazil-Russia-India-China four-some that is viewed as representing the next wave of economic power in the developing world. A sensible, balanced treatment of this economic transformation can be found in the work of Mauricio Font (2003) which covers the reforms of the Cardoso and Lula administrations in extensive detail. Brazil began to receive favorable assessments after the 1994 Plano Real, when then Finance Minister Fernando Henrique Cardoso instituted a brilliant series of monetary and fiscal policies that put a stop to Brazil's chronic double digit inflation, and produced 15 years of relative price stability. (Economist, "Brazil Takes Off", November 14 2009) This was fol-lowed by a dramatic boom in commodity and semi-commodity exports with oil and gas, iron ore, steel ingots, soybeans and sugar-based ethanol being particularly important. Brazil's manufacturing sectors also had a renaissance. EMBRAER, the Brazilian aircraft construction company, obtained a dominant position in the international market for mid-distance passenger jets. Given the general concerns about the quality of Brazil's educational system, it was surprising to see a Brazilian heavy industrialist obtain an international reputation of excellence on the basis of its own home grown technology. EMBRAER's success was echoed in the consumer products sector by Natura, which recently became a world-wide exporter of environmentally friendly cosmetics. (Exame, Melhores e Maiores Issue, August 2007)

In 2010, Brazil had the lowest unemployment rate in its history. (Istoé Dinheiro, July 21, 2010, p. 36) The real had doubled its dollar-worth relative to its low point in 2003. Its IMF debt had been eliminated since 2005. Its net international debt had fallen from 38 percent of GDP in 2003 to less than 2 percent of GDP. (Economist Intelligence Unit) GDP growth rates were higher in the 2000s than they had been in the 1980s and 1990s.

The new euphoria about the Brazilian economy needs to be tempered with the more pessimistic evidence that comes from making international contrasts. Its growth rate in the last decade was on a par with that of other Latin American nations, such as Argentina, Chile, Venezuela and Peru all of whom were experiencing similar booms in commodities. Brazil had the lowest growth rate among the BRICs, and it trailed the growth rates of most East Asian nations. However, Brazil's longitudinal progress has been impressive suggesting that at least some of the economic policies of the Brazilian governments of the 1990s and 2000s were beneficial in some way.

The present book does *not* cover the sectors that are discussed in the standard journalistic accounts of the new Brazilian economy. The reader will find little here on petroleum, soybeans, aircraft manufacture, or auto-mated banking machines. This is a book about multiplier effects – and increasing the amount of secondary employment that derives from an increase in a core industry – and not about core industries themselves. However, some of the principles that apply to the labor intensive sectors that are the main focus of the book are equally relevant to the core industries that comprise the more well-known components of contemporary Brazilian economic growth. The conclusion will take the lessons that have been learned from hotels, restaurants and barber shops, and apply them to the broader range of more famous Brazilian industries.

Hotels, restaurants, barber and beauty shops

Why study hotels, restaurants and barber and beauty shops? On one hand, the sector is relatively understudied. Most of the mainstream social sciences have essentially ignored the sector – although hotels and restaurants are belatedly getting some attention in tourism science. Secondly, the sector is large. These industries are present in every nation and within Brazil, in every state and region.

In 2000, each of these three sectors employed over 300,000 people, with restaurants alone employing over one million. These sectors contribute importantly to reducing disarticulation and social inequality. Much of the work in these sectors is semi-skilled but requires relatively little formal education. The lower salience of schooling requirements per se open up opportunities for lower class people who would face obstacles working in other sectors due to their low educational attainment. At the same time, each of these sectors pay relatively high wages for blue occupations – wages in excess of many occupations that would be otherwise available to the poor – a point which will be considered below. This makes hotels, restaurants and barber and beauty shops an appealing focus for the analysis of poverty reduction in the Third World.

These industries are also important because they are involved with important policies for increasing employment that are either relatively new or relatively under-discussed. Hotels and restaurants are two of the intended beneficiaries of programs in sustainable development. Sustainable development has put a fresh emphasis on tourism as a strategy for creating growth that is consistent with environmental preservation. The movement of economic development plans away from traditional heavy industry to tourism and services has been one of the major shifts in development policy in the 1990s. (Sinclair 1998, Hirnaux 1999, Cruz 2000)[1]

Barber and beauty shops are particularly important for the study of vocational education and urban redevelopment. Vocational education is one of the most common measures taken by governments to reduce persistent unemployment; hairdressing is one of the most common forms of occupational training that is provided. If workers are too unskilled to get jobs, give them the skills to make them more appealing to employers. These arguments are particularly popular in Third World settings where there is widespread concern about the low quality of education, and the inability of the labor force to meet the demands of technologically sophisticated global competition. Training in hairdressing does not increase a nation's capacity to compete in the world marketplace. However, in theory, trained hairdressers can serve the needs of the local population – allowing service sector jobs to absorb whatever surplus labor can not be used in export-oriented high-tech manufacture. These vocational programs are sometimes linked to the *economia solidária*, social programs that combine popular mobilization, anti-globalization protest, and explicit attempts by communities to reduce unemployment by patronizing the businesses of the local poor. (Singer 1998, França Filho and Laville 2004) As such, recent vocational education programs can combine the development of social capital with more traditional development of human capital, making such initiatives particularly interesting. Job training in the barber and beauty sectors has been at the forefront of these innovations.

Barber and beauty shops are also important in the consideration of the relationship between urban space use and employment. The zoning use of central city space is almost always regulated by the government – although usually a local rather than a national government is involved. The relationship between public space and small business receives extensive discussion in the literature on the mobilization of workers in the informal sector. (Cross 1998, Brown 2006) The relationship between the regulation of space and total employment, formal or informal, is generally undiscussed. However, access to the public is often a critical necessity for microentrepreneurs. In this regard, regulation of sidewalks is only a small part of a larger governmental rationing mechanism that includes zoning laws, building codes, and downtown redevelopment plans that determine the amount of space that will be available for commercial use in Third World cities – and what in what form and at what price that space will be available. Barber and beauty shops are particularly sensitive to the public regulation of the real estate market – making them a useful base for the consideration of otherwise neglected development questions.

False objection: Labor intense service sector jobs are pathological indicators of stunted economic growth – because the wages are low

The jobs in this study, those in the labor intense service sector, are often disrespected by social scientists because of their wages and conditions.

Jobs in the personal services are poorly paid. As such, these are positions of last resort taken by desperate jobseekers who can not find more lucrative employment in heavy industry or high-tech services. Wages and earnings in the personal service sector are so low as to make personal services a contributor to poverty rather than a solution to same. (Evans and Timberlake 1980, Kon 1997, Cardoso 2001)

Jobs in the personal services tend to be informal. Informal jobs tend to be poorly paid, because they lack the protections of government labor laws. Authors concerned about informality argue that exclusion from policies that protect workers intensifies the problems identified by Evans and Timberlake et al. making employment in the personal services particularly pathological. (Cacciamali 1983, Pereira Melo et al. 1998)

There is no doubt that work in hotels, restaurants and barber/beauty shops is less lucrative than being an oncological surgeon, a Linux programmer, or an automotive engineer. However, these jobs are by no means the worst in the Brazilian economy. Much of the labor force in all three sectors is semi-skilled rather than unskilled. Restaurants require chefs who know how to cook. Bartending is more than just pouring beers, particularly in a nation known for its sophisticated cachaça drinks. Beauticians are required to have a solid command of hairstyling techniques, coloration, and the use of chemical treatments. Brazilians greatly value glamour and personal appearance, and will not tolerate hairdressers who lack the skill to guarantee good results. (Dweck 1998) Hotels employ a large percentage of food service staff, with all of the cooking requirements of a restaurant. They furthermore hire substantial skilled and semi-skilled construction trade workers in order to maintain their physical plant. Even desk-clerks, a relatively low status hotel job, are required to be literate and in some cases, able to operate a computer system.

As a result, wages in these three industries are relatively high by Brazilian standards. We used Census data (the 25 percent Microsample for the 1991 and 2000 Censuses), to measure how the earnings of the workings in our sectors compared with typical Brazilian workers. We looked at all Brazilians who earned income and noted where hotel workers, restaurant workers, barbers and beauticians fell on the percentile rank of Brazilian earners. A 100th percentile score puts the worker at the top of the earnings pyramid; a 0th percentile score puts them at the bottom.

Hotel, restaurant workers and barber/beauticians do not have low earnings. In 2000, formal workers in the hotel sector were at the 52.6[th] percentile; formal restaurant workers were also at the 52.6[th] percentile and barber/beauticians were at the 67.7[th] percentile. Of course, employees in the formal sector with social security cards and fringe benefits are at the top of their field. However, informal workers do not do much worse. The earnings of informal workers in hotels in 2000 were at the 35.4[th] percentile; informal restaurant workers were at the 26th percentile and informal barbers and beauticians were at the 42.5[th] percentile. Self-employed workers might also be perceived as being at risk of low income. Hotel "self-employed" workers are in good shape because they at least own premises with a room that they can rent. However, a woman operating a lunch stand (a self-employed restaurateur) or a domestic beautician doing clients' hair in her living room can be fairly marginal. Nevertheless, the income data show these workers having fairly decent incomes. Solo self-employed restaurateurs earnings were at the 52.6[th] percentile – and the same figure applies to solo self-employed barbers and beauticians. Figures for 1991 are essentially similar except that they show higher incomes (40.4[th] percentile rather than 26.0[th] percentile) for informal restaurant workers.

Why are these numbers so high? Earnings for most of these workers are fairly modest. Self-employed restaurant and barber/beauticians workers in 2000 only earned 1.99 times the minimum wage; informal barbers only earned 1.66 times the minimum wage. Such wages will hardly make a person wealthy.

However, wages are so low in Brazil that in comparative perspective, these are actually good salaries. Over 50 percent of all Brazilian earners earn *less* than do informal barbers. So if you can take an unemployed worker, an agricultural laborer, a domestic servant, or a worker in a sweatshop, and you give them an informal position as a barber, you have improved their standard of living substantially. Everyone knows that "Brazil is poor". However, looking at the income data reminds us of the millions and millions of people in Brazil who do not even earn enough money to equal the minimum wage – and who nevertheless have to support families on such pittances. Giving these people double the minimum wage is very major poverty relief.

What government policies actually increased employment in Brazil?

The rest of the book lays out the detailed findings about what government policies raised employment in hotels, restaurants and barber/ beauty shops in Brazil. The basic claims of the book are reproduced here. This summary contains very little of the empirical or theoretical defense of these positions; the rationale for these conclusions is found in the analytical chapters themselves. However, it is easier to follow an argument when one knows in advance where that argument is going. So here in bald form, are the primary hypotheses and conclusions.

a)   Market factors are the dominant determinants of employment. Market models of employment work well – and analyses of policy that ignore these considerations do so at their peril.

b) James O'Connor is correct in that government construction of infrastructure is vital to economic growth, and is nearly always helpful. The state's role in the provision of these authentically public goods is irreplaceable.

c) James O'Connor downplays the role of the state as a corrective for failed capital markets – in contrast to much of the writing about Third World developmentalist states. There is a substantial subset of industries in Third World economies for which O'Connor's is correct to be skeptical about the "state as active investor". Generally, these are settings where, for some beneficent reason, capital markets have not failed.

d) Where capital markets have not failed, the provision of physical infrastructure is much more effective than is the public subsidy of individual investments. In the Brazilian hotel sector, public sanitation projects and transport infrastructure projects are more effective than publicly-funded hotel construction programs.

e) Airports produce dramatic economic benefits far in excess of their effect on the hotel and restaurant sectors. They have substantial growth effects on the economy as a whole, agriculture, retail and wholesale trade, and to a lesser extent, the services. Only heavy industry fails to benefit from airports, due in part to the "fixed location" of some forms of bulk production.

f) O'Connor argues that state provision of human capital through educational expenditure is also fundamental to creating growth. This can take the form of traditional schooling (primary, secondary and university education), or it can take the form of vocational education and job training programs. Vocational training is an effective strategy for creating employment. Regions that ran large vocational education programs had more employment at the aggregate level.

g) Vocational education programs are more effective in industries that have substantial scope for self-employment. In the Third World, employers can often train workers perfectly well by themselves. Vocational education creates jobs in part, by creating a stock of new microentrepreneurs who by starting their own business, and aggressively marketing their wares, increase aggregate demand for the products or services in their industry. Self-employment is a critical component of this mechanism.

h) O'Connor argues about the importance of fiscal crisis in hampering the ability of the state to produce development. In the Third World, this takes the form of debt crisis ... and the need to preserve national economic sovereignty, by avoiding unnecessary foreign debt. Indebtedness is a particularly serious issue in large infrastructure projects – which are, by their nature, expensive. Watching the cost of infrastructure projects is important; it is often possible to create substantial value with smaller projects that limit themselves to using cash on hand, avoid using borrowed funds.

i) O'Connor argues that fiscal crisis comes from insufficient taxation. The counter argument to this is that low taxes reduce financial burdens on business and stimulate employment. In Brazil, cutting taxes does not increase employment. In Brazil, evasion is widespread anyway, lowering the relevance of de jure rates. Even where taxes are collected, employers do not necessarily reduce either investment or jobs in response to tax burdens since alternative "tax-free" alternative investments may not exist – or it is possible pass the tax burden on to the consumer in the form of higher prices.

j) Some industries are very sensitive to rent and the availability of commercial or industrial space. It is possible to increase employment in these sectors by providing meaningful workspaces at affordable prices. Urban real estate dynamics, zoning laws and building codes have significant effects on the amount of commercial space that becomes available and the form that such space takes.

k) Surprisingly, economic expansion reduces the supply of commercial space available as cities move from being comprised of multiple small structures to limited numbers of large structures. These large structures often have higher rents, since concentrated ownership increases the negotiating power of landlords.

l) Rent control, and state construction of low rent commercial facilities, can provide a significant stimulus to the rent-sensitive component of the economy – although this needs to be balanced with other economic priorities.

m) Migration per se can be a significant source of employment. Migrants have significant needs that must be serviced while they are in transition – and require the creation of housing, stores and public services at their destination. This can provide a one-off stimulus to the receiving economy which is not counterbalanced by an equal loss in the sending economy. North-South migration in Brazil, a cause of significant slum development in southeastern cities, may not have been an entirely negative development.

n) In this light, frontier development in Brazil – and Brazil's practice of creating new capital cities for new administrative entities, may have had significant employment effects. This would hold even without the development of an export agriculture sector in the Brazilian center-west.

o) Pollution seriously harms the hotel sector – although it leaves other sectors unaffected. There is a clear public policy trade-off between support for heavy industry and the development of a tourism industry.

The following chapters will discuss these ideas in reference to the experience of Brazilian hotels, restaurants and barber/beauty shops. Because these conclusions are based on the properties of residuals from an economic model, the generation and details of that economic model are of key importance. The next chapter describes the results of an econometric analysis of the economic and social determinants of employment in hotels, restaurants and barber/beauty in Brazil from 1940 to 2000. These models represent our attempt to estimate what would have happened had the government programs of interest to our analysis did not exist. These what-if models do not comprise the main findings of the book, and represent the null factors that have to be removed from the analysis rather than the prime factors that underlie the analysis. The residuals from that analysis will form the foundation for the subsequent arguments.

2
What Would Have Happened If the Government Had Done Nothing

The previous chapter argued that it is impossible to estimate the effects of government policies to raise employment and income without having some sort of idea of what levels of employment or income would have occurred in the absence of government intervention. This implies using some sort of mathematical model to calculate the levels of employment or income that would have occurred purely from market forces. Because most studies of the effects of state intervention in the economy do not make such adjustments, it is often difficult to know if the policies being discussed were successful or not – unless the results are very extreme. Examining the state's capacity to improve economic conditions above those levels that would have been expected from market forces is a more rigorous test of state capacity than the mere capacity to seemingly raise employment over time. Such a test is necessarily a stronger test and provides a more robust confirmation of the value of state interventions than does the more traditional "post hoc ergo propter hoc".

In this chapter, we present the calculations of the base levels of employment that would have occurred in the absence of government intervention. We use these to identify what states or regions had employment in excess of market levels – and thus what states or regions might have had superior social or economic policies.

Statistical readers will recognize this type of methodology as a *residuals analysis*. We take the primary non-political determinants of employment and put them into a quantitative model. We estimate this model using an appropriate methodology for time series cross section datasets – in this case, regression with panel corrected standard errors.[1] This model is used to calculate expected levels of employment in various regions of Brazil. These figures are called the "predicted values". We then calculate the difference between the actual observed amount of employment and the predicted values. These are called the "residual values" or "residuals". They represent the employment that was caused by variables *other than* the variables in the model. Places with high residuals are places where there is some form of natural advantage that is producing superior rates of employment. Places with low residuals are places where there is some form of disadvantage or handicap that is lowering rates of employment. These advantages or handicaps could include government programs. In the later chapters, more rigorous tests are run to examine if government programs really do explain these differences in residual employment.

The models used to make the null model are theoretically eclectic. They draw from economics, sociology, tourism science and common sense. The cross disciplinary nature of these equations will be viewed as desirable by those readers who enjoy broad synthetic scholarship, and will be viewed as inelegant by readers who prefer tight derivations from a single set of theoretical principles. Employment in hotels, restaurants and barber/beauty is determined by a large number of different factors, not all of which are drawn from one discipline or one "type' of social scientific process. Using a medley of dissimilar variables was a measure taken in the interest of caution to assure that the analyses that follow would not be undercut by the inappropriate exclusion of a relevant non-political determinant of employment.

Previous attempts to model employment in our industries

Most of the pre-existing models for demand in hotels and restaurants have come from scholars with an interest in tourism science. There is a smaller contingent of models from scholars who study the service sector. The models that are tightly specified and practical to estimate tend to be drawn from microeconomic derivations. Other models have a broader and more attractive range of variables – but many of these pose implementation problems.

The simplest strategy for predicting employment in personal services or tourism is to simply extrapolate this from past trends. (Lundberg et al. 1995, Bailly et al. 1992) Alternative mathematical forms can be used to make the extrapolation very elaborate. Extrapolation is the weakest form of modeling because it assumes that present conditions will continue to pertain to the future – an assumption that is frequently violated. For our purposes, extrapolation is unacceptable. We need to be able to distinguish "market" causes of tourist employment from "political" causes of market employment. Just looking at past trends does not tell us which past trends were caused by economic forces as opposed to past political or social initiatives.

There are also attempts to list the attractive features that locations might have in order to attract tourists. (Vanhove 2005, Ritchie and Crouch 2003) These are models for the demand for services – and this book draws from that style of thinking. The Vanhove/Ritchie and Crouch approach is an "encyclopaedic" approach. They attempt to specify *all* the attractions that a location may have. Thus their models have lists specifying: ecological advantages, important sporting events, quality of hotel accommodations and other items of this kind. The individual components of the lists are all sensible. However, because of the exhaustive nature of these lists, their models have 30 to 40 different variables. Even if the data were available to measure all 30 to 40 variables – and generally such data are not available – most tourism datasets are too small to be able to support 30 to 40 predictor variables at the same time.[2] The present dataset, which is large by tourism science standards, has slightly over 1000 cases – far short of the mathematical demands of a variable list this large. For any model to be computationally stable enough to be useful, it has to be parsimonious theoretically.

Within the tourist literature, one strategy for obtaining parsimony is to use the "Delphi" system to sort through the complexities of multiple measures. In the Delphi system, a panel of experts is employed to consider the broad array of considerations that would impact tourism in an area and make a prediction forecasting future demand. (Seely et al. 1980, Green et al. 1990) This sounds good, but it is really no more than transferring the analytical task from the writer to the local informant. What local informants do which is of value is to identify the factors that are particularly important in their home setting – in essence cutting down the list of variables. Once you have this short list, Delphi tells you little about what to do with it. Delphi theorists are correct that all model-building is better if potential ideas are first vetted with well informed observers; however, once one has gotten intelligent advice one still needs to process that information in a rigorous manner in order to make concrete predictions. At some point, constructing a mathematical model will still be helpful.

In contrast to the previous approaches, microeconomic models of tourism demand are both parsimonious and quantitatively precise. Economists construct very rigorous mathematical models of tourism demand using a very small set of variables derived from one unitary intellectual tradition, the microeconomic theory of consumer behavior. (Baumol 2006, Case 2004) They argue that tourism employment at Destination X is determined by two factors: consumer income – and the price of travel to Destination X relative to other competing destinations. The literature that uses this type of model is vast. (Gray 1966, Artus 1972, Kliman 1981, Loeb 1982, Johnson and Ashworth 1990, Crouch et al. 1992, Sheldon 1990, Sinclair and Stabler 1997, Dritsakis and Athanasiadis 2000, Dwyer et al. 2000) These models have the advantage of being theoretically coherent and well integrated into other work on economic development. Furthermore, their argument on the key role of consumer income is entirely reasonable; we use that argument in the present work.

What is problematic is the excessive concentration on the claim that tourism is concentrated in areas where travel costs that are lower than those for competing destinations – and the single minded focus on finding better and more sophisticated treatments of travel prices. What are the problems with putting travel prices first and foremost?

1. Frequent flier programs have not been kind to neoclassical models of tourist demand. Many vacationers take their vacation with bonus tickets obtained by having flown a set number of miles for other reasons. The effective cost of these frequent flier tickets is zero. Because zero dollars can buy a ticket to many different cities in the airline's network, travel price becomes less salient to choosing a destination for a vacation.

2. Neoclassical travel models have very careful specifications of the relative cost of travel to destination X as opposed to destination Y. However, in a theory of consumer behavior, there are many other goods besides travel to destination Y that compete with a trip to destination X. Instead of going to destination X, the consumer could buy a consumer durable, make an investment, or invest in personal services in their home city. In principle, the cost of travel to X needs to be contrasted with the cost of ALL possible alternative expenditures. Such a project would be virtually impossible to do for both theoretical and practical reasons.

3. Neoclassical models make no attempt to model the relative attractiveness of different tourist locations. In this literature, Paris, France and Worcester, Massachusetts are equivalent tourist destinations and all that differentiates them is the price of the airfare. Vanhove (2005) or Ritchie and Crouch (2003) are surely correct in arguing that tourists prefer some destinations to others, and these preferences need to be somehow incorporated into the model.

4. Neoclassical tourist demand models have results that are inconsistent or hard to explain. Frechtling (2001, Chapter 7) argues that the

anomalous results are frequently the result of multicollinearity – a statistical problem in which models are made unstable by the inclusion of multiple predictors that are highly correlated with each other. Travel price indices are generally highly correlated with each other. This distorts the accuracy of the estimates both of the price variables themselves – and every other variable that is in the same equation with them. Frechtling argues that price data need to be excluded from models of tourism demand in order to provide robust results. Sinclair and Stabler (1997) in their exhaustive review of microeconomic models of tourism demand also argue that travel prices should not be included in models of tourism employment.

In this particular analysis of Brazil, data is simply not available on the price of hotels, restaurants or barber shops in the different locations nor is data available on the cost of travel to these different places. However, even if such data were to be available, the theoretical and statistical concerns of the preceding discussion might give us pause before automatically including such variables in the analysis.

The present model: What would have determined employment in the absence of government intervention?

This section describes the theoretical foundations of our base models. The exact sources and construction of the variables can find this information in the Appendix *Data and Sources*.

Reminder:

The variables and statistical tables discussed in this chapter do NOT represent the main argument of this book. These represent "trivial" non-political determinants of employment that will be statistically adjusted for as a strategy for identifying more important political and social causes of job creation. Readers seeking the main findings of the book are encouraged to consult the subsequent chapters.

All of the models attempt to predict employment in one of the three core industries in our study – hotels, restaurants or barber/beautician. The Census materials from which the data are drawn include all of the employees in the relevant industry regardless of occupation. Thus, a receptionist in an upscale beauty salon would be included, as would a cleaning person in a restaurant. The raw employment count is always divided by the population of the geographical unit being studied. Otherwise, large regions would always appear to have "more employment" than small states, simply by virtue of being bigger places. The unit of analysis is the state (i.e. province) for 1940–80. For 1991–2000, the unit of analysis is the Census Microregion, an area about the size of a US County.

We argue that in the absence of government intervention, employment in these industries would be predicted by the following list of variables:

1) *Per Capita Income.* Microeconomic theory argues that the demand for services – or for any other good – will be correlated with the disposable income of consumers in the market. (Baumol 2006, Case 2004) This is simple common sense. The more money people have, the more they spend on the good things in life. One can sell far more restaurant food in Beverly Hills than one can in a dying factory town.

   The link of income to volume of consumption and employment is also made in the literature on the rise of the service sector. Although there is mild controversy on this point, most authors on the rise of service employment cite Engel's law that argues that the share of household consumption that is represented by services increases with family wealth. Engels argued that consumption of basic necessities such as clothing and housing is intrinsically limited. As families reach the ceiling of potential expenditure on basic goods, they begin to purchase more luxuries; including personal services such as travel, and entertainment. (Kindleberger and Herrick 1977, p. 273, Marshall and Wood 1995, Illeris 1996)

2) *Infant Mortality.* We include this as a secondary measure of income. Wealthy areas are more likely to have lower infant mortality than poor areas. See the *Data and Sources* Appendix for a discussion of why including a second measure of income was necessary.

3) *Urbanization.* Urban areas should have more employment in hotels, restaurants and barber/beauty shops than should suburban and rural areas. Some of this comes from the well known truism that economic development entails a transfer of employment from the agricultural to the industrial and service sectors. (Kuznets 1966) Urbanization is a key indicator of economic development.

   A more sophisticated defense of this position can be found in the social demographic literature on the determinants of changes in national occupational structures. Residents of farms often produce their own goods and services domestically. This reduces all forms of consumption of market products in non-urban areas. (Kuznets 1966) Furthermore, the use of personal services is sensitive to travel time. People will be more likely to go to a bar for a drink if the bar is on the next corner than if the bar is 20 miles away. Population density reduces the geographical distance required to travel to personal service facilities and thus increases discretionary consumption. The demographic literature on occupational composition shows that urbanization is a very strong predictor of personal service employment both in the United States and Brazil. (Browning and Singelmann 1975, Dal-Rosso 1978)

4) *Unesco World Heritage Site*. Vanhove (2005) and Richie and Crouch (2003) argue that some places just have more tourism because they have spectacular natural or cultural attractions. It is hard to argue with such a position. So even if hotels, restaurants and barber/beauty are heavily driven by local consumption, some attempt needs to be made to measure the capacity of a location to attract tourists from distant locations.

Measuring the tourist potential of every square inch of Brazil is an unfeasible proposition. However, there are some regions with extraordinary attractions that are obvious stand-out locations for drawing tourists, such as Paris or Niagara Falls. Fortunately, a standard measure of the presence of an extraordinary attraction exists. Unesco has a program that lists significant locations which are part of the world patrimony of ecological and cultural resources. The list includes such well known treasures as the Grand Canyon or Mont Saint Michel. We incorporate this data into our measure by coding whether any given location has a single location Unesco World Heritage cite within it.

5) *Upscale Beaches*. The most famous tourist attraction of Brazil is its beaches. Brazilian holiday-making typically involves going to the shore, since Brazil has some of the finest beaches in the world. Beach development is a form of local consumption; the primary users of the beaches are residents of the state where the beach is located. Wealthy states have more developed seaside facilities. High income consumers are more likely to be able to afford middle distance trips to the beach. Once they are there, they have lunches in restaurants, spend evenings in cafes and pass nights in hotels. Our models indicate which locations are coastal and which are not. Coastal locations receive extra weight if they are in wealthy states.

6) *Female Labor Force Participation.* Female labor force participation is likely to increase the use of services. The literature on domestic political economy explains female labor force participation in terms of trade-offs in the relative utility of goods produced in the home versus goods produced in the marketplace. (Becker 1981, Smith 1980) As women become more likely to work, they become more likely to purchase services previously produced domestically from commercial sources. This argument is echoed in some of the European literature on service sector expansion which places heavy emphasis on women's paid employment reducing women's capacity to work around the home. (Illeris 1996, Gadrey 1992) Both restaurants and barber/beauty shops are substitutes for services that would be provided domestically, and as such should be correlated with female labor force participation. Female labor force participation also raises female income; income raises the demand for services.

7) *Year.* Time is included in the model. Time captures at least two different effects. In a developing nation, time often represents secular trends in economic development. Including year captures tendencies in economic development that may be missed by the income variables. Secondly, time also measures organizational ecological considerations discussed by Hannan and Freeman and their followers. (Hannan and Freeman 1989, Carroll and Hannan 2000) Their argument is that organizational populations pass through a two stage history. In the first half, the type of organization is new and not legitimated by the consuming public. As legitimation increases, people have to get used to the idea that having restaurants, or barbers is a good idea. Birth rates rise, death rates fall and the number of organizations grows. Subsequently, there is a second stage in which the ecological niche which supports the organizations becomes overcrowded. More entrants into the field produces greater competition for resources. This leads to lower birth rates, higher death rates, and lower rates of population growth. A year variable captures the maturation of a field from immaturity to acceptance to oversaturation.

8) *Excluded Variables.* We do not include measures of macroeconomic stability. In earlier analyses, data on GNP growth and inflation rates were included in the equations. The performance of these variables was surprisingly poor. In neither contemporaneous nor lagged specifications, and neither in static nor dynamic models, did any of these variables produce significant coefficients in the correct direction.

The core models in operation

So what non-governmental variables actually increased employment? The simplified results of our analyses are presented in Table 2.1. More technical readers who wish to see a full set of coefficients and significance levels can find these in the Appendix: *Details of Statistical Results*. The variables essentially worked as predicted. All variables work as predicted in at least one equation – while both urbanization and income (measured as either income or infant mortality) work as predicted in all six tests. No variable is ever significantly in the wrong direction.

Underneath each equation, we present a figure showing the percentage of variance explained – otherwise known as the R^2. This statistic measures how well the models fit the data. A model that does not fit the data would get a 0; a model that fit the data perfectly would get a 100. On equations such as these, 20 is a good performance, 35 is quite solid and anything over 50 is a very good fit indeed. The figures show that the goodness of fit of all the models is quite acceptable – and the fit for restaurants and barber/beauty is quite high indeed. The fit for hotels is adequate but less impressive for reasons that we consider below.

Table 2.1   Core Models of Employment in Selected Brazilian Industries

Hotels	Restaurants	Barber/Beauty
1940–80		
Infant Mortality (–) Urbanization Time (–)	Infant Mortality (–) Urbanization	Urbanization Time (–)
% Variance Explained: 58	% Variance Explained: 84	% Variance Explained: 71
1991–2000		
Income Urbanization UNESCO Heritage Upscale Beach Time (–)	Income Infant Mortality (–) Urbanization UNESCO Heritage Upscale Beach Time (+)	Income Urbanization Female Labor Force Participation UNESCO Heritage Time (–)
% Variance Explained: 27	% Variance Explained: 57	% Variance Explained: 72

All coefficients are significant and positive unless marked by a minus sign.

Note that there are important differences between the 1940–80 and 1991–2000 equations. Income can only be measured as "infant mortality" in the 1940–80 period. Likewise, the 1940–80 data is only available for whole states rather than microregions. This knocks Unesco Heritage and Upscale Beach out of the 1940–80 equations. UNESCO Heritage works in 100 percent of the equations in which it was included – while Upscale Beach works in two out of three of its equations.

In 1940–80, Infant mortality was negatively related to employment in hotels and restaurants. A negative coefficient for infant mortality shows that areas with higher standards of living, with better nutrition, more medical care and cleaner water – had higher levels of employment in hotels and restaurants.

Urbanization was positively related to employment in all three sectors. All three forms of service employment were more prevalent in urbanized states.

Female labor force participation was only related to barber/beauty employment and then only in the later period. The timing issue may reflect the fact that during the 1940–80 period some women may have continued to do their hair at home – using their income to procure the services of a domestic servant, or to purchase home beauty supplies for doing their hair themselves. In mid-century Brazil, a substantial proportion of hair care was provided in the home by either women themselves or by household staff. (Dweck 1999)

Overall, in 1940–80, not counting time, hotel and restaurant employment were determined by income and urbanization. Barber/beauty employment was narrowly determined by urbanization.

The more complete data of 1991 and 2000 allow for a testing of the full model. Overall, the findings are similar to those for 1940–80, with a small number of interesting minor differences.

Before considering the performance of individual variables, let us first consider the R^2. The R^2 for hotels is 0.27, for restaurants is 0.57 and for barber/beauty is 0.72. The explained variance for barber/beauty is nearly identical for the two periods – a remarkable coincidence. The R^2 for the remaining industries are respectable but lower. This reduction in explained variance reflects the fact that the 1991–2000 model is trying to explain variance in employment in over 500 microregions, while the 1940–80 model is explaining variance in 18 states. The 1991–2000 model has to target hotel, restaurant and barber location far more precisely geographically than does the 1940–80 model. A ten mile error in hotel location would count as a "hit" in 1940–80 but a "miss" in 1991–2000, since ten miles would easily move you out of a census microregion, but not out of a state. That said, an R^2 of 0.56 or 0.72 is very high, showing the models have good fit.

In both 1940–80 and 1991–2000, hotels had a lower explained variance than did restaurants and barber/beauty. This reflects the fact that restaurants and barber/beauty have a clientele that is overwhelmingly local. Hotels have some local business – but also serve a larger percentage of bona fide long distance tourists. As such, it is reasonable to expect that hotels will be less affected by local economic conditions – while restaurants and barber/beauty will be profoundly affected by local conditions. Because tourism is more important for hotels than for the other two sectors, economic policies that effect tourism will be disproportionately likely to effect hotels – and hotels alone – while more broadly-based policies will effect the three sectors together.

Income raises employment in all three sectors. This is precisely what would be expected from the microeconomic models of employment.

Where infant mortality makes a difference, it lowers employment – which is what would be expected if infant mortality was a measure of poor economic conditions. Restaurants are particularly affected by infant mortality. This may reflect microeconomics. It may also reflect the correlation of infant mortality with bad sanitation. Open sewers and foul water increase infant mortality; they are also very bad for the restaurant industry.

Urbanization increases employment in all three sectors. This is identical to the finding for the 1940–80 period.

Having a UNESCO heritage site raises employment for all three sectors. Recreational industries do better in settings with spectacular natural or cultural attractions. Note that having one's hair done does count as a recreational activity among Brazilians.

The upscale beach variable is positive for hotels and restaurants – meaning that in Brazil, the hospitality industry is more active on the coastline of wealthy states.

The female labor force participation rate was only significant for barber/beauty – but on barber/beauty the effect was quite strong. The increased effect of female labor force participation on barber/beauty probably reflects the decline of the use of domestic servants for hair care. Most middle class Brazilians still keep household workers to cook, clean and take care of children. However, having the maid do one's hair is becoming less common.

The time term was negative for both hotels and barbers, but positive for restaurants. The time coefficients are the same for both periods – showing the robustness of the model. The positive term for restaurants captures the explosive growth in taking meals outside the home. Restaurant use has been expanding dramatically both in Brazil and in the world as a whole. Eating out consumes an ever-increasing share of consumer budgets.

In contrast, hotel and barber/beauty use are declining over time. This means that increases in income are going to other types of expenditure besides hotels and barber/beauty. The obvious components of house-hold budgets that are increasing in relative size are automobile expenses and housing. Automobile ownership is now nearly universal among the middle class and not uncommon among the working class. At mid-century, automobiles were more limited to the upper classes. Housing quality is improving for the Brazilian population – allowing a larger share of the budget to go to the purchase and rent of larger homes or apart-ments – or for home improvement expenses for a working class which does a lot of "do-it-yourself". Consumer durables are also increasing as a percentage of household expenditures. Refrigerators, color TVs, washing machines and personal computers are becoming increasingly available to Brazilian consumers. All of these expenditures reduce the share of travel and grooming in the household budget – producing the negative trend over time.

Conclusion

The chapter reports the results of some new models of employment in personal services that draw from the literature in economics and sociology – but differ significantly from most empirical estimations of service or tourism employment. Most microeconomic tourism models focus on relative transportation costs. Most service sector models invoke a smaller number of variables than those reported here.

The equations work extremely well – with all except one specification having an R^2 of over 0.50. The coefficients are all in the correct direction and most work in the majority of tests.

Overall, service employment is a function of income (measured two ways), urbanization, female labor force participation, and the presence of attractions such as beaches or cultural landmarks. Economics, socio-logy and tourism science all make useful contributions to the models – showing that no one discipline has a monopoly of insight on these questions.

We have now established that market forces contribute to employ-ment in hotels, restaurants and barber/beauty. However, the larger question is what is the impact of government policy? The first policy we consider is the provision of physical infrastructure. Building roads and sewers is a fundamental responsibility of government, even if it is unglamorous. The residuals from market models show that these programs are important – and that they provide much more powerful benefits than do programs designed to invest directly in the industries themselves.

3

O'Connorian Models of Development: How States Literally Build Economic Growth

Chapter 1 made a strong argument that the state policies that create employment and reduce poverty in the Third World are often the same policies that create employment and reduce poverty in the wealthy nations. This is in contrast to models of "late development" where the role of the state is to compensate for some kind of handicaps that peripheral and semi-peripheral economies face when dealing with adverse market and political pressures from the core. This is **not** to say that these adverse pressures do not exist. Nor is it maintained that compensatory strategies do not work. There is a distinguished pedigree of outstanding analysis in development sociology and economics ranging from Alexander Gershenkron (1962), to Peter Evans (1979) to Dani Rodrik (2007) who have established without a doubt that there are unique developmental strategies that apply to poor nations and to specific poor nations ... and that these distinctive strategies can be very effective.

That said, an **exclusive** focus on "late development oriented" interventions can draw attention away from other effective state policies that are common to rich and poor nations alike. The porcupine may need quills in order to protect itself from the lion. However, both the porcupine and the lion have to breathe oxygen. This chapter focuses on the "oxygen", those common policies available to core governments and the peripheral governments alike that promote economic development.

A focus on common policy does not force the theorist into 1950s style functionalism or convergence theory. Nor does it require the analyst to ignore fundamental adverse trends within globalization that gut state effectiveness and inhibit the ability of local technocrats within the government apparatus to implement effective policies autonomously. Any serious analysis of state policy in the Third World has to be aware of international debt, has to be aware of fiscal crisis and has to be aware of the fact that European and North American governments have access to a panoply of financial and administrative resources that are not available to their counterparts in the global south.

That said, few macrosociologists, institutional economists, or Latin American specialists would want to argue that education has no effect on economic growth in the core or the periphery. Few macrosociologists, institutional economists or Latin American specialists would want to argue that state funded population control programs have no effect on economic growth in the core or the periphery. Comparable cases can be made for the Keynesian management of demand, the funding of research and development and – significantly for the analysis that follows – the provision of infrastructure.

Neglect of such programs can be justified if Third World states are in profound fiscal crisis. The literature on the Third World debt crisis argued that this type of program was exactly what was reduced by the need to make debt payments and that indebtedness made development strategies based on such garden variety programs non-viable. (Chossudovsky 1997, Potter 2000, Easterly and Serven 2003)

However, government programs in wealthy countries can be affected by budgetary crises as well. American academic readers are surely familiar with the fiscal crisis of public universities in the United States; primary and secondary schools in American inner cities have faced equally serious budgetary constraints. The great 1980s recession and its attendant fiscal crises in the European social democracies led to a dismantling or curtailing of the Welfare State in many of those nations. (Teeple 1995)

Economic growth in *both* the developed world and the less developed world are affected by government programs whose viability are dependent on the availability of public funding. If we wish to understand this process, it is useful to consider models of economic growth who consider the relationship between the state, capital accumulation and fiscal crisis.

The most obvious theorist for such a problem is James O'Connor.

James O'Connors 1973 *Fiscal Crisis of the State* lays out a general model of the role of the state in capital accumulation. The model is very simple.

1) States produce economic growth by constructing physical infrastructure that capitalists would never construct themselves.
2) States produce economic growth by investing in human capital that capitalists would never finance themselves.
3) States legitimate capitalism by providing welfare.

4) States maintain aggregate demand by with Military Keynesianism.

5) Limits on the ability to collect taxes produce a fiscal crisis that inhibits the state's ability to perform 1) through 4).

6) Monopoly capital expropriates most of the benefits of state spending since government programs disproportionately favor large corporations.

7) Monopoly capital effectively avoids taxation due to their influence on the tax code.

8) The tax burden thus effectively falls on petty capital and on individuals.

9) Once petty capital and individuals become fully class conscious about this process, they will mobilize against the state by refusing to pay taxes.

10) This will produce a fiscal crisis of the state – which will inhibit state capacity to provide the programs required for the reproduction of capitalism. Capitalism will fall not from catastrophic collapse but from slow decay.

Contemporary readers may notice the unsettling resemblance between this model and the current Tea Party mobilizations in the United States.

For the purposes of development theory, what matters is items 1) through 4), the specification of the routine "garden variety" government programs that generate development. O'Connor is all about building roads, building airports, building schools, supporting science, and running pension programs. Although O'Connor's work was early, and was drawn from a tradition of analytical Marxism, much of his logic anticipates later thinking about the state and development that emerged in institutional and development economics. One can find similar positions in the World Bank's 2002 report on the appropriate role of the government in responsible pro-capitalist development and in Joseph Stiglitz's heterodox prescription for state-led economic growth in *Making Globalization Work* (2006).

The O'Connorian perspective will used in several applications throughout this book. The present chapter focuses on point 1), the importance of infrastructure to economic development. A contrast is made between this and Point 0), an argument that does not appear in O'Connor at all:

1) States directly invest in strategic industries that will improve the long-term international competitiveness of the economy.

O'Connor is completely confident that monopoly capital will provide whatever investments are needed to fund any industry that would be intrinsically viable. Argument 0 is a key position of Celso Furtado (1983), Peter Evans (1979), and the developmental state theorists, but not of O'Connor. The purpose of this chapter is to show that O'Connor's emphasis is correct, and that, at least sometime, infrastructure provision is *substantially* more useful than is direct state investment.

Obviously, it would be too extreme to claim that proactive industrial policy is never effective. One can not dismiss the substantial empirical success rate of interventionist states notably in Europe and in East Asia. (Chang 2003, Amsden 1989) When state-led investment projects work, they work spectacularly well. However, a number of preconditions have to hold for industrial policy to have its desired goal. When all the right elements are in place, active state investment policies can be magic bullets. When all the right elements are not in place, simpler more O'Connorian programs can be more effective.

Infrastructure provision is easier to execute than is developmental statism. The most recent wave of sociological scholarship on the state and development has emphasized unsuccessful activist states, where local class structures and absence of endogenous bureaucratic capacity have undercut governmental attempts to promote development. (Chibber 2006, Lange and Rueschemeyer 2005) Capture of the state apparatus by the local bourgeoisie can be enough to undercut technocratic government planning. Unsuccessful developmentalist governments can turn into a neoliberal's stereotype of the rent-seeking state. Dani Rodrik (2007) argues that developmentalist states have to make strategic choices. Because seemingly similar countries can often have dissimilar problems, it is easy for governments acting in good faith to "guess wrong". The structural impediments to developmentalism identified by Chibber and Lange and Rueschemeyer, and the tactical impediments to developmentalism identified by Rodrik help explain why highly successful developmentalist states such as Singapore exist, but are relatively rare.

In contrast, it is not difficult to improve ports, pave roads, hire rural nurses, or open more high schools. Infrastructure provision generally provides some benefit, unless the country has become so developed that the public good in question is now in surfeit. Most developing nations are nowhere near the point where surfeit can be an issue. O'Connorian models provide a slow safe model for relatively incrementalist growth, while the more traditional world system models suggest formulas for high risk but relatively spectacular growth. Naturally, some of the most successful developing nations such as those in East Asia, use both strategies. However, when only one strategy can be implemented, the cumulative gains from steady incremental progress can be significant.

There is a second reason for sharing O'Connor's preference for infrastructure over state-led investment. State-led investment is meant to be a response to failures in capital markets. However, sometimes capital markets don't fail. Dani Rodrik (2007) makes this argument compellingly when he argues that every nation has its own particular strengths and weaknesses requiring individual solutions that reflect local characteristics; capital market failures may be present, absent or present only in a few sectors of a country. When capital markets *don't* fail, state-led investment accomplishes little, because the private sector is already providing adequate finance to appropriate industries.

Once again, infrastructure projects are less likely to have this problem. Most nations can use more infrastructure than they already have. Underdeveloped nations usually start with infrastructure levels far below the needs of their economy. Population growth requires the continuous addition of infrastructure to cover for ever increasing need. Furthermore, infrastructure deteriorates requiring substantial expenditure merely to maintain levels of service that previously existed. Thus, it is usually possible for economies to benefit from infrastructure in some way. Fernald (1999) offers an interesting analysis of the effects of adding infrastructure to a "high-infrastructure" case. In the United States, a nation well endowed with infrastructure, highway construction has always increased American manufacturing productivity. It has not always increased non-manufacturing productivity; furthermore, the size of the benefit to manufacturing dropped substantially after the completion of the Interstate Highway System. However, some industries always benefited from the construction of highways, even in the presence of substantial pre-existing capacity.

We demonstrate the utility of the O'Connorian perspective by testing the relative efficacy of infrastructure provision and direct state investment in promoting hotels and restaurants in Brazil.[1] We begin by reviewing the empirical evidence on the beneficial effects of infrastructure provision on growth in non-Brazilian settings. We continue by discussing why capital markets did not fail in Brazilian hotels and restaurants – and thus why it would be reasonable to expect industrial policy oriented towards correcting for market failure to be ineffective in this setting. We follow by an empirical test of the relative capacity of both types of programs to raise residual employment.

The state of the evidence on infrastructure and growth

We consider here the literature on the relationship between infrastructure construction and economic growth. For a discussion of the literature on the relationship between airports and economic growth, see the next chapter.

Nineteenth century governments constructed railways, and substantially stimulated industrialization by doing so. (Dobbin 1997, Hawke 1970, Reed 1969) In fact, the fundamental role of railways in stimulating early industrial growth has been a staple of traditional economic history. (Clapham 1930, Hobsbawm 1969) The role of railways has received somewhat less emphasis since Fogel (1964) published his contrarian position that econometrically railroads contributed little to US economic growth. Fogel could not be more O'Connorian. His main argument is that the United States already had a fully functional set of canals, making railways unnecessary. Canals were constructed by the state and federal governments and were a classic example of the public provision of infrastructure. construction is as O'Connorian as rail construction.

The largest body of systematic evidence on the role of infrastructure in economic growth comes from the work of development economists. Fedderke et al. (2006) do a long time series analysis of economic growth in South Africa to show the independent positive effects on GDP of railway lines, volume of rolling stock, telephone lines, paved roads, electricity provision and air passenger volume. Since reverse causation is a serious potential problem in such an analysis, they carefully rule this out by contrasting forward effects of external shocks in both variables. Even in this constrained test, all six infrastructure variables perform well.

Pereira (2000) did a similar time series for the United States. His dependent variable, private sector productivity, was related to aggregate public investment, energy and transportation systems (aggregated together for some reason), sewage and water supply systems, public buildings (a category that is dominated by schools and public hospitals), and a none-of-the-above infrastructure category.

Aschauer (2000) in a cross national sample of less developed nations found that private investment, secondary school enrolment and public investment had virtually identical positive effects on growth. In less developed nations which are not developmentalist states – which is most of them – public investment data would be dominated by infrastructure investments such as those discussed by O'Connor. An effect of public investment as least as large as that of private investment merits serious attention.

Esfahani and Ramirez (2003) find large effects on GDP growth within a large cross-sectional sample of countries of all income levels for increases in telephone availability and power generating capacity. Mitra et al. (2002) in an analysis of physical infrastructure and social infrastructure combined found that an index of roads, electricity, railroads, postal services, education and health, and banking correlated with differences in technical efficiency of manufacturing establishments in Indian states. Shioji (2001) estimates the effect of infrastructure growth and education on GDP growth in the US and Japan and argues that the effect of infrastructure improvements were substantially greater than those of education. Sanchez-Robles (1998) finds that measuring actual infrastructure constructed produces higher GDP effects than measuring expenditure on infrastructure; her methodology may implicitly correct for the corruption (and lost funds) that can be associated with infrastructure products, thus showing actual service delivery of public goods makes a difference. Easterly and Severn (2003) found that much of the decline in Latin American GDP that occurred in the 1990s was a direct result of reductions in expenditure on infrastructure. Mitra et al. (2002) find substantial effects of public capital on manufacturing efficiency in Indian states. Easterly and Rebeldo (1993) found large effects on infrastructure on growth in a cross-national sample – which particularly high effects for transportation and communication.

There is a small contrarian body of economists who argue that public spending on infrastructure is ineffective. (Holtz-Eakin 1994, Hulten and Schwab 2000) They present equations with low coefficients for the infrastructure variable, that either have a huge number of region and time dummies, or include private investment as a control. Any variable can be shrunk to insignificance by the inclusion of enough time and space dummies. Including private investment as a "control" ignores the fact that state investment in infrastructure provides favorable conditions for investors which increases their willingness to provide capital.

When are direct state investment programs most likely to not succeed?

While infrastructure generally supports economic development, direct state investment in particular industries works only some of the time. There is a substantial literature defending industrial policy; much of this is well thought out and compelling. However, the arguments in this literature can easily be turned on their head. Advocates of the developmentalist state identify cogently and reasonably a set of conditions that mandate aggressive government investment in strategic industries. On their home terrain, their arguments are well considered. However, if one took their preconditions for requiring aggressive state intervention in capital allocation and put a "**NOT**" in front of those preconditions, one would have an equally excellent list of preconditions for when states should eschew industrial policy entirely and rely on the wisdom and good judgment of the free market.

The literature on the mechanisms by which industrial policy works is vast; a discussion of *every* justification of state investment in firms would be a book unto itself.[2] Most involve some sort of failure of the private capital market. Some of the mechanisms that have been argued in the past to cause this failure involve empirically rare circumstances, such as a concentration of all investment competence in the state due to a lack of "modernization readiness" of the local capitalist class. (Rosenstein-Rodan 1943, Hoselitz 1963) However there are some important sources of capital market failure that do exist, and that would be remedied by well run programs of direct state investment. These include:

1) Impatience: Bias by private capitalists against viable investments which would require long maturation periods before becoming profitable.
2) Provincialism: Bias by private capitalists against viable investments in distant exotic locations.
3) Selfishness: Bias by private capitalists against investments that are intrinsically unprofitable but which provide critical inputs for the rest of the local economy.

Temporal Biases Towards Projects With Short-Term Payoffs. Private capital cannot tolerate projects that require long waiting periods before becoming profitable. Private investors generally require some sort of immediate return on their money. The state can consider projects that have 20 or 40 year gestation periods – because it is free from investor pressures to provide short-term returns. (Block 1987, Nove 1992, Streeck and Yamamura 2005, Szirmai 2005) Many viable infant industries do require long start up periods to become competitive – and only the state has the patience and resources to provide such protection. (List 1983, Papanek 1992, Adelman 2000) The empirical illustrations of the successful applications of this principle are well known: Japanese, Mexican and Brazilian automobiles, Taiwanese computers, and South Korean domestic appliances are just a few examples.

Note that there are two determinants of the time required for a potential investment to become profitable.

a) TECHNOLOGY THAT IS DIFFICULT TO MASTER. If a significant learning curve is associated with an industry, there will be a "training" period in which efficiency will be low, and costs will be high. Furthermore, product quality will be low, lowering sales and revenues. Industries with simple easy to master technologies do not have this problem.
b) SIZE OF CAPITAL STOCK. Big expensive projects require a longer time to recoup their investment. Part of the issue is that a significantly larger amount of money must be earned back before the break-even point is reached. Secondly, big expensive projects tend to be complicated. Even if the technology is essentially well known, there will be substantial construction and implementation delays.

Thus industries with complex technological content and large capital needs are particularly ideal for direct state investment programs.

Spatial biases towards home regions of investors. Even fully informed investors may have systematic biases against viable projects not in their home regions. Because there are more investors in wealthy than in poor areas, this can lead to over-investment in the center and under-investment in the periphery – even among projects of equal viability. A famous example of this can be found in Peter Evan's (1979) account of the origins of the Brazilian steel industry where American and European investors turned down opportunities to invest in virtually ideal steel-making facilities in Brazil preferring facilities in their own countries. Michael Hechter shows similar patterns of English investors overinvesting in England itself and under-investing in the Celtic periphery. (Hechter 1975)

There are several factors that can produce a bias towards an investor's own region.

a) EASE OF OVERSIGHT. Investments that require inconvenient travel may receive lower priority than those that can be supervised more conveniently. Doreen Massey (1974) has shown that American firms investing in Great Britain are disproportionately likely to locate close to Heathrow Airport – a pattern which was not replicated by British investors in the same industry.
b) LANGUAGE BARRIERS. Executives prefer interacting in their own language.
c) LEGAL PROTECTION OF PROPRIETARY TECHNOLOGY. Multinational corporations prefer to maintain the patent control of proprietary technology under the most favorable legal regimes possible. Generally this means

locating research and development facilities in their home nations, where their political influence is likely to be maximized. (Barnet and Muller 1974)

Subsidized inputs to other sectors. Governments sometimes invest in industries – not because they represent a potential for profit but because they provide critical inputs for other sectors of the economy. The energy industry is an obvious example of this type. Governments build power grids that may or may not be profitable; the purpose of the grids is to provide energy to the rest of the economy. Stiglitz (2006) notes that sometimes investments in heavy industry can serve this function. The government of Taiwan invested heavily in steel and plastics – creating large state-owned corporations to provide both. Neither firm was particularly profit-maximizing, but both provided other Taiwanese industries with extremely inexpensive raw materials. These subsidized raw materials were essential in helping the rest of the economy become capable of compete in global markets. (Stiglitz 2006)

Implications. Given the previous discussion, what types of industries should governments invest in?

Government investment in industry is most likely to increase rates of economic growth above those expected from market levels when the industries are subject to long delays before they attain profitability, when investors suffer from substantial regional biases, or when the industries are meant to provide subsidized inputs to other sectors. Table 3.1 illustrates these principles by considering the suitability for portfolio management of some different industries.

The accompanying table ranks seven industries by their suitability for government investment. Steel, computer, energy and automobiles are good candidates. Textiles, beverages and hotels are less promising. There should be few surprises on this list. Steel, computers, energy and automobiles have always received substantial state support either in the form of government-owned companies or subsidized capital. Textiles and beverages are less common investments although government programs in these areas are not unheard of.

All of the "strong" government investments require the mastery of new technology. They require specialized engineering and training which is generally unavailable from local universities and technical schools. The skills have to be imported from other nations – either by hiring foreign expertise, by training one's own nationals overseas and bringing them back home to work, or by reverse engineering imported products and attempting to induce appropriate manufacturing methods. This transfer

Table 3.1 Suitability of Industries for Government Investment

Industry	Long Delays Before Profitability	Regional Bias	Provides Inputs to Other Sectors
Strong Candidates for Government Investment			
Steel	Yes. Difficult Tech. Capital Intense	Yes. Most Steel Developed Nationally	Yes
Computer	Yes. Difficult Tech. Labor Intense	Yes. Patent Controls Discourage Globalizing R & D	Yes
Energy	Yes. Difficult Tech. Capital Intense	No. Heavily Globalized	Yes
Automobiles	Yes. Difficult Tech. Capital Intense	No. Heavily Globalized	No
Weak Candidates for Government Investment			
Textiles	No. Easy Tech. Labor Intense	No. Heavily Globalized	No
Beverages	No. Easy Tech. Labor Intense	50–50. Globalized Now. Historical Limits Based on National Tastes	No
Hotels	No. Easy Tech. Labor Intense	No. Travel Investors Work Globally	No

of knowledge is slow and unpredictable. Some nations never succeed in learning the new technology.

All of the "strong" government investments, except computers, are capital intense. Not only do they have long maturation periods until they become profitable, but the amount of money that has to be raised could conceivably tax local capital markets, if these are underdeveloped.

Steel and computers have national biases in investment. In steel, this comes from a) national differences in the properties of iron deposits making certain metallurgical techniques non-fungible, b) national differences in engineering schools – which sometimes have origins in path dependencies caused by differing national resource endowments and c) steel being critical to armaments and the war industry – which motivates governments to encourage steel development within their borders and discourage steel development in rival nation-states. The famous American and European rejection of Brazilian invitations to develop Volta Redonda has to be seen against the background of rising tensions of World War II – and the preparation of heavy industry for a potential major conflict. Computer investment tends to be regionalized because hardware and software companies are very concerned about maintaining patent protection over critical innovations.

All of the "strong" government investments except automobiles provide infrastructure. (One could argue that in mid-century, the automobile industry provided infrastructure for the defense industry, since truck builders were the primary constructors of tanks.)

In contrast, all of the "weak" government investments are labor intense, use simple well-known technologies,[3] are heavily globalized and provide no real infrastructural inputs to industry.

How does this apply to the present case of hotels and restaurants?

The tourism sector in general, and hotels in particular, are an unpromising sector for direct state investment – although a perfectly reasonable sector for infrastructural development.

a) The timeline for profitability in hotels is very short. The capital requirements are relatively modest. As an investment project, hotels are cheap – even if they are five star deluxe resorts. There is no arcane or difficult technology that needs to be mastered on a slow learning curve. Competition is somewhat restricted, since locations are imperfect substitutes for each other, reducing the capacity of strong global competitors to pre-emptively eliminate newcomers in other locations. Low capital requirements, easily accessible technology and partially restricted competition allow hotels to become profitable in a relatively short time period, eliminating the need for patient money.

b) Hotels and tourism are not subject to an investment process that is biased against exotic or Third World locations. Investors in many industries concentrate their investment on a small number of regions with known successes. Often this stems from the entrepreneurial pool emerging from a local source – with participants having strong social ties to a particular area. The role of Stanford University and MIT in producing technology clusters in their home cities is well known; the graduates of those institutions saw little reason to move. In contrast, travel industry executives are constantly scouring the globe for new locations to sell as vacation destinations. They travel throughout the world; linguistic and cultural differences pose no barrier for them. The cosmopolitanism of the hotel sector limits the degree to which regional bias would pre-empt investment in new promising locations.

c) The hotel sector does not produce vital inputs that are essential to the viability of other industries. Most workers live at home. Accommodating business visitors is a necessary but trivial component of commercial life. As such, the tourism sector is not like energy or steel or cement, where the rest of the economy requires access to large quantities of reasonably priced supplies that would otherwise need to be imported.

As a result, the hotel industry has none of the features consistent with the state outperforming the market in the making of investment decisions. If a location has reasonable potential to support either individual hotels or a tourism complex, the private sector is highly likely to provide the capital for such a project all by itself. Even in areas with weak or non-existent capital markets, the small size of hotel projects allows wealthy individual investors to engage in tourism development without recourse to bank loans or equity markets. Obviously the presence of fully developed capital markets increases the likelihood that such projects will be realized.

In contrast, hotels are extremely dependent on infrastructure. Hotels benefit from the valorization of private space by public action. (Harvey 1982, França 1999) The state constructs administrative centers, military centers, roads, airports, energy grids or recreational facilities, all of which increase the value of nearby real estate. Hotels benefit from any government expenditure that makes a location more attractive to visitors. They are particularly dependent on transportation infrastructure to bring in their customers, as well as electrical, water and sewage provision. This is particularly the case for "rural" resorts, which by their nature locate in remote and beautiful locations that could not be commercialized the provision of a minimum level of urban amenities.

Infrastructure vs. portfolio management in tourism development programs in Brazil's Northeast[4]

These principles can be illustrated with a consideration of the relative effectiveness of portfolio management and infrastructure provision in the development of a tourism sector in the Brazilian Northeast. State tourism policy in Brazil has alternated between two modes – one of the direct provision of capital for hotels, the other the provision of supportive infrastructure for the industry. Portfolio management was developed through two types of programs for the support of hotels: the provision of subsidized loans, and the provision of tax incentives. There were several programs that served these functions – and some combined loans and tax incentives in the same package. The primary hotel portfolio management programs were

1) FINOR – an all-industry regional development program adminis-tered by SUDENE – the national agency entrusted with the economic development of the Northeast and the Banco do Nordeste – the pub-licly-owned Northeastern regional development bank.
2) FUNGETUR – a national program for stimulating of tourism admin-istered by EMBRATUR – a national public corporation with respons-ibility for the regulation of tourism.
3) State tax incentives programs – Every Brazilian state had its own development plan and some of these involved tax subsidies for tourism.

These programs were primarily active from 1970–95 and used tax incen-tives and direct loans in order to stimulate investments in hotels. The number of different subprograms subsumed in these rubrics was extensive – and a wide variety of different types of public financing were available. However, legal technicalities aside, nearly all involved some sort of formal application to either Sudene, EMBRATUR or a provincial development agency for assistance in constructing a hotel. A staff of technocrats would review the application – with further review in the case of Sudene at the Banco do Nordeste. Assuming approval, there would either be the direct provision of funds, or a tax offset for documented expenses. All of these programs can be viewed as "reactive" portfolio management. The govern-ment never actually initiated a project – but by providing or withholding financing, the state second guessed which type of hotel investments would or would not be successful.

In the early 1990s, an alternative approach was introduced with the support of the Inter-American Development Bank. PRODETUR was an attempt to promote tourism by providing the infrastructure necessary to bring tourists to Brazilian vacation destinations – and to improve the quality and attractiveness of those destinations. Investments were made in airports, highways, bus stations, ecological reserves, historical reconstruction of colonial neighborhoods, parks, water and sewage systems, and infrastructure such as signposts for historical locations or visitors' centers. The scale of the project was enormous with over $700 million dollars being spent on infrastructure of some kind.

In principle, an infrastructure program that produces infrastructure that is unnecessary or unwanted should not produce much of an effect on growth. The PRODETUR project, however, was very well conceived. The infrastructure under discussion had been seriously lacking in North-eastern Brazil – and this lack had significantly impaired economic development. Air travel to the Brazilian Northeast was inconvenient, due to the poor quality of both airports and air service. Flights from the United States and Europe typically go through São Paulo first – making the trip to the Northeast relatively long. Before PRODETUR, some Northeastern airports lacked runways long enough to support modern jumbo jets. Passenger terminals were small and overcrowded; baggage facilities were primitive.

Basic sanitation was another issue. Open sewers and lack of hygiene is a significant deterrent to upscale travelers. I have had an excellent meal in a Brazilian café next to an open ditch with raw sewage – but this is not an experience I would recommend to fellow travelers. Raw sewage not only threatens the restaurant industry; it is a problem for marketing one's beaches as well. International travelers want clear, transparent, blue or green water. Water that is sullied or brown gets adverse reviews in tourist guides. Cleaning up the urban beaches was an important priority – and this involved the construction of major sewage systems.

Road access was an additional problem. Many excellent Brazilian beaches were too remote for travelers to reach – even by car. The Brazilian road network in the Northeast is relatively primitive by developed world standards. The primary commercial highway connecting the nine Northeastern states – BR 101 – is not a limited access freeway – but an ordinary two lane road, complete with potholes, bicyclists and livestock. Roads to beach locations were frequently unmarked and unpaved. Areas to be developed needed road improvement – or the construction of roads in the first place.

Improving surface transport meant not only building and paving roads, but improving public transportation as well. Working class Brazilians can be tourists as well. They are likely to travel by bus. Increasing the capacity of bus terminals was necessary both to increase the number of busses that could be served, and to insure that the waiting experience would not be so unpleasant as to discourage future travel.

The tourist destinations themselves also needed developing. Many areas of natural beauty were on private land and were unprotected from commercial development or squatter housing in any way. Squatter housing is a particularly significant issue in Brazil, where poor people construct shacks just about anywhere they can find vacant space. The most important scenic areas needed to be put into ecological preserves, with formal systems of conservation, legal limits on land use and protection for endangered species.

Urban areas also needed development. Many old colonial city centers had become rundown with age and lack of maintenance. Historical preservation of old buildings had been important in Minas Gerais, in the center of Brazil, which has a spectacular legacy of fine Brazilian rococo towns. In the Northeast, historical preservation had been a somewhat lower priority. The Northeast has several spectacular colonial settlements, notably Salvador, Olinda, Recife, and São Luis. Salvador and Olinda had received some previous, although partial, attention. Historic Recife and São Luis needed significant maintenance.

Developing urban parkland was also a priority. Many Northeastern coastal cities are dependent on a cultural complex based around the waterfront. This is known in Portuguese as the *orla*. The orla will typically be a series of seaside bars and cafes with good food, good drinks and lots of music. There will generally be a combination of parks and beaches to draw people to the orla. Standard features might include a beautiful paved walkway along the shore for exercise walking or promenading, playgrounds for children, volleyball and soccer fields, museums or aquaria, music stages for big public concerts, and a set of pretty places with benches and nice views for people to just sit and pass time. Recreational life revolves around the orla when one is available. Residential locations near the orla are highly valued. This often makes the neighborhood around the orla a preserve of the local haute bourgeoisie. However, social classes which generally do not mix in most forums of Brazilian life, mix routinely on the beach and orla, playing next to each other if not with each other. This creates an enormous demand for both upscale and down-market bars and restaurants. The vibrant social scene is attractive to tourists; the vibrant economic scene produces substantial employment.

There is a need for more minor forms of infrastructure as well. Building visitor centers, marking tourist areas, training tourist guides, and training public administrators in tourism promotion and marketing were all small scale jobs that needed doing.

None of these needs – be they airports, roads, sewers, ecological preserves, or visitor centers, were likely to be provided by the public sector – since these are not especially profitable endeavors. Thus there was ample space for PRODETUR to be successful.

The strategy of the analysis is to correlate public investments in FINOR, other state hotel investment programs, and PRODETUR with residualized employment from the models in Chapter 2. The material on FINOR was graciously provided by a local informant. The material on FUNGETUR and other public investments in hotels comes from the EMBRATUR annual yearbooks. The material on PRODETUR comes from the final report that was submitted to the Inter-American Development Bank. (Banco do Nordeste 2004) Data on FINOR investments and on PRODETUR activity is available at the level of the census microregion – the primary unit used in our analyses. The data on FUNGETUR and other government programs is only available by state.

Results for portfolio management programs: FINOR and FUNGETUR

Figure 3.1 shows the extent of state sponsorship of hotel investment for the 1980–2000 period by year. Altogether some 1283 hotels were built containing 44,228 rooms. FINOR was substantially less active in hotel investment than were FUNGETUR and the provincial economic development agencies. FINOR limited itself strictly to the Northeast, and put most of its money into agricultural and industrial projects. This is in contrast to FUNGETUR which was a national hotel development program with few other competing uses for its funds. As a result, FINOR only constructed 6 percent of the state financed hotels that were constructed in Brazil during the period.

The two types of programs also had different histories. FINOR entered hotel investment slowly and increased its involvement over time. The

Figure 3.1   Publicly Financed Hotel Construction in Brazil 1980–2000

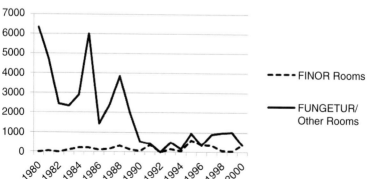

late 1980s and the mid-1990s represent periods of increased hotel investment for FINOR, the latter possibly being linked to the PRODETUR initiative. In contrast, FUNGETUR started with an extremely substantial amount of hotel construction which then declined markedly over time. There was a significant drop after 1985, and another drop after 1989. In the 1990s, barely 12 percent of the number of hotels were financed that had been financed in the 1980–91 period. Still by any objective measure, these programs were non-trivial. 1300 hotels and 45,000 rooms represent a fairly substantial investment, and one that in principle, should have had an effect on employment in the hotel sector.

However, all indications are that the effect of all this publicly subsidized hotel construction on actual hotel employment was trivial. To test the relationship between hotel construction and employment, we looked at the correlations between FINOR and FUNGETUR activity on one hand, and residual hotel employment on the other.

A Pearson correlation measures the extent to which two variables are related to each other. A correlation of 0 means the variables have no relationship to each other whatsoever. A weak relationship can be about a 0.20. A more serious relationship would be about 0.30 – with a strong relationship being anything 0.40 or higher. The maximum is 1.00 which would imply that the two variables are completely correlated with each other.

We correlated levels of hotel construction for FINOR (by microregion) and FUNGETUR/Other Programs (by state) with the *residual* level of hotel employment. Residual employment can be thought of as the "extra" employment that is not explained by the core models of Chapter 2. If government support for hotel construction had any effect on employment net of market factors, then it would affect the amount of hotel employment that existed after the market factors of the core models. The core models make a set of predictions about what they think the level of employment will be in each of the microregions or states. In government investment is also having an effect – it will move the observed employment above or below that expected value. This would make microregions with heavy public investment in hotels to have observed employment levels that are *higher* than the expectations of the model and microregions with little or no public investment in hotels to have observed employment levels that would be *lower* than the expectations of the model. That would produce a high solidly respectable Pearson correlation.

If the government programs don't have much of an effect on employment, then none of the conditions described in the previous paragraph would occur, and the Pearson correlation would be near zero.

In actual fact, the Pearson correlations are near zero. We looked at tests that correlated residual employment with finance activity by FINOR. We looked at tests that correlated residual employment with finance activity by FUNGETUR and the remaining government programs. We looked at tests that correlated residual employment with the number of rooms that were financed. We correlated employment in 1991 with government support in the 1980s. We correlated employment in 2000 with government support in the 1990s. We even looked at lagged specifications that correlated employment in 2000 with investment in the 1980s. We looked at residual hotel employment. We looked at residual restaurant employment – in the hope that the hotel investment might have produced a spillover effect in the tourist sector from which restaurants might have benefitted. In most of the tests, the correlations were dismally low. The technical reader who wants to see the actual Pearson r's is referred to the Appendix *Details of Statistical Results* where a full set of findings is presented. The bottom line is that a solid majority of the tests produce correlations of less than 0.10. Since even a weak relation would come in with a correlation of 0.20, Pearson correlations of less than 0.10 imply that there was no relationship between government financing and employment.

There were a handful of exceptions. We found one test, correlating FINOR financing in the 1990s measured in hotel rooms with residual employment in 2000 which had a correlation of 0.24 – tolerably acceptable. There was a cluster of three correlations that were actually high. The relationships of 1980s FUNGETUR/other hotels to 1991 restaurant employment was 0.54, 1980s FUNGETUR/other rooms to 1991 restaurant employment was 0.57, and 1990s FUNGETUR/other hotels to 2000 restaurant employment was 0.43. If these tests were the only tests of government investment in hotels and restaurant employment, they would show a strong effect of government investment.

However, this is only three out of the eight tests of FUNGETUR/other investment on restaurants. The other five tests all show correlations of less than 0.10. One test is so low that it is actually negative (–0.24) implying that FUNGETUR investment actually hurt restaurant employment. Plus none of the three positive restaurant tests had a parallel positive result for when the same test was run for hotels. How could hotel construction have increased restaurant employment without also increasing hotel employment?

Overall, out of 24 tests, one hotel test and three restaurant tests showed positive results. The remaining 20 tests showed a zero or negative relationship. The general sense of these results is that the subsidy programs for hotels run by FINOR, FUNGETUR and the states did not work.

Results for infrastructure construction: PRODETUR

While the portfolio management programs show results that are negative or at best, ambiguous, the PRODETUR results show solid positive findings. These findings manifest themselves both in the social benefits that came from the infrastructure provided by PRODETUR and from strong effects on residual employment. Restaurants typically did not benefit from PRODETUR. However, the effects on hotels were strong and these effects show up for a number of indicators.

Table 3.2 shows the physical accomplishments of PRODETUR. There can be no question that these results are impressive. The PRODETUR project reconstructed eight airports, built over 1000 km of new highways, laid over 742 km of new water and sewage lines – allowing for over 120,000 new households to be hooked up to a modern water system, created over 27 ecological projects and parks, and restored over 61 different historical buildings. The benefits were widely distributed throughout every state in the Northeast.

Table 3.2   Infrastructure Provided by PRODETUR I 1994–2005 (in millions of US dollars)

Infrastructure	Total
Airports Expansion of 8 Airports	**$223.4**
Highway Projects 1,025 km of New Highway	**$142.2**
Sanitation Projects 742 km of new water/sewage lines 122,043 new hook-ups	**$123.2**
Environmental Conservation 27 Ecological Projects and Parks	**$20.5**
Restoration of Historical Neighborhoods and Buildings 61 Classic Buildings Restored	**$44.1**
Total	**$729.9**

The table excludes various institutional development projects and various administrative expenses from the subtotals. Those items are included in the Total.

Even if PRODETUR had had no effect on tourism whatsoever, the project would have done a great amount of good. The general economic development of the Northeast was undoubtedly accelerated by the expansion of air and road transport capacity. Environmental concerns in the Northeast were greatly assisted by the ecological projects, and by the provision of formal sewer services to over 120,000 households. The sewage and water would have also had tremendous public health impacts, since the lack of sanitation is a primary cause of high infant mortality. The historical preservation and parks significantly improved the leisure options of Northeastern residents. In one particularly successful case, the building of the *orla* (waterfront park) in Aracaju, created a major recreational destination for the city along the beach at Atalaia. This stimulated a burst of new clubs and restaurants that became the major focus of nightlife in the city. However, even if there had been no direct benefit from the airports, the roads, the sewers, or the parks, PRODETUR would have had some beneficial impact through its significant stimulus of the civil construction industry. The sheer number of projects would have produced a significant increase in the short term demand for construction labor. Construction is labor intense and employs both semi-skilled and unskilled workers. Merely the multiplier effect from the wages paid to construction workers would have been an enormous stimulus to the Northeastern economy in the decade from 1995–2005.

However, did PRODETUR produce tourism employment which was the original point of the project? On balance, the record is strongly positive, although there were a few areas in which the effects of PRODETUR were more muted.

In terms of unadjusted statistics, tourism activity and tourism employment grew impressively. Between 1994 and 2003, the number of legally registered tourism establishments in the Northeast grew 485 percent, and the number of workers in tourism related establishments grew 26 percent. (Pedroza and Friere 2005) Between 1994 and 2004, the number of tourists visiting the Northeast more than doubled – increasing 127 percent. Every Northeastern state benefited from this increase, with the slowest growing state – Maranhão – still receiving a 67 percent increase in tourists. Tourist receipts increased 62 percent. Despite a 54 percent increase in the supply of hotel rooms in the Northeast, occupancy rates increased from 48 percent to 56 percent – and again these benefits were generalized throughout every state in the Northeast. (Teles 2005)

In contrast, a set of consultants paid by the Banco do Nordeste to evaluate PRODETUR found no significant employment effects of PRODETUR.

The outside evaluation concurred that the improvement in infrastructure was beneficial for the Northeast, and that raw tourism activity had increased. However, they argued that much of the increase in tourism would have occurred in the absence of PRODETUR. The stabilization of Brazil's economy with the Plano Real of 1994 led to a substantial increase in all forms of consumption including travel. Furthermore, the fall of the real relative to the dollar discouraged international travel and shifted the location of Brazilian vacation travel from overseas to Brazil itself. The Northeast would have benefited greatly from this transition. (Perraza and Tuazon 2006)

Perraza and Tuazon speak to legitimate concerns; however, the effects of PRODETUR were strong enough to be robust to these external considerations. Perraza and Tuazon make a variation of the argument that is made in Chapter 2: changes in employment are functions of exogenous changes in the economy as they are functions of government programs. Therefore, a period with favorable changes in the economy can cast doubts about whether government programs in that period have any independent effect on raising employment.

Put this way, Perraza and Tuazon don't go far enough. There were other important exogenous factors that were raising hotel and restaurant employment at this time. Between 1994 and 2005, the Northeast saw a substantial increase in personal income per capita. Much of this came from an energy boom associated with petroleum extraction in Northeastern waters; an additional factor as well were revivals of the textile industry and citriculture – due in part to other state-led initiatives. (Silva and Hansen 2001) The Northeast also urbanized during this period and with it secular increases in the demand for restaurant food. All of these would have increased the demand for recreational services – and for within-Northeast travel by Nordestinos – even in the absence of PRODETUR.

The strategy for addressing this is to explicitly control for the other factors and to test if PRODETUR made a difference net of these factors. This is difficult to do for volume of visitors, Perraza and Tuazon's dependent variable of interest, because they only have an N of nine – the nine Northeastern states for which tourist arrival data exists. The present analysis concerns employment – a measure of economic well being that is far more fundamental than is tourism arrivals. Having data at the level of microregions, we can consider 186 cases rather than nine and include statistical controls. The variables of the Chapter 2 model – notably personal income, speak to many of the concerns that Perraza and Tuazon raise, in their argument that changes in tourism activity result from exogenous increases in consumer budgets that would have facilitated greater domestic consumption.[5]

To test the effect of PRODETUR projects on employment, we estimated the correlations between the presence of PRODETUR projects that had been completed by the year 2000 and residual employment in hotels and restaurants. The test exactly parallels the test that was done of the effects of FINOR hotels on employment. Since both FINOR and PRODETUR were limited strictly to Northeastern states, only Northeastern microregions are considered. We examined correlations are reported for the presence of a completed water project, presence of a completed sewer project, presence of a completed environmental project (these are generally ecological reserves), presence of a completed road project, presence of a completed bus or hydro-ferry terminal project, presence of a completed urbanization project (generally historical reconstruction of downtowns or construction of urban parks), presence of a completed airport project, the presence of any completed project, and the number of types of projects that had been *completed*.[6] As before, a full summary of correlation coefficients can be found in the Appendix *Details of Statistical Results*.

The overall finding of the table is that PRODETUR had a very strong and favorable effect on promoting employment in hotels. This finding did not carry over into restaurant employment.

We consider the negative finding first – the low correlations between PRODETUR and restaurant employment. Out of nine correlations for restaurant employment and PRODETUR projects, seven out of nine are insignificant. Of the two non-zero correlations, one is positive (water) and the other is negative (urbanization). If these were the only findings, these would be dismal confirmation of the pessimistic worldview of Pedrazza and Tuazon.

These findings need to be tempered however, by the theoretical arguments made in Chapter 2. Restaurant employment is far more likely than hotel employment to be shaped by the economic health of local markets rather than by tourism policies per se. Most customers in restaurants are local residents rather than out-of-town visitors; the overwhelming majority of business for restaurants comes from local workers eating weekday lunches, families and friends having festive meals on the weekends or on weekday nights, or friends socializing in bars. Furthermore, many tourists take their meals in the hotel in which they stay, rather than in the broader community, reducing the impact on local restaurant employment. (This effect is likely to be particularly pronounced when tourists are staying in full service resorts.) Thus, it is not surprising that tourist policy did not have any impact on restaurant employment, and that this employment was determined overwhelmingly by the economic well being of local residents.

The picture is completely different for hotels, a sector that is profoundly affected by the influx of tourists. Out of nine reported correlations, six are positive and statistically significant and a seventh is positive and almost statistically significant. The two observed negative correlations are completely reasonable and represent peculiarities associated with the types of projects involved.

Sanitary infrastructure had particularly strong positive effects on hotel employment. The completion of a sewerage project had the greatest effect of all the projects considered: a correlation of 0.46 between project completion and employment. Water projects had the third strongest effect with a correlation of nearly 0.32. Sewage and water projects promote hotel employment through two obvious mechanisms. Firstly, sanitation makes a place pleasant for visitors. Few upscale tourists want to spend their vacations next to open trenches of untreated waste. Secondly, the provision of basic infrastructure makes hotel construction viable in locations that might otherwise be nonviable for reasons of remoteness. While a small bed and breakfast might be able to tolerate an informal septic tank system, a four or five star hotel with banquet facilities will need substantial quantities of fresh water along with the capacity to dispose of the gray water of a large population.

The second most effective intervention was constructing infrastructure for transportation. Airports, roads and bus terminals had the three most positive correlations with employment, after sanitation improvements. Airport improvements correlated 0.32 with residual hotel employment. Both roads and terminals correlated at 0.21 with hotel employment. The fact that such parallel projects had nearly identical correlations is worthy of note.

It is important for visitors to be able to travel to a tourist location easily. Airports facilitated the arrival of international visitors – and also facilitated travel from distant parts of Brazil. International visitors were particularly valued by PRODETUR because their expenditures help to increase foreign exchange reserves. Not only do airports bring in distant visitors, but they raise the brand awareness of a region's attractions. As will be shown in the next chapter, airports also stimulate non-touristic employment in the rest of the economy. Increased accessibility increases the potential integration of local producers into world markets; this increase in long distance commerce produces a steady flow of business travelers to the region. Visiting business travelers become aware of leisure as well as the commercial potential of the areas that they are visiting. A business traveler in year 1 can become a tourist in year 2, after he learns about the interesting things to do in the region.

Road and terminal projects also increased accessibility and with it hotel employment. Road construction facilitated the development of tourism in rural areas. Airports only deliver tourists to central places. The development of a balanced tourism sector with multiple locations requires road grids to get visitors to these other settings. Road projects also facilitated within-Brazil tourism for visitors who wished to travel by car, a realistic consideration for a middle class that can not always afford airfare. Terminals promoted "popular" tourism, i.e. tourism by lower class visitors. The Brazilian working class generally travels by bus. Better bus facilities promoted "economy class" vacations as rural workers could use public transport to enjoy weekends and holidays in the city.[7]

Microregions with multiple types of projects tended to have higher employment than did microregions with a narrow focus or with no improvements at all. The correlation between the number of types of projects and residual hotel employment was a respectable 0.27. Having any project (one or more versus zero) was correlated at 0.13 with hotel employment. This figure, significant at 0.07 is not very strong, but shows that most PRODETUR projects made some difference in increasing the stock of jobs.

The two types of projects that did not increase employment were environmental projects (with a correlation of −0.23) and urbanization (with a correlation of −0.20). Both of these interventions lowered employment; this drop was statistically significant at the 0.05 level. How does one explain these seemingly perverse effects?

The environmental finding is not perverse at all. The environmental projects generally involved the creation of ecological reserves. The whole point of ecological reserves is to protect an area from commercial development. Ecological reserves promoted tourism not by generating hotel employment in the microregion being preserved, but by creating hotel employment in neighboring microregions which would carry the tourist infrastructure for the area being preserved.

The urbanization finding represents the reality that the urban conservation projects were among the most difficult and slowest programs to implement. Reconstructing an entire historical district is a complex and time-consuming enterprise – with every building requiring separate specialized attention. A historical city center has a lot of buildings. One consequence of this is that rebuilding a downtown generates a lot of construction sites. Even after one has built the new market, refurbished the old cathedral and put new facades on 12 eighteenth-century buildings, there are still a vast number of buildings left to upgrade. Most of those will still be in transition. This means scaffolding and plastic everywhere, the building hidden from view by plywood barriers, trucks coming and going during the day and construction noise that can be a block away. Neighborhoods that are being rebuilt are not especially pleasant places to spend time.

I had an extended visit to Recife in 2006 – after the completion of PRODETUR I and during the execution of a follow-up project: PRODETUR II. Both PRODETURS had scheduled major improvements for the historical center of the city. The center of Recife in 2006 was, frankly, an ugly place. The historical downtown had a few pleasant streets, a wonderful new folk art mall and some charming refurbished buildings. However, there were construction sites everywhere – looking as unappealing as construction sites always do. Where there were no sites, there were rundown buildings that had not yet received their renovation; these were looking more than a little dingy. Even with the lovely products of PRODETUR I, downtown Recife was not a prime tourist location. I have little doubt that when the urban renewal of Recife is finished, the historical center will be gorgeous. However, such complex transformations can take longer than a decade to come about; while these changes occur, the reconstruction process reduces the attractiveness of the older city as a tourist location.

It is worthy of note that PRODETUR ran from 1995 to 2005. The data reported here reports employment in the year 2000 – and correlates it with the effect of projects completed before that date. This means that those PRODETUR projects that were completed after 2000 are undiscussed in these analyses.

The effects of these unfinished products are hard to assess. It could be that including later projects would lower these correlations. Projects that are finished quickly are likely to be well run, well administered projects that faced few administrative difficulties. Problematic projects are more likely to take longer to reach completion – and may be associated with weak effects based on the intrinsic limitations of the project.

Counterbalancing this is the consideration that projects with longer set up times allow for better integration of the publicly provided infrastructure with private sector plans for real estate development. Such "embeddedness" could have produced better designed, more effective private sector responses to the PRODETUR stimuli – leading to a greater impact on employment and growth.

Another counterbalance is that slower projects are likely to have been larger. Larger projects are likely to have a greater impact on local labor markets.

Given the presence of both positives and negatives, it is likely that the effects of the PRODETUR projects completed after 2000 was not that different from those completed before 2000.[8]

Conclusion

The present chapter is the first of a series of analyses that will show the utility of the O'Connorian perspective for analyzing development in the Third World, and in Brazil in particular. O'Connor argued that the provision of infrastructure by the state was a general prerequisite for capitalist development. He placed significantly less emphasis on state correction of failed capital markets. We argued that in the industries we analyzed, Brazilian hotels and restaurants, there was no particular capital market failure. Therefore we predicted that state financed direct investment in firms would not significantly raise employment, while the public provision of infrastructure would have much stronger job creation effects.

For hotels, the data showed this precise pattern. Hotel construction programs had no effect on hotel employment. Infrastructure programs raised hotel employment substantially. Two types of programs, environmental and urbanization, did not have positive effects. However, water programs, sewage programs, airport construction, road construction and terminal construction all raised hotel employment noticeably. Public sanitation raised the attractiveness of potential tourist areas. Water provision made the construction of hotels more feasible. All forms of transportation improvements had positive effects on the hotel sector. Whether visitors were brought in by air, by private automobile or by bus, increasing the accessibility of the city to tourists increased the volume of tourist activity.

The picture is somewhat more complicated in the case of restaurants. Nothing consistently raised restaurant employment. All of the results for restaurants had zero effects, except for portfolio management programs not administered by FINOR in 2000 (but not in 1991). Except for one seemingly aberrant exception, both portfolio management and infrastructure provision programs did not create jobs in restaurants. This reflects the strong sensitivity of restaurants to local economic and market conditions, and the limited potential of any tourism promotion program regardless of strategy to increase demand very much in this sector.

The analysis presented here however, significantly *understates* the impact of infrastructure. This is because we only consider the effect on the tourism sector per se without looking at any spillover effects to other industries. The next chapter looks at the beneficent effects of airport provision on the economy as a whole. We then return in the remaining chapters to other O'Connorian perspectives on employment growth in Brazilian hotels, restaurants and barber/beauty shops.

4

Major Infrastructure and the Larger Economy: The Central Importance of Airports

(with Jessica Schuett)

This chapter takes the O'Connorian argument that states promote economic development by building infrastructure – and expands it beyond the hotel and restaurant sector to the economy as a whole. Nominally, the programs discussed in Chapter 3 were tourism development programs. However, PRODETUR in a deeper way was an infrastructure program, which was meant to have an impact on reducing poverty in Northeast Brazil as a whole. Far more money went into general infrastructure than went into any project that was strictly "touristic". The largest single financial component of PRODETUR was airport construction – representing 30 percent of the total expenditures. The next three largest components were road building, water projects and sanitation. Transportation and sanitary infrastructure have far more effects on an economy than the mere support of tourism; they are critical stimuli to the development of entire economies. Transportation is essential for facilitating agriculture, industry, trade and export. Water and sanitation are critical supports for the housing industry.

Such thinking was explicitly on the minds of the development bankers of the Banco do Nordeste when they commenced designing the PRODETUR initiative. Before the 1990s, most serious development work in the Northeast involved either providing irrigation to combat drought in the Northeast, or providing support for heavy industry. (Banco do Nordeste 1974, Oliviera and Vianna 2005) Tourism was seen by bank functionaries as a private special interest with negligible multipliers into the rest of the regional economy. (Perazza and Tuazon 2006) By the 2000s, there was a more substantial appreciation of the multipliers associated with tourism. However, in the 1990s when PRODETUR was being developed, tourism was largely seen as a vehicle for developing infrastructure. The seven volume document that set out the Development Plan to be used for the Banco do Nordeste in the 1990s had only one thin (although very good) essay on tourism itself. That essay has very little discussion of infrastructure per se. (Friere 1995) A full volume – and a very long one at that – was devoted to infrastructure. That volume calls for extensive development of airports, roads, water and sanitation. This became precisely the main focus of the PRODETUR initiative. Most of the work on developing the PRODETUR initiative came out of the infrastructure branch, rather than the branch on commerce and services per se. (Oliveira and Vianna 2005, Informant Banco do Nordeste 2006) It is not too much to suggest that the linkage of infrastructure to tourism per se was an opportunistic one, designed to make the use of attractive opportunities coming out of the Inter-American Development Bank. The larger goal of the Brazilians was to maximize development overall rather than tourism per se.

Assessing PRODETUR in this light requires considering the general benefits to the economy that accrued from significant additions of infrastructure. The analysis here will only consider one non-tourist effect, an effect however, which is crucial. The present chapter considers the effect on the expansion of airports on economic growth.

There has been little analysis of the effects of airports on growth, even within development economics. The significant exception is the sociologist, John Kasarda. (Irwin and Kasarda 1991, Kasarda and Sullivan 2006) Kasarda essentially correlates employment growth with the volume of air traffic in and out of metropoli. In theory, this ought to be a completely artifactual correlation, since there is an obvious relation between volume of economic activity and the volume of air traffic that is caused by that economic activity.

What makes Kasarda's findings important, and what rescues them from spuriousness, is the use of the hub system by American and foreign airlines. Airlines do not fly point to point between all centers of economic activity; air traffic is channeled to strategic central airports, where both cargo and passengers change flights in order to get to their final destination. Therefore, cities with hub airports receive volumes of air traffic far in excess of that volume needed to support their own locally generated arrivals and departures.

It is this excess traffic that is correlated with job growth and GNP growth in the future. Excess traffic is implicitly a measure of infrastructure. In order to have a hub airport, a city has to invest in substantial runway space, passenger terminal space and cargo terminal space to support the transshipment function. By the standards of physical infrastructure projects, airports are relatively expensive, since they tend to require large amounts of contiguous urban or suburban space, most of which has to be obtained at a premium price. Those cities that have made such an investment have tended to prosper.

Intuitive support for Kasarda's argument comes from the rise of Atlanta at the expense of New Orleans. In the nineteenth century, both cities were equally important centers of Southern commerce and service. Neither city has a locational advantage such as Pittsburgh or Houston, that puts them near stocks of physical raw material used in manufacture. While some of Atlanta's early advantages came from its status as a rail junction, its gigantic take-off in the late twentieth century was centered around the construction and dramatic expansion of Hartsfield Airport, with Delta Airlines using Atlanta as its main hub. New Orleans airport development was desultory, and the city is not associated with any major airline.

Work by the Marxist geographer, Doreen Massey (1974), provides further support for Kasarda's argument. Late twentieth century Britain was marked by a movement of employment away from traditional manufacturing centers in Northern England and Lower Scotland to Souteastern Britain in the area around London. This could not be accounted for by any objective economic advantage of the London area – such as access to population or labor, access to raw material, transportation costs relevant to continental export, or access to an educated labor pool. The key factor was proximity to Heathrow Airport. In the postwar era, there was substantial multinational penetration of the British industrial structure, with American firms buying up a large percentage of important UK employers. The American executives wanted easy physical access to their offices and production facilities and did not want to travel extensively once they arrived in Britain from the United States. So they tended to relocate offices and production centers to facilities within easy commuting distance of Heathrow Airport in West London. This created a substantial secondary wave of British-owned firms relocating to Southeastern England in order to be able to service and work with these key American-owned companies – with the end result being the dramatic de-industrialization of the Northern England.

The present analysis

This chapter follows Kasarda and Massey in analyzing the effects of airports on the economy as a whole. This requires a temporary respite from the methodology used in the rest of the book of analyzing residual employment. It is hard to build convincing models of "what would have happened in the event that no airport had been built". Entire economies, even regional economies, are too complex to model exhaustively. Certainly some control variables could be added to a model, but partially specified models can be more misleading than no models at all. They provide an artificial illusion of scientific precision – that is belied by the large volume of missing variables operating under the surface creating systematic errors.

Therefore, the relationships that are reported are the bivariate relationships between airport expansion and GNP straight up. Any reader can easily identify dozens of variables that could have also affected GNP and would have also contributed to the behavior of the dependent variable. We attempt to deal with these extra variables by a "semi-experimental" analysis. We contrast growth in the same state before and after the construction of an airport, and growth in matched pairs of similar states, where only one member of the pair received an airport. By limiting our contrasts to highly similar cases, we reduce, although do not eliminate, the role of exogenous factors producing a correlation between airports and economic growth. Overall, the balance of cases in both types of contrast shows that airport expansion was helpful; when an airport was expanded, states grew faster than they did before, and faster than did similar states with no airport assistance.

The analysis considers all of Brazil from 1997 to 2004. These years includes the entire period of PRODETUR activity, but also includes states with and without airport expansions in the entire country. Although we only report national findings here, smaller analyses that just limit themselves to the PRODETUR states show results not dissimilar to those in this chapter.

The GDP data are the standard economic indicators that are available from the IPEA (Instituto de Pesquisa Economica Aplicada), (www.ipea. gov.br) the official federal economic research institute for Brazil. The data are available by state and are price corrected (which is extremely important). Series are available for total GDP, agricultural GDP, manufacturing GDP, service GDP (excluding trade) and GDP in retail and wholesale trade. Following Portuguese language conventions, we use the term "commerce" to refer to retail and wholesale trade and "services" to refer to all services except those subsumed in commerce. This is one matter in which Portuguese industrial classification systems are superior to our own.

The airport discussion requires a little understanding of the technical properties and history of Brazilian airports – material that has a few non-intuitive aspects.

Brazilian airports: An introduction

Measuring the capacity of airports raises non-trivial complexities. Most complex institutions have multiple bottlenecks, and airports are no exceptions. An airport can be too small because it does not have enough runways, because those runways are too short for certain types of aircraft, because it lacks the navigational systems to permit the landing of planes in rapid succession, because it lacks cargo capacity or because it lacks passenger terminal capacity. Congonhas, the domestic airport for São Paulo, is shoehorned into the middle of urban development on four sides. It has been historically plagued by a shortage of freight terminals – and excessively short runways which end dangerously close to apartment complexes. Santos Dumont airport in Rio de Janeiro is sandwiched between the city's commercial district and Guanabara Bay with water on three sides. This location made enormous sense in the era of hydroplanes – but when Santos Dumont was the only airport in Rio de Janeiro, it left Rio with some of the shortest runways in Brazil. A second airport, Tom Jobim, was constructed in Rio to compensate for Santos Dumont. It has the longest runways in Brazil. (Gazeta Mercantil 1997)

Table 4.1   Significant Passenger Terminal Expansions in Brazil 1997–2004

Year of Airport Expansion	Airport	State
1997	Porto Seguro	Bahia
1998	Fortaleza-Pinto Martins	Ceará
1998	Imperatriz	Maranhão
1998	São Luis-Marechal Cunha Machado	Maranhão
1998	Pelotas	Rio Grande do Sul
1998	Boa Vista	Roraima
1998	Aracaju-Santa Maria	Sergipe
1999	Rio Branco	Acre
1999	Rio de Janeiro-Galeão/Antonio Carlos Jobim	Rio de Janeiro
2000	Salvador-Dep. Luís Eduardo Magalhães	Bahia
2000	Curitiba-Afonso Pena	Paraná
2000	Natal-Augusto Severo	Rio Grande do Norte
2001	Belém-Val de Cans	Pará
2001	Porto Alegre	Rio Grande do Sul
2002	Juazeiro do Norte-Cariri	Ceará

Source: See Text.
Airports are listed by City Name and then when appropriate by Airport Name.

Airports can be handicapped by more than just terminal capacity and runway length, however. In 2006–2007, air traffic in Brazil was nearly paralyzed by a capacity shortage brought on by underdevelopment of the national radar control network. (Wikipedia, Apagao Áereā de 2006)

The measure used in this analysis is passenger terminal capacity – the number of passengers airport terminals can process in a single day. Passenger terminal capacity is an extremely important bottleneck. It is not hard to land many planes on a small number of runways – but it is harder to find space for those planes to load and unload once they are on the ground. In the 1990s and 2000s, passenger terminal size was the critical factor limiting the expansion of air travel in the Brazil; The Gazeta Mercantil of 1997 noted that terminal overcrowding was a critical issue at most Brazilian airports – while runway provision was in most cases adequate.

The period between 1997 and 2004 saw the biggest wave of airport reconstructions in Brazilian history. The contrast with previous history was striking. In the 1950s and 60s, there had been isolated construction projects in very large cities, such as São Paulo and Rio de Janeiro, along with the development of modest airfields in regional centers. Over the next two decades, these airports grew, with a few of the largest Brazilian cities getting a second airport. However, none of this relatively slow growth came close to the near explosion of airport construction that occurred in the late 90s and early 2000s. Starting in 1997, there were no fewer than 15 major airport expansions in eight years, implying growth at the unprecedented rate of two major projects a year. These expansions occurred in every region of Brazil, both rich and poor, both urbanized and frontier.

Very few of these expansions involved new runway construction – or runway expansion. All of them involved new terminals. The increases in capacity were generally very substantial – raising the potential flow through of passengers 50 percent to 100 percent. This was often associated with other significant efficiency measures like the introduction of snorkels rather than outdoor ramps for disembarkation, and the addition of mechanical baggage systems.

Since most of the historical changes in airports during this period involved passenger terminals, we use passenger terminal improvements as our measure of airport upgrades. To measure the history and timing of terminal upgrades, a variety of sources were consulted. Nearly all sources of information are partial and nearly all sources contain some errors, requiring careful cross-checking to generate consistent valid estimates. The primary data sources is the Infraero website http://www.infraero.gov.br/usa/aero.php which contains statistical summaries and histories of every major airport in Brazil. The Gazeta Mercantil (1997) published a history of Brazilian airports that has exhaustive information on the largest Brazilian airports. EMBRATUR, the Brazilian tourism ministry, published its own collection of airport data in 2001. Lastly in the Northeast, the final report for PRODETUR has complete information on the airport improvements financed by that program.

Historical contrasts of states before and after airport expansion

One of the most logical tests of the effects of airport expansions on GNP, is whether the GDP growth rate increases after the airport has been expanded. Before and after contrasts within states that received terminal expansions test to see if the airport had any noticeable effect.

To get an intuitive grasp on the issue, graphs were produced showing changes in GDP rates over time. To simplify the analysis, all state level annual rates of change in GDP were recalibrated so that the "average" rate of change among all states was treated as 0.[1] These simplified graphs showed clear successes, clear failures and a number of ambiguous cases.

Figure 4.1   Paraná: An Example of a Success Case

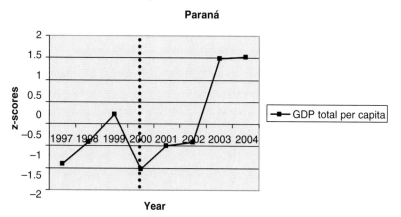

········ *Paraná's airport Curitiba-Afonso Pena received a new passenger terminal in 2000, which allowed for a passenger capacity to expand from 800,000 to 2,500,000.*

Figure 4.1 shows Paraná which was a clear success case. The airport was constructed in 2000 – when growth rates for the state were declining. The rate of decline was immediately reduced; by 2003 and 2004, decline had turned into strong dramatic growth. In contrast, the years before the airport construction in 2000 showed mediocre growth with only one exception, a good year in 1999. Overall, growth rates were much better after the airport than before the airport.

Figure 4.2   Fortaleza-Pinto Martins: An Example of a Failure Case

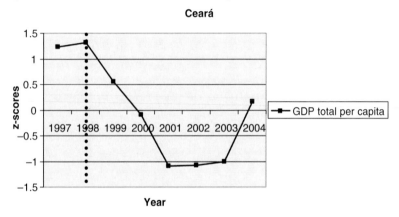

········ *Fortaleza-Pinto Martins received a new passenger terminal in 1998 that allowed the passenger capacity to increase from 900,000 to 2,500,000.*

Figure 4.2 shows a clear failure case, Pinto Martins airport, in Ceará in Fortaleza. The airport expansion was in 1998, the year with the highest growth rate of the period. Growth rates immediately declined after that, turning negative for most of the post 2000 period.

Not all cases lead to unambiguous interpretations. Some cases have to be treated as "neutral" because the data do not allow for even a crude bivariate judgment of whether airport expansions are associated with improving or worsening GNP. This can occur when there is extreme instability on both sides of the airport expansion; however it is more likely to occur when there is a consistent trend upward or downward in growth rates that continues on through the airport expansions.

Figure 4.3 shows an ambiguous case – the case of Natal-Severino in Rio Grande do Norte. Rio Grande do Norte has been enjoying consistent improvements in the rate of growth of their GDP. On one hand, all rates of growth after the airport expansion were higher than the

Figure 4.3   Natal-Augusto Severo: An Example of an Ambiguous Case

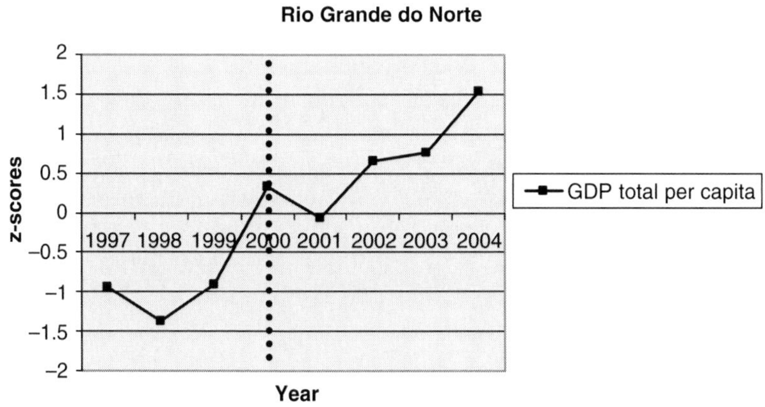

Rio Grande do Norte

·········· *Nata-Augusto Severo received a new passenger terminal in 2000 that allowed for the passenger capacity to increase from 550,000 to 1,500,000.*

rates of growth before the airport. However, the rate of improvement was high before the airport, making it unclear whether the airport or some exogenous factor produced the growth. In cases such as these, there was little choice but to remain agnostic and treat the state as an indeterminate finding.

Graphs were drawn for all states with airport expansions and for total GNP and GNP in agriculture, commerce, industry and service individually. There were 14 cases overall, since out of 15 airports, two were built in the same state in the same year – Maranhão in 1998. Using the criteria described above, graphs were coded as showing success, failure or representing ambiguous cases.

For every sector except services and industry, a majority of the cases were clear successes. 64 percent of all the analyses of total GDP, agriculture, and commerce showed higher growth rates after the airport expansion than before the airport expansion. The finding is still positive but weaker in the industry sector: 50 percent of all the cases were successful – but only 43 percent of the cases were failures, leading to more successes than failures. In contrast, in services industry only 36 percent of the cases were successful, while 64 percent failed. Note that not only did the majority of tests show clear success, but on the most important measure, total GNP, the majority of cases showed clear success. For total GNP, there were three times as many successes as failures.

Overall, the record on the in-state analyses is fairly positive.

Matched state contrasts

Historical before-and-after analyses are informative. However, they include no information on states which did not receive airport expansions. How can material on non-expansions be incorporated into the analysis?

In this section, airport states are matched with similar non-airport states – to determine if the state that received an airport outperformed its own clone. Analyses of this nature are useful but not perfect. There are no identical twins among Brazilian states; each state is as unique as a fingerprint. Thus all pairings are intrinsically pseudo-pairings – and differences between members of a pseudo-pair could reflect some intrinsic difference rather than airport expansion per se. The credibility

Table 4.2   State Matchings with Justifications

State with Airport Expansion	State without Airport Expansion	Reason for Pairing
Acre	Rondonia	Small Amazonian states – Southern tier
Bahia	Pernambuco	Both industrialized northeastern states
Bahia	Espírito Santo	Neighboring oil states
Bahia	Minas Gerais	Industrialized states with sertão
Ceará	Piauí	Neighboring Northeastern states
Maranhão	Piauí	Neighboring Northeastern states
Maranhão	Tocantins	Neighboring Amazonian states (Maranhão has both sertão and Amazonian forest)
Pará	Amazonas	Large Amazonian states
Paraná	Santa Catarina	Wealthy neighboring states
Rio de Janeiro	São Paulo	Very large industrialized states in southeastern core
Rio Grande do Norte	Piauí	Neighboring northeastern states
Rio Grande do Sul	Santa Catarina	Wealthy neighboring states
Roraima	Amápa	Small Amazonian states – northern tier
Sergipe	Alagoas	Small Northeastern neighboring states

of the matched analyses depends on two factors: a) the degree to which the reader agrees with the pairings that are made and b) the number of tests that are run. The more tests that are run, the less likely it is that a positive result is the result of all of the outside factors "just happening by coincidence", to produce a pro-airport finding, and the more likely it is that the airport expansions themselves are producing the observed differences.

Table 4.2 shows the state match-ups that were made. Fourteen different pairings were made of airport and non-airport states. Neighbors were matched with neighbors of the same size. Industrial states were matched with other industrial states of the same region.

For each pair, contrasts were made in every sector that was included in the previous section. In all cases, growth rates for each observed year were contrasted with the growth rate of the year that the airport was expanded in the airport state, so long as the observed year occurred after the airport expansion in the airport state. For each airport, all possible matched pairs were considered, and data for all years after the airport reconstruction was used. Since every state had five different measures of GDP, there were 70 possible tests overall. Not all cases allowed for unambiguous interpretation. Life was simple when one state outperformed another for most of the years that were contrasted. Life became more complex when there were years with true ties – or when one state outperformed the other in some years but not others. As a result, we consider simple and complex cases separately.

Overall, the contrasts using total GDP show that airports dramatically increased overall economic growth. Consider total GDP first. In the simple cases, where one state outperformed the other for most years, 80 percent of the cases showed airport states outperforming states without airport expansions. There were 57 of these. Furthermore, all of the complicated cases that were not dead heat ties had airport states out performing non-airport states. There were four complex cases of this nature. There were no ties here. (There would be ties on other tests.) Thus looking at all the cases, strong, weak and tie alike has 76 percent of the cases showing an advantage to states which received airports.

The findings are also basically positive in agriculture. Sixty-nine percent of all unambiguous cases were showed airport states outperforming non-airport states. Sixty-four percent of all cases showed a good result for airports.

Airports also improved performances in services. Seventy-five percent of all unambiguous cases were positive; 71 percent of all cases were positive.

The findings for commerce are much weaker but still supportive. Fifty-five percent of all unambiguous cases were positive. Fifty-seven percent of all cases were positive.

The one true adverse outcome was in industry. In industry, only 36 percent of all unambiguous cases were positive. Only 29 percent of the complete set of cases were positive.

The majority of matched state tests showed positive effects of airport development. Sixty-three percent of all unambiguous cases showed airport states outperforming non-airport states. Sixty-one percent of all cases showed the same thing. The overall findings – plus the very strong positives reported for total GDP, the most important measure in the study, provide confirmation of the results for the within-state comparisons: airports promoted economic growth.

What sectors benefited from airport expansion?

Table 4.3 summarizes the results of the previous analyses by indicating whether airports had a positive, ambiguous or negative effect on GDP growth – for each sector and for each type of test.

Airports clearly raised total GDP, and GDP in agriculture. Most tests showed a positive relationship between airports and GDP.

GDP had a positive effect on commerce in within state analyses and a weak ambiguous effect in the matched state analyses. Probably overall, the effect of airports in this sector are positive but not markedly so.

The situation in services is very indeterminate with within state analyses showing negative results and across state analyses showing positive results. Nothing more on this question can be said for services.

Table 4.3   Summary of Results by Sector: Relationship of Airport Expansion to GDP Growth

	Total GDP	Agriculture	Commerce	Industry	Services	All Tests
Within State Analyses	+	+	+	?	–	+
Matched State Analyses	+	+	?	–	+	+

Industry showed a probable negative effect. The effect was strongly negative in across state analyses – and at best ambiguous in within state analyses.

Overall, the important finding is that airports promoted total GDP and that the majority of all tests were positive. However, considering which sectors benefited airports provides useful information about how airports produce growth. The strongest effect was on agriculture. This is highly consistent with airports facilitating the development of export agriculture where freshness and perishability are of prime concern. The Northeast during this period experienced a significant diversification of its agricultural output, with significant moves away from the traditional monoculture of sugar and from subsistence agriculture, towards new export crops, notably of fruit. Rapid air freight out of the Northeast – that can avoid preliminary transshipment to the major airports of the Southeast – significantly improves product quality and makes Northeastern fruit far more competitive in world markets.

The effect on industry was significantly lower. Note that Brazil does not really emphasize maquiladora-style cheap labor-based light manufacture for export. Maquiladoras are an important component of the economy of the state of Amazonas, where Manaus has an important free trade zone. (Mueller 1981, Despres 1991) However, this represents a negligible share of total Brazilian industry. Maquiladora production benefits from the capacity to rapidly export lightweight products. Textiles, computer components and small appliances benefit from airports. However, most of Brazilian industry is in sectors for which air transportation is less important. The most important Brazilian industries are oil production, steel production and automobile manufacture. Oil production and steel production locate their facilities next to sources of raw ingredients. (Estall and Buchanan 1965) Airports have no effect on moving iron or gas deposits. Automobiles are heavy and are generally moved by surface transport. In Brazil, this often means water transport, since many of the most important centers of population are conveniently located on the Atlantic Coast. Access to airports is relatively unimportant for this industry as well. If Brazil's industrial composition had been different, industry might have been more responsive to airport construction. However, the pre-existing industrial mix lowered the relevance of air transport.

Both commerce and services showed some positive responses. The ambiguous nature of their findings probably reflects heterogeneity within each sector, as some sub-industries are likely to be more responsive to airports than others. In commerce, wholesale trade is likely to benefit more from airports than retail trade. Wholesale trade is likely to be more responsive to airports than retail trade, particularly wholesale trade that is focused on international markets. Warehouses are likely to be located next to critical export facilities; having good airport connections to the outside world justifies building distribution centers near centers of air transport. In contrast, retail trade is likely to be responsive only to changes in population and income – which will have only indirect links to airport expansion.

Services are likely to have very heterogeneous responses to airport access. Tourism greatly benefits from access to airports – as was shown in the analyses of Chapter 4. Financial, information and media services may benefit from airports, when the rapid movement of key personnel is judged to be an important dynamic of that sector, Note that services that take care of corporate headquarters are particularly likely to benefit from such dynamics. Other services seem likely to be less responsive. Government employment will depend on population size per se, particularly to the extent to which such public service involves providing for the needs of local residents. Education, policing and state supported medical services all fit this description. Other forms of service such as domestic cleaning, security, and barber/beauty also seem to be linked to population size.

Conclusion

So airports benefit the economy as a whole. They affect some sectors of commerce and services. They have a very substantial effect of commercial agriculture, and the sectors that have multiplier links to commercial agriculture. This shows that "tourism" policy had effects on far more than merely the tourism sector. It also supports the main argument of Chapter 4 that building infrastructure is a critical mechanism by which governments produce economic growth – and raise employment above levels that would have been expected from market forces alone.

The discussion thus far has narrowly focused on physical infrastructure. However, O'Connor writes about social infrastructure too. Education and human capital formation are fundamental responsibilities of the state – and are central to maintaining economic growth. The analysis now turns to education – and specifically – a form of education that is highly germane to employment policy – vocational education. Job training programs are a key state policy for reducing unemployment. Did such policies work in Brazil?

5
How Brazilian Vocational Education Reduces Poverty – Even If No One Wants to Hire the Trainees

One of the most important public policies for the reduction of unemployment is the promotion of job training and vocational education. Of all the O'Connorian state interventions, Vocational training is one of the most appealing. Education is clearly correlated with favorable labor market outcomes; workers with more education are consistently more likely to be employed and more likely to enjoy higher incomes. (Becker 1964, Blau and Duncan 1967)

There is also substantial concern that many Third World nations are uncompetitive in world markets because the quality of their education is so low. (Ferranti et al. 2003, Urani 1997, Pochmann 1999, Londono 1996) Raising the quality of the human capital of the labor force usually means simultaneous attention to primary, secondary, university and vocational education. The vocational education has the advantage that participants in such programs enter the labor force with shorter lag times than students in primary, secondary or university education – and that such training is often tightly linked to actual productive skills.

Vocational education is relatively inexpensive. This is especially important in O'Connorian logic because the primary threat to the state reproduction of capitalism is fiscal crisis. Inexpensive programs are a reasonable defense against fiscal crisis. The amount of money necessary to run training programs is far less than that required to construct physical infrastructure or support a capital intensive infant industry. In fact Bartik (2001) argues that the costs are so low that even if the effects of vocational training were to be very weak indeed, the cost efficiency of these programs would more than justifying their continuation and support.

Furthermore, vocational education is under the control of the state itself. Unlike many other programs that may require extensive assistance from actors external to the state, such as capitalists, governments have the full capacity to create whatever vocational education programs they like at will.

As a result, vocational education figures prominently in the employment policies of most countries. It plays a prominent role in the active labor market strategies of Scandinavia and Central Europe. (Streeck 1992, Lynch 1994) State financed job training is in fact a nearly universal feature of governmental responses to unemployment in advanced capitalist societies and in the underdeveloped world. (Heckman Lalonde and Smith 1999) The International Labor Office has identified over 26 Third World nations with highly developed systems of vocational education (Galhardi and Mangozho 2003) There are substantial international differences in the balance of public and private training – and equally important differences in how these programs are organized. (Muller and Gangl 2004) Likewise, there are importance differences in the level of funding of these programs, and the degree to which some programs are integrated with the preferences of local employers. Some authors have reservations about the effectiveness of programs that are underfunded, or are poorly integrated with local industry. Even with these reservations, there is still widespread consensus that, properly executed, vocational education is effective and can be an important component of any active labor market program. (Heckman et al. 1999, Bartik 2001)[1]

This chapter will argue that vocational education is a useful tool for job creation in the Third World. However, it does not always work in the stereotypical way that most academics imagine. Normally when we think of job training, we think of giving workers skills – and they use these skills to obtain employment in firms that require advanced skills. The dynamics of vocational education in underdeveloped countries are completely different from those that pertain to advanced industrial economies. In particular, in the Third World:

1) Job training does not need to raise the human capital of trainees to be effective, although it may do so, and the skill upgrade does no harm.
2) Job training is not especially effective at increasing employment in capitalist firms.
3) Job training works by increasing opportunities for entrepreneurship and self-employment.

4) What increases employment is the mobilization of social capital to support recent trainees which in turn increases aggregate demand in the field in which vocational education was provided.

In principle, job training works in a manner similar to the *economia solidária*, the new wave of alternative economic mobilizations in Latin America intended as a counter to globalization. In the *economia solidária*, communities attempt to increase aggregate employment by explicit attempts to provide help and assistance to local workers to allow them to maintain their jobs in a harsh economic environment. Such support is generally mobilized under the rubrics of social movements making nationalist or progressive ideological appeals. (Singer and de Souza 2000, Dal Ri 1999)

However, family and friendship can be as strong of a basis of mutual support as any invocation of any invocation of the defense of a national or regional economy. In this case, vocational education works, because it provides an inducement for family and friends to support the newly trained worker. Such social support is irrelevant to an employee in a capitalist firm – but very important for a self-employed worker who is trying to keep his or her fledgling enterprise alive.

Most readers will be somewhat surprised by the claim that job training does not always work by raising the technical capacity of workers – and will be even more surprised by the claim that it is not very effective in the capitalist sector. To understand why job training is so effective using non-standard mechanisms, it is necessary to understand why the standard mechanisms associated with job training tend to fail. So this discussion of the enormous positive potential of job training starts – ironically – with a discussion of its weaknesses.

The cynical case against vocational education

Most authors agree that vocational education raises the employment and income prospects for workers. The doubts that exist in the literature concern the mechanism by which this occurs. There are questions about whether the positive results achieved by job training reflects the selective recruitment of more able students into vocational education programs, rather than any teaching provided by the programs themselves. There are questions about how well these programs are articulated with the hiring needs of local employers. There are questions about whether the benefits of receiving training are short or long term. These questions about "how job training works" have substantial implications for how those programs ought to be organized to guarantee the maximum impact. (Heckman et al. 1999, Bartik 2001, Ryan 2001, Stern et al. 1995, Orr et al. 1994, Rios-Neto and Oliveira 2000, Lafer 2002)

A significant question is whether success of a program is defined on an aggregate or on an individual basis. *Aggregate success* on the aggregate level would mean that a vocational education program raises employment in the region where it is implemented. There would be more jobs in places with job training than in places without job training. *Individual success* means that students who enroll in vocational training have better labor market results than students who do not. A comparison of recipients of training with a control group would find higher rates of employment and income for the experimental group than for the control group.

Note that the presence of individual success does not guarantee that a program is an aggregate success. This is because of the possibility of a "displacement" effect – the threat that workers who have received vocational training may be hired by employers who then fire or don't hire workers without the training. The total number of employed people would remain the same. All that the vocational training would do is to reallocate a fixed number of jobs among a different set of job-seekers. The displacement effect has been documented in previous evaluations of vocational education (Heckman et al. 1999, Calmfors 1994, Davidson and Woodbury 1993), making the difference between individual and aggregate success a legitimate issue.

From the standpoint of politicians who are self-interested office seekers, all that needs to occur is that a job training program be an individual success. An individual success produces a happy set of job holders who can attribute their good fortune to participation in a job program. Because the people who do not get jobs are likely to attribute their misfortune to bad economic conditions or general hard times for employers, a job program that is an individual success produces a body of voters who are very satisfied with government programs, and no body of voters who are necessarily displeased with government programs. This is a net electoral gain. This consideration alone virtually guarantees that governments will invest in job training programs of one kind or another.

From the standpoint of politicians who are interested in public policy and reducing poverty, the standards are higher. A job program needs to be an aggregate success – making the district objectively better off. Aggregate success is the criterion for evaluating vocational education that is used here – since the definition of state effectiveness used here is raising employment and income above market levels. This implies that a large percentage of the literature evaluating job training is somewhat irrelevant for present purposes – since those studies exclusively involve comparisons of the labor market experience of trainees and non-trainees, a measure of individual rather than aggregate success.[2]

What conditions would lower the aggregate effectiveness of state financed job training programs? Vocational education is particularly likely to produce no increase in aggregate employment – when the provision of government financed job training does not increase the overall total amount of training that is provided in an economy. This occurs when state financed training substitutes for training that employers in the private sector would have provided anyway.

Such trade-offs are likely to be particularly common in the Third World. This is because the amount of training that employers provide is directly related to the size of the reservation wage. The reservation wage is the minimum wage that a worker would accept in order to participate in employment. It is not necessarily the same as the legal minimum wage. If the legal minimum wage is $8 an hour, but some workers would work for $4 an hour then $4 is the reservation wage. In the Third World, reservation wages are very low. This makes the cost of training workers very low. The low cost of training workers makes it economically rational for employers to do all of their training themselves, eliminating much of the relevance of government financed job training programs.

In a perfect neoclassical labor market, employers provide all the training they need. Under conditions of perfect competition, workers' wages equal marginal productivity (Hicks 1963). Training has the effect of lowering a worker's productivity. It can lower productivity because the worker is not producing while he receives instruction, because an under-trained worker produces scrap during the learning process and because other workers and resources have to be committed to training the worker as opposed to producing output directly. However, if wages can be reduced to reflect the low productivity associated with the training process, then there is no economic obstacle to the employer providing such training.[3]

In advanced economies, government job training is necessary because workers have reservation wages that are higher than the marginal wage necessary to justify their employment during the training period. These reservation wages are maintained by minimum wage laws, and where applicable, by union contracts and labor scarcity. Because there is a floor below which wages cannot fall, there are some forms of training that are uneconomic for employers to provide. They are thus dependent on the state to make up for this shortfall.

There are few barriers to low wages in the Third World setting. On paper, most Third World nations have generous labor laws that specify minimum wages and generous fringe benefits. (De Soto 1989, Pastore 1997) In practice, these can be easily evaded. The most common strategy for avoiding minimum wage laws is to hire workers informally. (Rakowski 1994, Thomas 1992) Alternatively, employers can register their workers and misrepresent their working conditions – or register their workers and count on weak enforcement of labor codes. Any of these strategies permits the payment of sub-minimum wages.

The presence of a substantial reserve army of labor produces vast numbers of workers who would be willing to work at any wage – and a large population of firms who would have no compunctions about paying extremely low wages. (Behrman 1999) Third World employers can thus easily finance the costs of training by having workers absorb these costs in the form of lower earnings.

In this case, the risk of displacement, and of job training programs being ineffective at the aggregate level is very real.

The previous arguments have empirical backing. Heckman et al. (1999) reviewed the empirical literature on the effectiveness of job training programs in the United States and Europe. A consistent finding of their review is that experimental designs that measure the relative attainments of individual trainees against a control group show far greater effects for job training programs than do more ecological designs that test whether job training increases aggregate employment or income. This is highly consistent with the existence of widespread displacement.

They also found significantly greater effects for job training programs in Europe than in the United States. Some of this may be due to better funding for European programs or better integration of those programs with employer short-term needs. However, it is also consistent with reservation wages being linked to the effectiveness of state financed job training. Reservation wages are likely to be higher in Europe than in the United States due to the more extensive welfare state that exists in Europe. Europe also has a broader and more inclusive social safety net, and higher minimum compensation packages once mandatory fringe benefits are included. All three factors would lower the willingness of a European to work for a substandard wage. This makes it necessary for the European governments to subsidize vocational education. In the United States, there are lower reservation wages, and as a result, employers do more training on their own. This produces the empirical result of American job programs being less effective.

Claudio Dedecca (1998) has proposed an interesting alternative form of this argument. He argues that job skill demands in Brazil, if not the Third World as a whole, are falling. Even if in principle, the national economy would be better off with a skills upgrade, the de facto occupational mix implies declining employer demand for skill. Thus, even though the recipients of government financed job training have a higher likelihood of obtaining employment, this merely reflects Thurowian screening (1975) or Spencian (1975) signaling – the tendency of employers to hire the most educated workers available regardless of whether that education increases productivity in the workplace. Dedecca argues that declining skill profiles imply that employers already have sufficient human capital at their disposal and that government financed job programs will have no effect on aggregate employment.

Both the cynical argument presented here and that of Dedecca suggest that job training would provide no improvement in overall employment and income.[4] However, the analysis that follows will show that these vocational education was a powerful tool for raising aggregate employment. What mechanisms exist that can counteract these otherwise discouraging forces?

Third World job training as social capital rather than human capital

The previous section assumed that all of the positive effects of vocational education are subsumed in their effects on human capital. However, vocational education can provide stimulate significant development of social capital that is in and of itself a tool for economic expansion. The previous section also assumed that the graduates of job training programs seek employment as employees in pre-existing firms – i.e. they go to work for someone else and they are not self-employed. The entire logic of the analysis changes when graduates become self-employed.

If the graduate of a vocational education program becomes self-employed – and through his or her efforts they can increase the overall demand for products in their industry – then there is no displacement, and vocational education raises aggregate employment.

Self-employed graduates expand the demand for products in their industry by exercising social capital.

The problems of the previous section can be averted if vocational education creates new jobs through the creation of new firms. A trainee who becomes self-employed replaces no workers in the pre-existing firms. This eliminates the one fundamental cause of displacement.

For displacement to not occur, it is also the case that new firms must not cannibalize business from pre-existing firms. Otherwise this would displace employment from old firms to new. To avoid cannibalization altogether, the new firms must expand the demand for the products of the industry, creating a positive-sum game in which workers in old and new firms both benefit. Thus, in essence, employment grows because new entrepreneurs enter the field and these entrepreneurs expand the total production and sales of the sector.

Vocational training works by increasing the social capital of entrepreneurs rather than the human capital of employees. Social capital is not increased when the student actually takes the vocational training courses – but social capital is increased afterwards, when the student uses his or her social network to support a new fledgling business.

It is well known that social capital helps struggling jobseekers obtain jobs (Granovetter 1985, Fernandez 2006) and provides networks of assistance for established businesses. (Uzzi 1996, 1999) The same relationships apply to infant entrepreneurs trying to start their own microenterprises. In this case, friends and family of graduates of job training programs assist the entrepreneurs in starting their new business by contributing capital or by serving as customers. These voluntary contributions represent new investments or new consumption that helps to increase aggregate demand and expand the industry in which the graduate was trained.

Consider the job prospects of new vocational trainees. Some lucky individuals will obtain formal or informal employment in pre-existing firms in their chosen industry. However, not all trainees will be this fortunate. The students who do not obtain employment in a pre-existing firm have only two choices. They can leave the industry, thus losing their investment in training – or they can start a new firm as a microentrepreneur.

Neither of these are particularly attractive options. For members of the lower working class who have extremely limited resources, tuition fees for job training programs can represent a very sizable financial investment. Leaving the industry would mean taking what for them is a very substantial monetary loss.

Starting a new firm is a very hazardous proposition for a recent trainee. Microenterprises by nature involve significant risk. More than half of all new firms die in their first year – a fact which is as true for Brazil as for the rest of the world. (SEBRAE 2004) The new entrepreneur is going to need a place of business, equipment, supplies, and a set of customers, much of which is going to require investment in order to obtain.

Microentrepreneurs who choose to stay within the industry may need a great deal of help in order to survive. This is where social capital becomes important. Graduates of training programs who have friends and family with financial resources can turn to them for assistance in setting up their new business. Parents and friends can buy equipment; they can buy supplies. They can volunteer space in a home or a workplace where the student can do their work. They can purchase goods and services from the student.

The purchase of goods and services by family and friends hoping to assist the student represents a form of Keynesian expansion of the economy. If the members of the social support net would not have purchased these goods or services in the absence of a personal connection to the microentrepreneur, then the act of social support represents an increase in aggregate consumption that would not have occurred otherwise. Increasing consumption increases overall economic activity and stimulates aggregate employment.

A related argument applies to the solidaristic provision of equipment, working supplies or space by family and friends to the student starting a business. To some extent, the purchase of equipment or supplies that would not have been purchased otherwise represents another form of expansion of demand via increasing demand for capital goods.

More importantly however, the new business receives its capital stock at a substantial subsidy. Part of the business person's working capital has been provided at no financial cost. The lower cost profile allows the new business to lower prices. By lowering prices, his or her goods and services become more attractive to the general public. Discounting increases the volume of goods and services that are sold – possibly providing enough economic activity to keep the fledgling enterprise in business.

Clearly, the use of social capital to provide subsidized inputs to allow for the survival of new firms through discounting implies relatively low earnings at the beginning of the microentrepreneur's career. Discounting may become less important when the new firm becomes established, and the student has a regular stock of customers and can pay for equipment and materials with earnings – but it does not get around real questions of financial hardship during the initial phases of the creation of a firm. Furthermore, the presence of discounting may lower income in other more established firms, as they have to compete with the prices set by new trainees.

However, if the overall income potential of the industry is sound, the social capital investments made by family and friends provide a way for a larger stock of workers to share in the market and enjoy stable employment. The increased sales from discounting do represent a positive sum gain for workers in the industry.

Note that none of this is available to sectors characterized by capitalist employment. Family and friends do not have to purchase equipment or material for a new employee starting a regular job.[5] Likewise a capitalist firm would not have a stock of goodwill donations that would allow it to lower costs and hire more workers. People call on solidaristic aid when they are in trouble. An adolescent starting a career with no experience or assets, or a poor man or woman trying to start a business out of nothing, can generate some sympathy from people in their social network who might want to help them. The desperation associated with these two vulnerable groups legitimates requests for what is frankly charity. An established business which wishes to expand is typically not viewed as a legitimate recipient of philanthropy. Some family businesses may be able to invoke ties of mutual assistance. Entrepreneurs in strong ethnic networks may agree to exchanges of mutual investment. However, established firms are less likely to be able to count on the receipt of outright gifts.

The gift relationship is what facilitates the survival of the weakest of microentrepreneurs. Vocational education represents a commitment mechanism that produces a stock of potential microentrepreneurs who need gifts and support. The stock of gifts represents a supply of subsidized capital – and this increased investment increases demand and raises employment.

The present analysis

This chapter illustrates these principles by showing that that vocational training worked differently in hotels, restaurants and barber/beauty in Brazil. This contrast matters because these three industries differ significantly in the opportunities they offer for self-employment. We then show that in the industry where vocational training had the most effect, barber/beauty, that social capital and the use of social network support was critical for the survival of barbers and beauticians who were struggling after obtaining their initial training in hairdressing skills. We interview a number of successful and unsuccessful barbers and beauticians in Sergipe, a state with an extremely ambitious and large-scale program of hairdressing training. The successful ones survived by generating financial contributions from members of their social networks. The unsuccessful ones were left to their own devices and were ultimately driven from the industry.

Hotel workers have less access to self-employment than do the other two sectors and thus the sector is less likely to show positive employment effects associated with job training. Hotels have substantial capital-based barriers to entry – since to start a hotel, one must have a building with rooms to rent for lodging. Some lower class families do take lodgers into their home – but generally, access to a structure nice enough to support a bed and breakfast, or a full fledged hotel is beyond the means of most working poor.

Restaurants have greater opportunities for new entrepreneurs. A food and beverage operation catering to working class customers can be very modest. In Brazil, a microentrepreneur can go to a vacant lot, put up a tarpaulin shade, set up some chairs and tables, a sound system, a barbecue grill and a cooler full of beer, and he or she has the makings of a humble but successful outdoor café. Furthermore, many cities provide subsidized spaces in places such as public markets and bus stations, where very small businessmen can set up a stand with a grill and a cooler and sell food and beverages to the passing crowd.

The barber and beauty sector has the greatest capacity for independent entrepreneurship. This is because hairdressers don't even require an official place of work to ply their trade. Hairdressers if need be can operate out of their own homes. Some of the beauticians who are interviewed in this chapter, in fact do just that.

In the nineteenth century, all commercial hairdressing in Brazil was provided in this manner; the development of barber shops and beauty salons in commercial settings was a twentieth century phenomenon. (Dweck 1998, Wynne 1973) Since young hairdressers do not need to acquire a place of business, they can acquire their capital stock slowly purchasing one piece of equipment at a time as their microbusiness grows. Not only does this provide ample scope for self-employment, but it provides opportunities for the types of assistance from family and friends that increase the viability of Third World vocational education.

The chapter considers the effect of SENAC training on aggregate employment in the three industries for 1991 and 2000. SENAC is the primary source of state supported vocational education in the service sector in Brazil. A brief introduction is given to the history of SENAC and the extent of its training programs. In particular, the argument is made that the quantity of students participating in SENAC service sector programs increased dramatically at the end of the twentieth century raising a significant potential risk of displacement. We then show the statistical correlates of SENAC training with employment at the aggregate level. We then provide qualitative support for the social capital interpretation of these findings by presenting the results of interviews given to hotel entrepreneurs, barbers and beauticians and administrators of SENAC itself showing the complexities of the linkages between skill acquisition, social support and survival in a harsh economic environment.

A brief history of SENAC training in hotels, restaurants and barber/beauty

Vocational education in Brazil originated in the nineteenth century with the founding of military schools designed to teach the making of armaments and, later on, the founding of railroad schools designed to train railroad operatives. (Franco and Drona 1984) However, since the 1940s, most of the public adult vocational education has been provided by the "three S's", SENAI, SENAC and SEBRAE. SENAI does industrial apprenticeships, and specializes in heavy and light industry. SEBRAE is the small business administration and teaches courses in entrepreneurship oriented towards small business owners. SENAC provides training in the services. SENAC provides courses for the three sectors of this study – hotel, restaurant and barber/beauty shops – and also provides training in health sciences, computer science, and finance. Their emphasis is on introductory courses that would permit adults to obtain entry level jobs in these sectors. The division of labor between SENAC (services), SENAI (industrial apprenticeship) and SEBRAE (entrepreneurship) is long standing and well institutionalized. There is almost no duplication of tasks between these three agencies. In the 1990s, there was a very small amount of new non-SENAC training in the service sector coming out of some new programs administered by PLANIFOR and PRODETUR. However, SENAC continues to provide well over 95 percent of the federally funded vocational training in the services for Brazil and can be viewed as being the sole provider of such training for most analytical purposes. (Ministerio do Trabalho 1982, 1987, Urani 1997, Campino et al. 1985, Horowitz 1985)

These programs are highly respected and well reviewed by outside evaluators. Urani (1997) notes the very high cost efficiency of SENAC and SEBRAE.[6] Individual participation in training in the three S's generally correlates with higher probability of employment.[7] Minor complaints exist. Some authors wish there were more funding and more course offerings. (Ammana and Schacter 1985) SENAI has been accused of neglecting microenterprise. (Alexim 1993) Some states are viewed as having better training programs than others. (Azeredo 1998) Some authors wish that government training programs had better integration with the skill needs of employers. (Fogaca 1998, Markert 1997) Some authors would prefer less of an emphasis on classroom training. (Trevizan 1985) However, on balance, SENAC, SENAI and SEBRAE are highly respected by policymakers, by academics and by the general population of Brazil. Given the cynicism felt by most Brazilians about their public institutions, the esteem in which the three S's are held is in and of itself an extremely substantial and non-trivial accomplishment.

Figure 5.1   Matriculants in SENAC Training Programs: Brazil 1967–2000

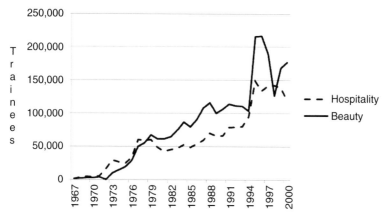

Figure 5.1 shows the number of matriculants in SENAC classes in Brazil in the subareas of Hospitality and Beauty. "Hospitality" refers to the tourism preparation program which offers courses in hotel and restaurant studies. Courses are offered in such areas as waiting on tables, cooking, front desk management, and hotel marketing. "Beauty" is the program for barbers and beauticians. Courses are offered in such areas as hairdressing, coloring, manicure and depilatories.

The graph shows the extremely dramatic increase in SENAC training that has occurred in hospitality and beauty between 1967 and 2000. In 1967, Brazilian economic development policy was primarily oriented towards the promotion of heavy industry. (Abreu 1989) As a result, there was very little state interest in the promotion of services. SENAC which was the training program for the service sector was quite small in comparison with the industrial training program, SENAI. As the graph shows, in 1967, both the Hospitality and the Beauty programs trained fewer than 1500 students in all Brazil.

However, this number steadily grew between 1967 and 2000. There were dramatic ratchet jumps in the size of SENAC in 1972, 1977, and 1995. Between these years, there was steady incremental growth. In the ten years between 1967 and 1977, there was a fiftyfold increase in the number of hospitality students and a more than thirtyfold increase in the number of beauty students. Between 1977 and 1987, the number of hospitality students remained the same. However, the number of beauty students more than doubled. Between 1987 and 1994, the number of beauty students remained nearly the same. However, the number of hospitality students almost doubled.

The Cardoso administration which took office in 1994, expanded SENAC to an even greater extent. It is no understatement to refer to increase in enrolments that occurred between 1994 and 1995 as the "Cardoso Explosion". In one year, hospitality training increased more than 50 percent. Beauty training more than doubled. Increases of 50–100 percent were not uncommon in the early years of SENAC, when the programs were starting from a low base. However, these doublings were occurring when SENAC enrolments were at some of the highest levels in their history – with each program training over 90,000 students a year. In one year, the size of the hospitality program moved from 95,287 to 149,282. The beauty program grew from 103,856 to 215,845. In the case of barber/beauty, SENAC was doubling the number of new job trainees entering the market every year.

Such a dramatic increase in occupational training ran the risk of creating serious absorption problems. One indicator that this may have occurred is that SENAC began to retreat from this supervolume of training and to reduce the size of its hospitality and beauty programs. The hospitality program fell back from 149,282 in 1995 to 134,776 in 1996. It hovered at about 140,000 for the rest of the decade and then fell again to 120,417 in 2000. The number of beauty matriculants increased slightly between 1995 and 1996 – going to 216,737. Then it too saw a rollback, down to 189,755 in 1997, and 127,270 in 1998. However, it rapidly began to rise again at the end of the decade and by 2000, it was up to 177,129.

Neither program in 2000 was at the maximum size reached at 1995. However, 2000 levels were still near historical highs. Both programs were approximately three times as large as they had been in 1980, and were over 50 percent (for Hospitality) and 100 percent (for Beauty) higher than they had been in 1990. Most of the increase in enrolment that occurred during the "Cardoso explosion" was maintained.

Note that it is extremely unlikely that the demand for hotel clerks, waiters or beauticians grew at a comparable rate during this period. Increases in labor market entries of 50–100 percent in a single year must have taxed the absorption capacity of employment markets dramatically. Displacement must have been a significant risk during this period, especially during the super-expansions of the 1990s. The threat of overcrowding was very real, making the new entrants very vulnerable and in need of social support – and raising the risk that this new investment in training could produce no aggregate increase in employment whatsoever.

Statistical results

To evaluate the impact of SENAC training on aggregate employment, the effect of the number of SENAC matriculants on the residuals from the models in Chapter 2 were analyzed. The effect of vocational education is hypothesized to be much weaker in the hotel sector than in the other two.

For this analysis to be valid, hotels in fact do need to have lower self-employment rates than the other two sectors. We expected this on a theoretical level because the hotel industry has high levels of barriers to entry – since a hotel owner has to own a building or a residence with rooms nice enough to be suitable to rent to customers. Restaurants have lower barriers to entry due to the capacity of Brazilian restaurateurs to start with food shacks or with street corner operations, and lower still for barbers and beauticians who can work out of a single room or even a driveway in a rented home.[8] However the question is whether the expected differences exist empirically.

The next graphs display census data to show that workers in hotels have far lower opportunities for self-employment than do restaurants or barber/beauty. Figure 5.2 shows the percent of workers in each industry that are self-employed for 1991 and 2000. In 1991, fewer than 4 percent of all workers in hotels were self-employed. In contrast, 35 percent of workers in restaurants and 70 percent of workers in barber/beauty were self-employed. These relative rankings persisted in 2000. Although the percentage of self-employed in hotel role to nearly 20 percent, it still lagged behind restaurants and barber/beauty.

Figure 5.3 presents another indicator of the capacity of each industry to support microentrepreneurship. Data are presented on the percentage of workers in each industry who work in their home or the home of a customer. The self-employed are disproportionately likely to work in houses at the beginnings of their careers, because they cannot afford

Figure 5.2   Percent of All Workers in Selected Brazilian Industries Who Were Self-Employed With No Employees: 1991–2000

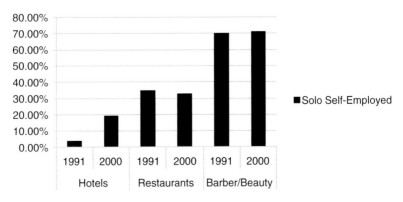

Figure 5.3   Percent of All Workers in Selected Brazilian Industries Who Worked at Home: 1991

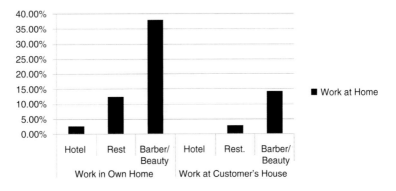

the rent required to obtain a dedicated commercial space. This variable was not collected for the 2000 census, so data are only available for 1991. Note that fully 37 percent of barber/beauticians worked in their own home. 12.5 percent of restaurant workers worked in their own home and only 2.6 percent of hotel workers worked in their own home. Furthermore, 14.3 percent of barber/beauticians worked in the customer's home, 2.7 percent of restaurant workers worked in the customer's home, and not surprisingly, 0 percent of hotel workers worked in the customer's home. The data on self-employment and locus of employment both support the notion that hotels have significantly fewer opportunities for entrepreneurship than do restaurants or barber/beauty.

To analyze the relationship between SENAC training and employment, we calculated for every year between 1980 and 2000 by state, the number of students who matriculate in courses in the relevant areas. Obviously, it would be preferable to use data on completion of vocational courses rather than the commencement of vocational courses, since not all students complete their training. However, a preliminary methodological analysis performed by the author on a subset of years for which both matriculation and graduation data were available found that these two measures of participation in vocational education correlate at well over 0.90. As such, the matriculation data while imperfect, are an excellent proxy for graduation data, and are used in that capacity here.

In the statistical analysis, we took the core equations of Chapter 2 for the 1991–2000 period and added the data on participation in vocational education.[9] The actual numerical coefficients, significance tests and goodness of fit statistics for these equations can be found in the Appendix *Details of Statistical Results*. The goodness of fit of these models was similar to that of the core equations – with acceptable goodness of fit for hotels and excellent goodness of fit in the other two sectors.

The essential finding was that SENAC training had no effect on employment whatsoever in hotels – but a substantial positive effect on employment in barber/beauty and in a ten-year test, but not a two-year test, restaurants. The effect of vocational training was tested two ways. In one test, we looked at the short-term effect of SENAC training by relating employment to the number of students in SENAC courses in the same year and the one just before it. This would pick up any immediate effect of training on the job market. Since it is reasonable to argue that the job training may have a very durable effect on employment, since once one is trained, one has those skills for much of one's life, we also ran a long-term test in which employment was related to all of the job training that had been provided by SENAC in the previous *decade*. In other analyses we don't report in the Appendix, we tried a number of "middle-term scenarios" with lags that were intermediate to these two extremes. In nearly every test, the effect of the job training variable for hotels was one tenth of the size of the job training variable in the other industries. In every test involving hotels, the effect of SENAC training was statistically insignificant. In every test involving the barber/beauty, the effect of SENAC training was generally highly statistically significant and the substantive coefficients were large. For restaurants, long-term tests produced a positive SENAC effect while more short-term tests were more likely to be insignificant.

The superior performance of SENAC in the long-term tests probably suggests a two-part sequence of training in which students acquire basic skills in vocational training – which are then seasoned by the acquisition of years of experience in a kitchen. The SENAC training is essential to creating the stock of "kitchen-ready trainees" who can then start establishments – and then build them up as the quality of their cooking improves over time. The ability to start one's own establishment guarantees that the training will not be lost – even if pre-existing restaurants are not hiring at the time of graduation.

Displacement potential in Brazilian beauty labor markets

A critical claim in the theory section of this chapter is that the training programs are more likely to be ineffective when there is a potential risk of trainees displacing already employed workers in the labor market. But how important is displacement really? If older workers never lose their jobs to competition from recent graduates of job training programs then orthodox discussions of vocational training would be correct – and the concerns of this chapter would be misplaced.

To really validate the discussion in this chapter, it would be helpful to actually measure the amount of displacement that occurs. In an ideal world, we would actually count the number of workers who have lost employment because they have been replaced by a recent graduate of a vocational training program. That plan would be impractical because it would involve a large, difficult and very expensive survey of all the workers – displaced or not – in a major labor market.

However, there are indirect measures that could suggest the presence of displacement. These might include identifying places with levels of training activity far higher than those of socio-economically similar settings, identifying places where training is increasing at a greater rate than the market potential for the target occupation, or identifying places where workers complain about competition from recent trainees.

We use such indirect measures to show that the threat of displacement was a real issue in Brazil. For simplicity, we confine the discussion to a real life "worst case scenario" – the labor market for barbers and beauticians in the Cardoso regime. The displacement issues here were particularly severe – and was much more severe than what was experienced in the restaurant sector. The level of increase in SENAC training in barber/beauty between 1967 and 2000 was almost 150 percent that of hospitality. At the same time, the demand for barber and beauty services was relatively stagnant, particularly in contrast with the booming increase in restaurant employment.

This discussion focuses on a number of localities where such problems seem to have been very serious. By identifying such labor markets, we can identify settings where one can observe trainee survival strategies at work and assess the relative importance of social capital.

How might one identify what labor markets might have a displacement issue? We looked at multiple indicators – and then to be conservative, only selected places that scored high on *every* indicator of displacement we could find. If we had included every location that scored high on at least one measure of displacement, our list of labor markets with displacement risk would have been much longer.

Four indicators of potential displacement were considered:

a) the volume of SENAC barber/beauty training in the 1980s,
b) the volume of SENAC barber/beauty training in the 1990s,
c) the rate of increase in the volume of SENAC barber/beauty training between the decades,
d) the gap between the rate of increase of training and the rate of increase of the capacity of the market to absorb new trainees. The capacity of the market to absorb trainees is estimated from the core models.

A state is only considered to have serious displacement problems if it is *substantially above the Brazilian average* on all four indicators. This methodology is a conservative methodology because it assumes that the average Brazilian state did not have problems absorbing SENAC trainees.

The five states were displacement issues in the barber/beauty labor market were probably severe were Sergipe, Rio de Janeiro, Rio Grande do Sul, Brasilia and Amapa. In the 1980s, all five of them had more trainees per capita than the national average. Rio de Janeiro in particular, was training twice as many barbers and beauticians per capita than the national average. All five states increased the gap between themselves and the Brazilian average in the 1990s. Rio de Janeiro continued to excel with a training rate nearly 250 percent of the national average. However, the other four states were training 170–180 percent of the national average. Note that Rio de Janeiro was training far more barbers per capita than was São Paulo – a substantially richer state. Sergipe in the 1990s had the second highest training rate of any state in Brazil – despite being a poor Northeastern state with an underdeveloped economy.

All five states substantially increased their training activity during the Cardoso Explosion – even though their training rates were already high. Sergipe led the nation – by more than doubling its barber/beauty training activity in a single decade. But even the slowest growing state of the lot, Amapa, increased its training by 25 percent.

More significantly, however, all five states raised their training rates at a rate greater than their barber/beauty markets were increasing. Amapa and Rio Grande do Sul raised their training rates over twice as much as their latent markets were expanding. Rio de Janeiro raised its training rate more than three times as much as its market was expanding.

The standout case, however, is Sergipe. Sergipe increased its training over five times as much as its economy was increasing! The rate of SENAC training went up 121 percent when the barber/beauty absorption capacity was increasing only 24 percent. Even had Sergipe been able to absorb all of its barber/beauty trainees in 1991 – a strong assumption given its high level of training activity – the increase of 121 percent in a market that was increasing only 24 percent implies that some 80 percent of the new trainees were facing a strong probability of being excluded from the labor market – or of displacing a previously employed worker.

Note that an increase in the rate of SENAC trainings does not in and of itself imply displacement. A rate of SENAC training growth faster than the market may be justified if a state had previously been a laggard who was under training in barber/beauty. Pernambuco fits this description. It had a SENAC growth rate over four times as great as the rate of growth of its barber/beauty market potential. However in 1991, it had been training 41 percent as many barbers and beauticians as the national average. Because of its relatively underdeveloped vocational education programs in personal hygiene, it could easily absorb a rapid increase in SENAC training; even in 2000, it was training fewer barbers and beauticians per capita than the national average.

It is also worth noting that at the national level, the rate of change of SENAC training was not terribly out of line with the national increase in market potential. For Brazil as a whole, SENAC barber/beauty training rose 46 percent between the 1980s and the 1990s, while market potential rose 41 percent. Displacement was probably a localized phenomenon. However, cases like Sergipe, with rates of training growth five times greater than changes in market potential, suggest that there were some localities where the risk of displacement was extremely severe.

The paradox

The alert reader at this point has probably noticed a paradox. The theoretical discussion argued that job training was likely to be ineffective in many settings in the Third World. The displacement analysis suggested that labor markets with high levels of job training could put older workers at real risk of displacement. However, the statistical analysis paints a completely different picture. The statistics show – and show robustly – that in restaurants and barber/beauty, regions with especially large amounts of job training were likely to have higher than expected employment. The very locations that are "overtraining" and putting out more students than the labor market could support nevertheless *increased* their aggregate employment. Somehow, these "overtraining" localities had some sort of technology for "packing the workers in" and creating permanent jobs where such jobs seemed not to exist. What were the secrets of job creation in these places where displacement was a particularly serious risk? To understand the secrets of job growth in overloaded settings, let us consider the details of the survival of entry level job entrants in one of the most crowded of Brazilian barber/beauty labor markets: Sergipe.

Economic survival strategies under conditions of displacement: How barbers and beauticians coped in Sergipe

To understand the dynamics of how vocational education works under conditions of high potential displacement, I did two waves of interviews with barbers and beauticians in Sergipe. The first wave consisted of in-depth interviews with six older experienced barbers and beauticians who entered the labor market in the 1960s or 1970s. The second wave consisted of 11 interviews with recent SENAC trainees who entered the labor market after 2000.

The older barbers/beauticians were firm about the fact that they perceived SENAC trainees to be flooding the market and creating employment problems for others in the field. Here is a selection from older barber M:[10]

> *Barber M had been discussing hard times for barbers and had just concluded a discussion of the "long hair era", the period in the 1960s and 1970s when longer hair styles became fashionable for men, reducing the demand for haircuts significantly.*
> *Barber M: "Nowadays we have unemployment, reductions in salary, everyone without a job … [the problem is] the school for barbers: Senac. … On*

every corner you have someone trying to survive … [This has caused] unem-
ployment, reductions in salary, the economic power of people has fallen.
Now everyone is looking for other cheaper salons … This occurs as a func-
tion of unemployment. Many people go to the school, SENAC, where they
prepare professionals, and then they begin to fill up [the market]. Every
neighborhood, every corner, every little place has a person at least trying to
learn [the trade] …"
Interviewer: Had this occurred in other periods?
Barber M: "No. Not to my knowledge. The school had always func-
tioned at a proper level … [Senac] had always functioned, but it was very
small. Its influence on today's problems firmed up, I suppose about 1997,
1998."

Note that 1997 and 1998 were a few years after the Cardoso explosion,
after several supersized cohorts of trainees had entered the beauty market
nationally.

The overcrowding problem also existed for beauticians. Beautician E
spoke to this issue.

Interviewer: Is there more competition than there was before?
Beautician E: Yes. Much more.
Interviewer: When did this begin?
Beautician E: About five years ago.

This would have been 1997, the same year for which Barber M reported
an increase in the barber population.

Beautician E: I'm telling you. A neighborhood like this , I would not have
imagined fifteen [beauty shops], which I'm telling you, I have seen. …
Look, there is one next to us. Two. Over, there, three. Four. Five. This stretch
of the street has another, six. On this street altogether, there are ten, and
there are five others as well.
Interviewer: Why is there so much competition today?
Beautician E: Because today it is so easy to get courses at SENAC … and
each student takes a chair, a scissors, a mirror, a dryer, a comb and a brush
and starts up a beauty parlor.

Most of the other hairdressers reported some sort of concern with over-
competition as well. Not all informants felt personally threatened by
SENAC trainees. Barber V, for example, reported concerns with SENAC,
but was relatively optimistic about the ability of experienced barbers to

survive. His concern was about the economic prospects of new barbers entering the field.

> Barber V: *"There are many [weak salons]. People take courses at SENAC, put up a little salon in their house, usually very simple, and they are trying to get people to switch salons. ... [The barbers] are inexperienced because they are just starting and have not acquired clients. ... They leave the course without practice.... The SENAC courses are good, but the students leave the course without experience. ... The older barbers are suffering but they are going to manage to come back from this. ... The new ones if they don't have clients, they are dependent on family and friends. If someone gives them a hand, they will pass through this".* (Emphasis mine)

Barber V's analysis is extremely revealing. None of the older experienced barbers or beauticians reported being driven from the field themselves or having friends in their cohort that were driven from the field. The older workers *do* report wage competition and diminished income, although their employment is more or less secure. However, the prospects for younger workers were substantially bleaker, with many semi-established young workers being driven out of the field by the highly competitive environment, and pressure from rival salons. Displacement manifested itself in job competition among the young, with some worsening of wages for all age groups.

Barber V's concluding remarks are also worthy of note. He explicitly argues that social networks and social capital are the key to survival. The young workers without a pre-existing client base need support from family and friends. Those who have support become established. Those who do not are in economic jeopardy.

The interviews of young market entrants in the 2000s confirm Barber V's analysis – and the opinions of the other barbers. Nearly all of the interviewees reported substantial competition, and very real obstacles to making a living in the barber/beauty field. Several were driven from the industry, a few more than once.

Social capital was important to the survival of young barbers and beauticians. This is illustrated in the experience of Beautician A. Beautician A made two different attempts to set herself up in the world of personal hygiene. Her first attempt failed; the second attempt succeeded. She took her first SENAC course over the explicit opposition of her parents. Her father was a career military professional and had set his own rigid occupational plans for the entire family. Beautician A was from a family of

15 children. Every one of the boys was to become a stonemason. Every one of the girls was to become a housewife. Beautician A was the only child out of 15 who did not follow the family formula.

As a result, she was cut off by her father. She had to establish herself on her own. After her first SENAC training, she was able to find employment in a downtown salon. However, a dispute with her boss cost her that position, and she had no capacity to set up shop on her own. As a result, she was driven from the field.

She returned to personal hygiene several years later. This time, she had the financial support and the (lukewarm) blessing of her father. Her father purchased her equipment for her. With her equipment expenses covered, she was able to afford the rent on a storefront in a working class neighborhood. The salon was an immediate success, and she quickly developed a list of clients. At the interview, she reported that her father intends to buy a building with family money to allow her to have her to have a rent-free location for the salon. She was extremely optimistic about her future.

Beautician A represents a natural experiment of the same person with and without family support. Most other cases represented workers with one condition or the other, with or without network support.

Beautician B was able to set up a successful business in her home – not only providing services but selling lots of hair products on the side. Her army husband paid for her SENAC training and bought all of her equipment. Furthermore, her customer base was entirely founded on pre-existing friends and family. She had no "new" business from strangers. However, her social network was very large and rich, allowing her to generate enough volume to require keeping an appointment book and restricting access. For her to get started, she needed to discount extensively at the beginning – a practice which was made feasible by the absence of rent and capital expenses from the investments made by her husband.

Social capital played a tremendous role in the success of Beautician L. Her salon is in one of the few true favelas (slums) in Aracaju – but it is the best appointed and most upscale salon in the neighborhood. Throughout her career, she had tremendous support from her family. Her first store was in the house of her mother – in a different favela; the current salon is in a building owned by her father – where he keeps another business. Her father provided half of the capital needed for the salon – which has better equipment than many of the domestic salons visited in the study.

Beautician L also benefited from another form of support from social capital. Approximately half of her customers did not use commercial hair services before they began to work with L. These customers had very low disposable income, and had been doing their own hair at home as a way of saving money. Beautician L used her personal connections to these customers to induce them to come and help her out. They stayed with her as customers, building her business. Note that in L's case, her survival was dependent on increasing the total consumption of commercial hair services in her neighborhood – and that her entrepreneurship represented a stimulation of consumer demand in her industry.

Beautician D illustrates the important of outside support – not all of which necessarily comes from social capital. He entered the personal hygiene field after being laid off from a job in a store. He had had formal employment at the store and thus had access to the full set of legal protections specified in Brazilian employment law. Thus, when he was laid off, he received a generous severance benefit, which he invested in SENAC hairdressing training. Upon completion of his training, his mother bought him all his equipment, and gave him a space in her house to open his salon.

With these substantial economic advantages, it would have been expected that he would have done well. In fact, he struggled throughout his entire career as a hairdresser. He reports that he has very few repeat clients, and that his friends refuse to be his customers. Although the informant did not say so, such a pattern is consistent with Beautician D not being a very skilled hairdresser. Beautician D reports that he has only survived on the basis of extensive discounting – and that he has never been able to raise his prices. As of the interview, he was currently studying occupational safety, hoping to leave the hairdressing field and get a formal job as a safety officer.

Beautician O resembles D in everything except the capacity to obtain help from her friends. Like D, she worked in a salon in her parent's house. Like D, she used occupational money to make her initial investments, in this case, money earned on a job as a nurse's aide. However, she has been able to induce her family and friends to make her their primary hairdresser. Her network was not large enough to allow her to work full time as a beautician; however, she earned non-trivial income as a part time hairdresser. Like D, she had to discount to initially attract business, but she had been able to raise prices over time.

Beautician C illustrates the problems faced by starters with limited assistance from members of their social network. Beautician C was a highly skilled artist and hairdresser – who had worked successfully in graphic arts and in making artificial flower settings. The graphic arts job was enough to pay her bills. The artificial flower business had no shortage of willing customers; it however died from cash flow issues linked to an over-extension of credit to slow paying customers.

Although she would have preferred to be a beautician, her hairdressing business closed in three months. Her mother was poor and could contribute nothing to the business. Her romantic situation was unstable – with few relationships lasting long enough to move to the point where financial support would have been feasible. Her house was in a very remote location – the most inaccessible of any in the study – at the end of a long dirt road in a sparsely settled rural suburb. Although she had many friends through political activities, few lived close enough to provide support. With no financial transfers and few friends as customers, the business did not do well.

Beautician S is another example of how new entrants with weak financial support from their network can face real obstacles. Her husband was a casual day laborer who could contribute nothing financially to the business. She was able to obtain some space in the house of an aunt – but had to provide everything else herself. She nearly went out of business on more than one occasion – and on various occasions had to seek labor or small contributions from her sister. However, the business finally caught on, and she is operating in rented facilities currently.

Some starters look at the level of competition and decide to avoid the rat-race altogether. Beautician H was in a SENAC class in which all seven students failed to open a salon. After taking her course, Beautician H got cold feet when she realized that there were eight competing salons within a few blocks of her house. Fortunately, her husband was an oil worker earning a comfortable middle class salary. Rather than compete, she chose to withdraw from paid employment and the labor market.

Beautician N did similar calculations – but lacked a prosperous husband to support her. In order to attract customers, she had to discount very heavily – earning almost nothing for her efforts. Seeing potential problems, she only invested lightly in equipment. She used family support not to buy hairdressing equipment but to pay for a pathology course to get out of hairdressing. She now works as a lab technician and is planning a future career in computers.

Not every new entrant required social capital in order to survive. High levels of human capital could substitute for social capital. There were two clear cases of highly talented SENAC students who used artistic skill to establish themselves quickly. Beautician T had been an artist before she went to SENAC, and had given up a successful doll-making business to follow her husband. T took a very large number of SENAC courses in a very short time, and used her own money to set up a salon at home. The salon is very modest but is on a busy street in a densely settled urban neighborhood – an ideal commercial location. She passed around fliers once advertising for her new salon, and business took off quickly. All indications are that she is extremely skilled. She reports getting frequent offers of formal employment from established salons – and routinely turns away business.

Beautician F is one of two sisters who founded a highly successful salon in the richest neighborhood in the city. She only studied manicures at SENAC and was largely self-trained at another salon. She established a solid reputation at her old salon and was able to bring her old customers into her new business. The two sisters paid for both rent and equipment out of the profits of their activities – and have been able to hire eight other workers besides themselves. Their neighborhood has a high density of competing salons, including three in very close proximity. Although there are obvious social capital factors linked to starting any business with a member of one's own family, the dominant consideration in the success of F's salon would seem to be personal talent – and human capital obtained from on-the-job training.

What do these stories illustrate overall?

a) Most of the successful barbers had some sort of capital infusion, either in the form of donated SENAC tuition, donated equipment, or most commonly, donated commercial space in the home of a relative.

b) Workers who received limited support from their networks, either because their social networks were small, or because the members of their social networks were poor or because members of their social networks opposed their career in the beauty field, had severe problems surviving in the market. This is illustrated strikingly in the natural experiment represented by Beautician A who failed when she lacked social network support and succeeded when that support was forthcoming.

c) Discounting was widespread, and was observed for nearly every case in which the respondent did not report high personal skill and ability. Where there were capital or space subsidies, the discounting was feasible and the business was able to survive. When social capital support was limited, and workers were paying full costs for their inputs, discounting severely threatened the viability of the enterprise, encouraging the worker to leave the industry.

d) In a limited number of cases, the struggling barber was able to increase aggregate demand by getting customers who had done their own hair care to use commercial services. However, this process was rare.

e) Social capital was less important for a small number of highly skilled practitioners who enjoyed instant success in building a reputation and a client base. This group however, was a small minority of all trainees.

Conclusion

We have seen that vocational education was an important tool for raising employment in Brazilian personal services. However, it was not effective in sectors which were dominated by formal employment relations – namely hotels. It worked better in industries with self-employment, such as restaurants and barber/beauty.

It was argued that Third World employers can easily afford to train their own workers, since the cost of training is very low when wage levels are very low. Reservation wages are very cheap in countries with substantial labor surpluses – allowing employers to offer low wages during training periods and still have wages equal marginal productivity.

Vocational education worked by training workers to enter self-employment – and allowing these new entrepreneurs to expand the demand for their sector. Thus areas that "over-trained" their populations relative to the capacity of the labor market to absorb workers – actually did their workers a service by stimulating an expansion of that market's capacity to absorb labor. Even if massive overtraining gave the appearance of trying to pour a gallon of water into a shot glass – the students entered these highly overloaded labor markets trying to survive in some way, took actions that increased the demand for services in the industry. The shot glass turned into a tumbler.

The primary mechanism for increasing demand was the use of social capital to induce investment in the industry. Friends and relatives of new trainees invested money in the student's new start-up. The most common provision of service was space in a home. However, equipment or tuition was often donated as well. This subsidized capital allowed workers to lower their prices while still remaining economically viable. Widespread discounting produced substantial bargains for consumers and could have easily motivated expansion of the sector through increased purchases.

What does this imply for social policy?

1) Vocational education is a good investment in increasing employment and income in poor populations. It is relatively inexpensive and it works.
2) Vocational education is especially effective if it can be linked to increased opportunities for entrepreneurship.
3) Brazil already has extensive institutionalized support for micro-entrepreneurship in the form of SEBRAE – the Brazilian version of a Small Business Administration. SEBRAE specializes in microfinance, entrepreneurial education and the provision of technical assistance to start-up firms. Although SEBRAE was not explicitly studied in this setting, the thrust of the argument here suggests that this type of program would be very effective.
4) The critical key to the support of nascent entrepreneurs was social capital and social network ties. Any mechanisms that increase solidarity among the poor and increase the capacity of willingness of groups to contribute voluntarily to the well being of others can help to reduce poverty. The primary links of solidarity here were family and friendship. Any other such bonds, such as ethnicity, or community spirit could have a similar effect. The new initiatives of the *economia solidária* that attempts to create economic growth by inducing voluntary contributions from locals to help locals, could be a promising application of the principles discussed here. The analysis of SENAC showed that the key to increasing employment was getting workers to voluntarily help other workers. Anything that permanently and robustly stimulates such principles of communitarianism is likely to be helpful in increasing self-employment and producing economic growth.

The analysis thus far has supported O'Connor's arguments about the importance of the state in providing physical infrastructure and human infrastructure. However, the essence of O'Connor's argument concerns fiscal crisis – and the importance to capitalism of the state having sufficient revenue to do its job. Fiscal crisis has been a chronic problem in Latin American development. This problem became particularly acute in the 1980s and 1990s. How does fiscal crisis affect employment in the industries that are the main basis of this study? It is to this question that we now turn.

6
Government Effectiveness in the Face of Debt

The fundamental claim of O'Connor's *Fiscal Crisis of the State* is that when the governments are deprived of financial resources, they are unable to fulfill their natural function of reproducing capitalism. This argument seemed very foreign to O'Connor's American leftist readers of the early 1970s. The United States was the dominant superpower of the world. "Big Government" was aggressively addressing social problems, notably racial discrimination and urban decay. Federal support for university and scientific funding was flush. Keynesian stimulation of demand was largely effective. The prediction that the American state could lack the fiscal ability to support capitalism seemed implausible.

However, fiscal crisis is a very real issue for Third World states. These take the form of *debt crises* rather than tax revolts per se. Taxation is not irrelevant to the problem of international indebtedness; that issue will be addressed in the next chapter. However, the phenomenon of indebtedness undercutting state capacity to stimulate the local economy, and economic development suffering as a result, is a fundamental feature of world-system dynamics in the semi-periphery and periphery. Christian Suter (1992) has shown that debt crises have been a serious problem in Latin America, Asia, the Middle East and Subsaharan Africa since 1820, and that each new wave of crises gutted the resources of the debtor states and seriously undermined local economic development. The crises of the 1980s, 1990s and 2000s are simply the most recent examples of an endemic limit to growth in underdeveloped nations. The importance of debt has been noted by many observers. (Furtado 1983, Hoogvelt 1997, Chossudovsky 1997, Potter 2000) The critical issue is to integrate the problem of indebtedness to the general theory of the role of the state in economic development.

One of the most successful debt-informed analyses on the role of the state came from Albert Fishlow, an economist. Writing in 1990, just after the Fall of the Berlin Wall and just before the onset of the Washington Consensus, the question of the role of state versus market in economic development was particularly salient. The failure of command economies was particularly fresh in people's minds; radical free-market-ism and minimizing government constraints on the private sector seemed particularly attractive. Neoliberalism was about to go on the march. (Fuhr 1993, World Bank 1993)

Fishlow's approach to the question avoided the polemic extremes of his time, and was eminently sensible. He argued that there are a wide variety of government interventions in the economy. Some are valuable. Some are not. Governments have a lot of choices as to how they structure their economic policies – and many alternatives can produce favorable results.

What matters – is that the government avoid international debt. The critical limit on Third World government's intervention into the economy is that budget deficits be kept low. Once the government becomes a debtor to international capital, they no longer control their planning agenda and future government programs will be compromised by the needs to service foreign creditors. As long as the government could limit its expenditures to its own resources in hand, it could choose any of a number of viable economic strategies. Once the state incurred debt, it lost all autonomy.

Significantly, Fernando Henrique Cardoso, distinguished underdevelopment theorist and former President of Brazil, has come to the same conclusion. In a reflective essay on the theoretical lessons of his experience as President, his key point is that all other state imperatives are secondary to the key priority of staying out of debt. (Cardoso 2009) As we shall see from the analysis that follows, the policies of his own administration did not always follow this dictum. But Cardoso agrees with O'Connor, that avoiding fiscal crisis is everything.

How does debt alter the calculus of what types of state economic interventions are feasible?

The best answer to this comes from another Brazilian academic/statesman, Luiz Carlos Bresser Pereira, an economist who was the Minister of the Treasury in the late 1980s when Brazil was first responding to the exigencies of the debt crisis. According to Bresser Pereira (1992), the financial limits placed on Third World governments did not eliminate the capacity for activist economic policy; they simply required a rethinking of that policy:

Even under debt, state developmentalist programs can be effective so long as they are CHEAP.[1]

There are many economic policies that don't cost very much to implement. Tourism development, small business support, vocational education, or state support of international marketing are all relatively inexpensive – and within the capacity of even the most financially strapped governments. Government-owned steel mills, automobile factories, or computer hardware companies are not cheap. A government that restricts itself to relatively inexpensive options can avoid the worst limitations of externally imposed debt repayment plans. Stale formulaic policies that throw money at factories that are persistent money losers are not viable in times of limited budgets.

In a world without debt, one of the strongest cases for state-centered rather than market-centered development strategies is that governments can take on projects with longer gestation periods than could the market because governments are not bound by short-term considerations of profit maximization. (Nove 1992, Papanek 1992, List 1983, Streeck 1992, Szirmai 2005) This logic changes completely when the state is under a stringent internationally imposed debt repayment plan. An indebted Third World nation is usually required to maintain high domestic interest rates in order to ensure the payment of the debt by encouraging the entry of foreign capital and reducing the rate of inflation. High domestic interest rates dramatically reduce employment by severely curtailing private sector investment. In some cases the damage done to employment by high interest rates can dwarf the benefits of individual state programs. Thus under a debt repayment program any government expenditure that is designed to increase employment implicitly has to raise employment more than the number of jobs that would have been lost from the raising of interest rates necessary to service that debt. The employment costs of debt service are rarely zero. Debt adds a short-term pressure to government programs that is wholly analogous to the short-term pressure placed on private sector investment. if interest rates are high, then state policies become "impatient" just the way that private sector policies are "impatient".

Cheapness reduces the problem of impatience. When programs are not costly, it is not absolutely essential for government investments to "turn a profit" in the first year. By reducing the interest payments associated with public investments, the state can regain its ability to plan strategically and can provide funding for critical initiatives for the long term.

What does this imply for the infrastructure arguments of the previous chapters? That question can be answered more rigorously by considering the actual costs of infrastructure programs in detail.

The costs of the infrastructure programs of PRODETUR

We have already established in the previous section, that the infrastructure programs of PRODETUR were effective government investments that raised employment in the hotel sector and had substantial spin-off effects on the economy as a whole.

How much did PRODETUR cost – and who paid for it?

Table 6.1 shows the money that was applied to the PRODETUR initiative and the sources of those funds. Specifically, the table shows whether those funds came from Brazilian government itself or were paid for by foreign debt.

Table 6.1   Origins of Funds Used by PRODETUR I 1994–2005 (in millions of US dollars)

Infrastructure	Brazilian Funds	Debt	Total
Airports Expansion of eight airports	$114.8	$108.7	$223.4
Highway Projects 1,025 km of new highway	$32.3	$109.9	$142.2
Sanitation Projects 742 km of new water/sewage lines 122,043 new hook-ups	$36.2	$87.0	$123.2
Environmental Conservation 27 ecological projects and parks	$14.2	$6.3	$20.5
Restoration of Historical Neighborhoods and Buildings 61 classic buildings restored	$9.1	$35.0	$44.1
Total	$331.2	$398.7	$729.9

The table excludes various institutional development projects and various administrative expenses from the subtotals. Those items are included in the Total.

PRODETUR cost approximately $730 million dollars. Some 55 percent of these expenses were financed by debt. Forty-five percent of the expenses were covered by the Brazilian government. All in all, the Brazilians absorbed nearly $400 million dollars in new debt as a result of engaging in PRODETUR.

What is remarkable however – is that a number of scenarios existed in which Brazil could have had most of the benefits of PRODETUR without incurring any foreign debt at all!

Table 6.2 uses data from the actual PRODETUR final expenses to calculate the cost of a number of smaller projects. The actual PRODETUR I used $331 million of resources already at the disposal of the Brazilian government.

Table 6.2   Alternative PRODETUR Designs that Involve Zero Debt: (Expenditure Plans that Only Use the $331 Million the Brazilian Government Spent from Its Own Funds)

No-Debt Alternative 1:
Maximize the Total Number of
    Projects Executed
	100% of the Highway Projects
	100% of the Sanitation Projects
	100% of the Ecological Projects
	100% of the Historical Preservation
	    Projects
	No Airports
	Cost: $330 Million

No-Debt Alternative 2:
All Projects for Three Most
    Populous Northeastern Cities
Plus Three Largest Enclave Resorts
Including Airports and Highways
	100% of Projects for Salvador
	100% of Projects for Recife/Olinda
	100% of Projects for Fortaleza
	100% of Projects for Porto Seguro
	100% of Projects for Rio Grande
	    do Norte South Coast
	100% of Projects for Suape/Porto
	    Galinhas
	No Other Cities or States
	Cost: $326 Million

Table 6.2 constrains the total price of the PRODETUR project to $331 million – the money that Brazil paid with its own resources. By limiting expenditures to this amount, Brazil would have incurred zero debt as a result of the project. There are two different ways that this could have been accomplished – and both methods seem superficially attractive.

No-debt Alternative 1 attempts to maximize the total number of PRODETUR projects that could be completed for $331 million. The surprising result of this calculation: *nearly ALL of the PRODETUR projects could be fit under a zero debt scenario!* $331 million allows one to construct 100 percent of all the highways, 100 percent of all of the sanitation and sewer projects, 100 percent of all of the ecological projects and 100 percent of all of the historical reconstructions. The only item that gets cut are the airports. Airport construction is clearly desirable. Chapter 4 showed that the airports clearly contributed to the economic development of the region. However, the airports were incredibly expensive compared to the rest of PRODETUR – representing over 55 percent of the cost of the project. The highway, sanitation, ecological and historical reconstruction elements each produced enormous benefits for the Northeastern economy and population – and all of this could have been had debt-free.

However, airport construction produces significant benefits for the economy. Would it have been possible to generate a cheaper version of PRODETUR that would have still been cost-effective and allowed for some of the economic advantages of airport infrastructure? No-debt Alternative 2 limits the number of locations which received PRODETUR inputs. To maximize the humanistic and economic benefits of the program, this second alternative fully finances six prime locations: the three most populous cities in the Northeast – which would have the largest populations who could benefit from PRODETUR improvements. It also finances the three largest rural enclave resorts in PRODETUR. These were the "most important" resort investments in the package – those that were anticipated from the beginning to have a major impact in increasing employment in tourism. Making dual provision for large cities and for large resorts, balances the equally legitimate needs of serving poverty populations in large cities and producing the largest employment effects in tourism per se. Concentrating on large cities also facilitates the inclusion of airport projects which generally serve a larger area than the actual metropolis itself.

If PRODETUR had concentrated on six prime locations – the three large cities of Salvador, Recife and Fortaleza, and the three large resorts of the Rio Grande do Norte southern coast (Pipa), Suape (Porto Galinha) on the Pernambuco coast and Porto Seguro on the southern coast of Bahia, they could have financed *every* project associated with these areas – including three very expensive airports. Even in this scenario, they would not have had to take on a penny of debt. Note that there even would have been a spillover of five million dollars that could have been used for smaller ecological reserves, historical reconstructions or some of the administrative reforms financed by the project.

Debt, democracy and the size of PRODETUR

The sociological question thus becomes, given the relative attractiveness of a smaller PRODETUR, why was such an option never implemented? Explaining the absence of counterfactuals is always by nature, speculative. However, the role of democracy and the weakness of the Brazilian state suggest obvious possibilities.

The relative weakness of Brazilian presidents relative to Congress and to legislators is well known. State congressional delegations are controlled by the governors of the states – as opposed to by political parties. (Mainwaring 1999) These governors direct the voting even of members of their delegation from other parties. Although it is possible for the executive branch to take on state governors and win – one famous case being Cardoso's imposition of the Law of Fiscal Responsibility on governors with runaway budgets – in general, Brazilian social policy is consultative with federal policymakers having take local political sensibilities very much into account.

The substantial power of subnational units in Brazil would have eliminated any prospect of regional rationing of PRODETUR. It is no accident that every single state in the Northeast was invited to participate in the project. Excluding any state would have posed a political problem that would have produced "payback" problems on some sensitive issue for which the President would have needed support from the congressional delegation of the unfunded state. The presidents of the 1990s, Collor, Franco and especially Cardoso, were all navigating sensitive economic and neoliberal reforms through their legislatures. Creating an acrimonious regional issue over exclusion from a public works project would have been counterproductive for the attainment of other national priorities.

Could Brazil have run an all-small-project PRODETUR with no airports? Here the resistance could have been either technocratic or political. Planning officials could have easily argued that increasing airport capacity would have produced economic gains to far more than the tourism sector – and that the airports should be obtained if at all possible.

However, it is probably the case that political factors played a role as well. The airport contracts were the financially, the biggest component of PRODETUR. Private sector developers and contractors would have been keenly eager to see the implementation of the terminal expansions because these represented enormous and highly lucrative contracts. The developers would have been completely indifferent to the debt consequences of such projects.

Local politicians would also have been reluctant to see the airports cut from PRODETUR. Brazilian local elections are frequently determined by the incumbent's ability to deliver large public works to their district. Governors put their names not only on the works themselves, but on all the signage associated with the works. Streets are decorated with big banners to the effect of "Thank You Governor X for the Provision of this Y!" Perceived relative performance of candidates is often determined by how much they were able to bring in for their state. This would make most governors very enthusiastic about an airport project – particularly when airport infrastructure can be legitimately viewed as being favorable to development.

Finally, transnational financial organizations would have not have necessarily been in favor of a plan that did not involve debt. The Inter-American Development Bank was a key player in originating PRODETUR, shaping its strategic direction, and using managing the technical details of the execution to pursue larger bank initiatives. Nearly all of the IDB's concerns were constructive, progressive and prosocial. They helped to design the well conceived overall strategy of the program. They insured that the program would have an ecological component and would be consistent with transnational ideals concerning sustainable development. They worked aggressively to insure that the program would be relatively free of corruption and highly transparent. The public documentation for the expenditures of PRODETUR is far more open and extensive than is the documentation for nearly any other development initiative in Brazil. The Inter-American Development Bank was able to use its leverage to shape Northeastern development to the terms of a transnational agenda – an agenda that on the whole was extremely beneficent. The progressive nature of the PRODETUR project as a whole, and prosocial manner in which it was executed belies facile stereotypes of multinational financial organizations as only doing harm to Third World nations.

However, the IDB would have not had any influence on this process whatsoever if PRODETUR had been completely self-funded. It was only the provision of foreign monies that gave transnational policymakers any input into how Northeastern Brazilian development would occur. It was because the program was financed with debt that the Inter-American Development Bank could use tourism development as a vehicle for constructive social change.

A no-debt PRODETUR would have been opposed not only by developers and construction interests, but by local governments and by the international financial community. Under these circumstances, it is easy to see why PRODETUR grew to a size that would require debt financing.

Taking on debt given the realistic unknowns about the consequences of projects

In an ideal world, these contradictions could be avoided. International organizations would promote economic development through grants rather than loans. Alternatively, governments would have enough money to finance internal development without having to rely on international capital markets. However, those ideal circumstances are unrealistic. Real governments have to make real decisions about major projects – and some of those major projects may require loan commitments.

In the present case of PRODETUR, it is not necessarily the case that no debt should have been taken on whatsoever. As long as the economic return on a state investment is greater than the job loss that will occur because of loan repayment, the benefit justifies the cost. Calculating this cost benefit ratio however can be complex. Consider that

a) No one in economic life ever really knows the rate of return of investments before one invests. This is true even of a simple bond, let alone the state construction of infrastructure.[2]
b) When a project consists of both state and borrowed funds, the relevant question is not the earnings that would be obtained from the best project in the proposed portfolio. The question is what are the earnings from the best project in the debt financed portion of the portfolio. If five projects could be funded from local sources and projects six through ten would need debt financing, identifying which projects six through ten are the least remunerative, let alone the rates of return for projects six through ten, would be a difficult challenge for any state technician.
c) It is politically difficult to exclude components from large expenditure projects when regional political interests have political leverage – or when contractors and other private parties have legitimate interests in seeing a project become implemented. The calculations that matter to statemakers on a given day may not be the cost-benefit ratio for a project – but the vote count in a key parliamentary dispute, or the outcome of forthcoming gubernatorial elections.

These considerations tie the hands of policymakers. That said, some lessons may still be drawn from these calculations.

1) Cheap projects are better than expensive projects. Reducing costs often makes sense
2) Projects with long-term payoffs are more feasible when interest rates can be kept low – Reducing the job loss effects of government expenditures
3) Autonomous policymakers have greater capacity to keep the expenses of viable projects under control. Insulation of development technical teams from short-term political pressures from special interests can help keep debt loads low

Debt, however, is not the only source of fiscal crisis. A more fundamental source of fiscal crisis is low state revenue due to inadequacies in the taxation system. Brazil is a nation known for high nominal tax rates and widespread tax evasion. How do taxes impinge on employment creation in Brazilian hotels, restaurants and barber shops?

7
Why Reducing Taxes for Employers Does Not Raise Employment

The previous chapter showed that development expenditures should be financed from some sort of public funding that avoids international debt. An obvious source of such monies is tax revenue. Thus, in principle, insuring that the state has adequate financial resources to perform its functions would seem to be a fairly high priority. This would imply a commitment to assessing and collecting taxes.

However, one of the most common policy recommendations for increasing employment is for governments to cut taxes. Advocates of tax cuts, both in the developed and non-developed world, argue that lower tax rates create employment by making business more competitive. Employers and employers' associations are long standing critics of mandatory fringe benefits, claiming that social charges raise the cost of hiring workers and lower rates of job creation. (Lahóz and Caetano 2001, Whalen 2001, Walker 2003) They sometimes have support from anti-statist members of the academic community. (De Soto 1989, Rabushka and Bartlett 1985) Of particular note, in the Brazilian context is José Pastore (1998) who has published a highly visible body of work linking reduction of government mandated payroll taxes to a substantial potential increase in employment. This claim is frequently echoed in the Brazilian business press. In Europe, Gosta Esping-Anderson (2000), customarily a strong Marxist critic of neoliberal reform, has provided empirical evidence that social charges have had a substantial effect on inhibiting employment particularly for youth.

The case for tax relief is extremely simple. Taxes raise costs. Cost increases raise prices. Price increases reduce consumption. Reduced consumption lowers employment. The result is an overall deadweight loss. (Auerbach 1985, Harberger 1974, Kehoe and Serra-Puche 1983) The models used to generate these results often incorporate fairly rigid neoclassical assumptions of a competitive market. However, in some settings, those assumptions are not unrealistic. Large firms can face substantial competition from foreign rivals. Small firms generally face price competition at home. Some of these enterprises may in fact be highly vulnerable to the adverse effects of price increases – and thus the case for tax relief in these settings might seem plausible.

As a result, in practice, many forms of industrial policy make explicit use of tax relief in order to stimulate employment. This is particularly the case for legislation designed to stimulate small business. Brazilian microenterprise policy has always included some form of tax relief. In the 1980s, small firms were exempted from a large number of federal taxes. Parallel cuts were made in many state and municipal taxes. These tax cuts were implemented at about the same time that the Brazilian congress created SEBRAE the federal agency charged with supporting small business. (Sanders 1985) Ecuador has a tax relief program similar to Brazil's. Morrison and Oudin's (1984) survey of microenterprise in underdeveloped nations found de facto tax relief for small businesses in every country they examined with the one exception of Algeria.

The argument here is that the link between taxation and employment is weak. The damage that comes from reducing government revenues far exceeds any job gains that may come from lowering the tax burdens of firms. More specifically, the economic literature on taxation and employment argues that tax reductions do not raise employment. The empirical findings from Brazilian hotels, restaurants and barber/beauty shops support this literature by showing that tax burdens have no correlation whatsoever with employment. Because tax burdens do not correlate with employment, and tax cuts do not raise employment, state officials should be firm about defending the public treasury – and seeing that the state has sufficient resources to provide the public goods that are essential to the process of capital accumulation.

Theoretical arguments for weak tax-employment relations

The enthusiasm of business lobbyists for tax cuts has not been matched by most academic economists. Although there are divisions of opinion on this issue, the bulk of the scholarly literature on the relationship between tax cuts and employment in the Third World argues for little relation between the two.

The traditional arguments made by economists who are skeptical of the relationship between taxation and employment is as follows:

1. *Tax increases stimulate employers to invest in order to recoup the lost revenues from taxation.* The literature on public finance maintains

that taxation produces two contradictory effects on investment and employment, one an income effect and the other a substitution effect. The claim that taxation reduces investment involves a *substitution* effect, an implicit argument that lowered profitability induces capitalists to move capital to other investments or to prefer to hold cash. However, this is counteracted somewhat by the *income* effect. In the face of a tax, entrepreneurs who have a given goal of making a fixed amount of money increase their investment to compensate for their lost revenues. It is difficult a priori to specify which of the two types of effects are likely to predominate. Stiglitz suggests that without a theoretical specification of the relative magnitude of income and substitution dynamics, the effect of taxation on business activity becomes almost impossible to predict. (Musgrave 1959, Stiglitz 1988)

There is some empirical evidence that in some settings, the income effect dominates the substitution effect. Vroman (1967) found that employers react to increased social charges by raising product prices. In situations where demand for the product is price-inelastic, such cost increases may not reduce sales or employment. In other cases, employers simply tolerate lower profit margins. Neoliberal reforms in Morocco had negligible effects on employment, due to oligopolistic employers reorganizing production to raise productivity. (Currie and Harrison 1997)

2. *Tax write-offs reduce the effect of crude tax rates of seemingly high magnitude.* A second consideration is the effect of tax write-offs for business losses. When adverse business results produce counter-vailing relief in tax obligations, this reduces the risk inherent in making investments. When tax write-offs are explicitly included in models of investment, the introduction or raising of taxes *increases* rather than decreases entrepreneurial risk-taking, because the state is inherently insuring against adverse results. (Musgrave 1959, Stiglitz 1969) This consideration is not germane to taxes that must be paid regardless of firm profitability. It is however, relevant to corporate income tax, a tax which is often reduced in policies designed to stimulate microenterprise. (Sanders 1985)

3. *In the case of payroll taxation, employers can counteract the tax by reducing wages if labor demand is inelastic.* Writers on payroll taxation address its impact on employment by considering the question of incidence. If the burden of the tax can be shifted on to workers rather than employers, then payroll taxation should not reduce employment. The seminal discussion of the incidence of payroll taxation is that of Brittain (1972). Using static analysis, Brittain claimed that in principle,

a payroll tax would reduce both wages and employment. However, in practice, most of the tax is passed on to workers in the form of lower base salaries. This transfer of the burden of payroll taxation to workers is due to high observed levels of labor supply inelasticity. Most payroll taxes do not push salary levels below worker's reservation wages, and therefore most workers are forced to accept the adjusted wages predicated by the existence of payroll taxes.

Most empirical analyses of the incidence of social charges show some percentage of those taxes being recouped in the form of lower wages. However, this does not rule out the existence of an employment effect. The range of estimates of the percentage of these charges that are absorbed by workers varies wildly from 0 percent to 100 percent of the tax. The median estimate is approximately 30 percent (Hamermesh 1993). The employment interpretations of a 30 percent incidence are ambiguous and subject to differential interpretation. Without explicit estimation of employment effects per se, any conclusion concerning employment by a pure analysis of incidence alone is necessarily speculative. (Hart 1984)

It is worth noting that if shifting of the payroll tax on to workers were to minimize adverse employment effects, the Third World would have a weak relationship between taxes and employment, because it is in the Third World that such shifting is particularly likely to occur. The relative scarcity of employment combined with high levels of poverty reduces the elasticity of labor supply, because workers are simply desperate for work. Furthermore, the Third World is free from some of the institutional rigidities in the developed world that restrict the ability of employers to reduce wage rates at will. The labor markets of wealthy nations are characterized by union contracts and minimum wage laws. Because poorer nations are characterized by flexible labor markets, weak unions and uneven enforcement of labor laws, it should be particularly easy in these settings to preserve employment by lowering wages. (Camargo 1996, Harrison and Leamer 1997, Barros and Mendonça 1996) Gruber (1997), for example, in a study of Chile found payroll taxation had large negative effects on base wages but almost no effects on employment.

4. *The effective burden of taxation in the Third World on small and middle sized firms is sufficiently small as to not be sufficient to effect employment.* The literature on Third World taxes maintains that de jure tax rates in the Third World are often high. However, high tax rates are often not sufficient to generate a significant tax burden due to widespread non-compliance with the tax code. The capacity of Third

World treasuries to collect the full range of taxes that are due to them is limited. Tax offices are generally understaffed; administrative support is often inadequate; collection efforts may be undercut by corruption or by weak support from the judiciary. This allows many small businessmen to underreport their liabilities knowing that the odds of being audited are relatively low. (Bird 1992, Burgess and Stern 1993, Surrey 1958)

This argument is particularly relevant to the Brazilian context. Anti-tax writers claim that the Brazilian rates of payroll taxes are so excessively large, that they thwart any reasonable attempt of companies to shift those costs. The simplest version of this argument is to simply take the potential legal obligations of an employer, add up all the charges as a percentage of base salaries and show that this figure is objectively large. (Pastore 1998, Bacha et al. 1972, FIESP 1993, Santos 1973) As a result, some Brazilian critics cast doubt on the utility of tax cuts in employment policy by providing alternative accounts showing that the size of tax burdens is more modest than would appear from a superficial reading of the relevant laws. (Pochmann 1999, Dos Santos 1996)

These considerations induce most writers on Third World taxation to de-emphasize any effects of tax structure on development. Burgess and Stern, for example, reviewed the field of taxation and development for the *Journal of Economic Literature* in 1993. Nowhere does there appear any argument linking economic growth to the overall size of the tax burden. Such an argument is also missing from Richard Bird's 1992 monograph *Tax Policy and Economic Development* and Ahmad and Stern's 1989 discussion of taxation in the *Handbook on Economic Development*. To the extent, there is any discussion on the effects of taxation on employment at all, it is confined to a consideration of the viability of hiring subsidies.

5. *Other factors play a far greater role in small business survival than do taxes.* Taxes are not the only cost facing entrepreneurs. Very often other concerns are far more pressing. Schmitz's (1982) ethnography of small-scale Brazilian businesses notes that access to cheap raw materials is the make-or-break factor for domestic manufacturers – with all other costs including taxes being relatively unimportant. SEBRAE, the Brazilian small business administration, has a long standing series of studies of mortality and survival among microenterprises. A consistent finding of these analyses is that lack of working capital or inadequate sales are far more important causes of firm failure than are tax payments. (SEBRAE-SP 2005) Durand and Rodrigues (1979)

in the first large-scale study of successful and unsuccessful micro-enterprise in Brazil noted that tax problems were almost never cited by failed entrepreneurs as a reason for the loss of their business.

6. *If tax cuts raise employment at all, they will only work in a limited number of industries.* A line of analysis that is often missed in traditional discussions is that taxation may not have the same effect on employment in all industries. There are various considerations that raise or lower the degree to which a tax is likely to reduce consumer demand for an industry's products. Three considerations are particularly germane.

I) TAXES ARE LESS LIKELY TO LOWER THE SALES IN AN INDUSTRY WHEN THAT INDUSTRY'S PRODUCTION IS NOT DIVIDED AMONG DIFFERENT GEOGRAPHICAL JURISDICTIONS WITH DIFFERENT TAX RATES. In this case, it becomes possible for consumers to purchase goods from the less taxed region, reducing sales and employment for firms in the region with the higher tax. In contrast, in a case where all firms in a market are concentrated in one region with a unitary tax, the question of losses of sales to rivals from lower priced regions becomes moot. An example of this would be personal services, such as primary medical care, or restaurants which must provide those services close to the residence of the customer, eliminating any possibility of cross-regional tax competition.

II) TAXES ARE LESS LIKELY TO LOWER THE SALES IN AN INDUSTRY WHEN THE TAXED INDUSTRY DOES NOT COMPETE WITH MAKERS OF UNTAXED FUNCTIONAL SUBSTITUTES. When the price of a product increases, consumers typically turn to alternative products that are less expensive. This reduces demand for the taxed product and lowers employment. However, if no such products exist, and the need for the product remains, consumers may have no choice but to continue purchasing the original product at a higher cost. An example of this would be firms in basic necessities such as food, which have few good functional alternatives.

III) TAXES ARE LESS LIKELY TO LOWER THE SALES IN AN INDUSTRY WHEN THE PRICE DIFFERENTIAL BETWEEN THE TAXED PRODUCT AND ITS SUBSTITUTES IS DETERMINED BY FACTORS OTHER THAN THE TAX. The tax is likely to have a maximum impact when the two competing products are similarly priced, and only the tax itself determines the overall price difference. In contrast, when the price difference between the products is determined by differences in the price of other factors (such as labor or material costs), these differences can exceed those produced by taxes alone and produced no significant change in consumption patterns. An obvious example would be goods produced in multiple nations with widely varying base wages.

The consequences of factors I) through III) taken together is that there is a large subset of industries that would experience significant sheltering from the effect of a tax. Tax cuts would only work in industries where **none** of these conditions apply. This implies a very limited domain of applicability.

7. *The empirical basis for claiming that taxes decrease employment is quite weak.* There is very little empirical literature showing any effect of Third World taxation on the reduction of employment. The only direct test of the effect of tax burden on Third World economic development is Rabushka and Bartlett (1985). Their empirical analysis of 49 Third World nations showed a perverse positive and statistically significant correlation between aggregate tax rates and per capital economic growth. The literature on the effects of payroll taxes on employment generally produces negative findings. (Harrison and Leamer 1997)

Incorporating taxes into the previous analyses

Because of the importance of tax policy to most discussions of the generation of income and employment, estimates of the effects of taxation and payroll taxation were added to the core models of Chapter 2.

Unfortunately, this cannot be done for the 1991–2000 data that have been the basis of the discussions in Chapters 2–6. There simply is no good material on the taxes paid by firms for personal service firms in the period under discussion.

In contrast there is excellent data for 1940–80. These tax data come from the Service Censuses of 1940, through 1980.[1] What is lost in convenience of periodization is more than compensated for in data quality. The Service Censuses measure the amount of taxes actually paid by firms, and not de jure tax rates per se (which are what appear more typically in the literature). De facto measures of actual tax payments are superior to measures of taxes based on de jure tax rates, because they include the legitimate reduction of tax burdens that would come from the available deductions in the tax code, and also include any reduction in burden that would come from intentional underpayment.

The Service Census also provides separate estimates of the total amount of payroll taxes that are reported as being paid by reporting firms. All social charges are included in this measure, including social security, unemployment insurance, contributions to vocational education, and workmen's compensation.

The Service Censuses provide estimates of the total amount of taxes that are reported as being paid by reporting firms. All taxes are included in this measure, including corporate income tax, property tax, sales tax on raw materials, and most importantly, ISI, the sales tax on services. Taxes are divided by receipts to provide a measure of the degree to which taxation provided an overall burden on the revenues of the firms. Dividing through by receipts also removes inflation and monetary distortions from the measure, since price levels are included in both the numerator and denominator of the index, canceling each other out.

A reasonable objection can be made that tax payments are misreported in survey data; many employers may make false claims about their payments as a strategy for concealing tax evasion. While undoubtedly self-interested misrepresentation occurs, this does not invalidate the use of these data for our purposes. Firstly, the direction of any bias stemming from misrepresentation is known: estimates of tax payments will be too high. No one claims to pay *less* tax than they actually paid. This means that any reported levels of tax payments will be maxima, and true levels will be lower than those reported here. Furthermore, the propensity to misrepresent tax payments is probably somewhat constant across the population and can be treated as random noise. While individuals may vary in their relative honesty, it seems less likely that the over-reportage of taxes varies systematically by date or by region.

A brief history of de jure taxation in Brazil

The structure of taxes was more or less consistent throughout the 1940–80 period. Firms paid a corporate income tax, which was set and collected by the federal government.

There was also the ICMS which was a sales tax on raw materials. Food was subject to this tax, if it was used to produce a commercial product. ICMS was nominally set and collected by the states; however federal legislation and budgetary policies somewhat restricted the autonomy of the states in the administration of this tax. ICMS was a true sales tax, as opposed to a value-added tax, in that raw materials that were used in multiple stages of production were charged the ICMS at each stage. This produced the famous *cascada* (cascade) of repeat taxation which has been a long-standing feature of the Brazilian corporate tax system.

Service firms, such as those in this study, would have also paid the ISS, a tax on service receipts. This was a municipal tax, although as with ICMS, federal law limited the capacity of cities to vary the implementation of ISS.

Finally, firms would have paid local property taxes. Unlike ICMS and ISS, these were relatively unregulated, with tax rates varying substantially across regions. In this study, barbers would have primarily paid ISS and property tax. Although restaurants and hotels would have paid these taxes as well, their primary burden was ICMS, due to the taxes paid on the groceries required for their food service operations. (Andersen 1976, Amed 2000)

The payroll taxes that the firms in this study would have been legally obligated to pay were not unlike the payroll taxes that characterize contemporary Brazil. In 1940, service employers would have had to pay for the following social charges: *Previdência* (Social Security), paid vacations, holiday bonuses, provision against medical infirmity, unemployment insurance, workers compensation and union dues. In 1946, small charges were added to pay for SENAC, the government vocational training program for the services, and for SESC, community recreational facilities.

In the 1960s, social charges became substantially more expensive. A thirteenth month of pay was mandated as were family allowances. The unemployment insurance program was dramatically restructured and required higher contributions (in part to provide a source of capital for government housing projects). The workers compensation program was revamped and a small program of schooling subsidies was added as well.

In the 1970s, there was an additional tax to finance government industrialization efforts, and a small charge as well to pay for the CEBRAE (later SEBRAE), the organization which services small business. (Campanhole and Campanhole 1983, dos Santos 1996, Nascimento 1975, Santos 1973)

De facto taxation: Low effective burdens despite high nominal rates

Despite the presence of a legal regime with high de jure rates and cascading multiple taxation of the same items, the level of taxes actually paid by Brazilian firms in the personal services during this period was surprisingly low. The Service Census data show that between 1940 and 1980, non-payroll taxes never exceeded 3 percent of total receipts. For hotels, the burden was just under 3 percent. For Restaurants it was 2 percent. For barber/beauty, it was a mere 1 percent.

Payroll taxes were of about the same order of magnitude – generally less than 3 percent of revenues. In hotels, the burden was virtually the same as for non-payroll taxes, just under 3 percent. Restaurants paid only 1 percent of their revenues in payroll taxes. Barber and beauty shops had a payroll burden that was greater than the non-payroll burden, but it was still modest. Only 2 percent of their revenues went to payroll taxes.

Even when the two items are combined, the overall tax burden does not amount to much. It was heaviest for hotels, where just under 6 percent of their revenues went to taxes. In restaurants and barber/beauty, employers paid 3 percent of their receipt in taxes.

There is no doubt that the numbers reported here are significantly lower than what would be expected from the Brazilian tax laws of the time. Undoubtedly, significant tax evasion was occurring, and that these numbers could have been increased with greater enforcement by the fiscal authorities.

However, that said, it would seem that Brazilian firms were able to effectively neutralize the adverse effect of taxation on their businesses. One would expect that such low rates of taxation would have had very little impact on the levels of employment in these firms – and that is in fact what seems to have occurred.

Statistical results

The effects of non-payroll, payroll and all taxes combined were analyzed for hotels, restaurants and barber/beauty. We ran simple analyses of the core model plus taxation. We also ran more complex analyses in which primary costs for each industry were added to the equation. The exact mathematical results can be found in the Appendix *Details of Statistical Results*. The clear majority of runs show no adverse effects of taxes on employment – although there are individual exceptions to this case. For simple equations with no control for other industrial costs – all of the restaurant analyses showed zero effects for taxation. Most of the barber/beauty runs showed zero effects for taxation – including the summary equation where the total tax burden of payroll and non-payroll taxes combined is considered. (The equation that considers non-payroll taxes alone did find a negative effect for taxation.) Hotels in contrast did show more robust harm from taxation. The equations for all taxation – and for payroll taxes by themselves did show taxes lowering employment. There was no adverse employment effect for non-payroll taxation.

The previous equations however methodologically *over-estimate* the effect of taxation. This is because no other business cost is included in the model. Taxes are not the only cost incurred by small businesses. Borrowing from the results of the chapter to follow, we ran a series of equations including the core variables, taxation and the single largest non-labor cost relevant to each industry. Including such a correction in the model incorporates the common sense that areas where taxes seem high can be areas where overall prices are high – and that factor prices rather than taxes per se are the primary obstacle inhibiting business growth.

The dominant factor cost in hotels and restaurants is raw materials. In both cases, the raw material is food. Restaurants sell food as their primary product; hotels' restaurant operations increase the importance of food as an input. In Brazil, nearly all hotels offer a complimentary breakfast with every overnight stay. Most also have in-house bars, and many have in-house restaurants – some of which are justly famous. President Collor was known to have been particularly fond of the special Saturday *feijoada* at the Rio de Janeiro Hotel Caesar Park.

The dominant non-labor factor cost in barber/beauty shops is rent. This relationship is elaborated further in the next chapter.

When exogenous costs are including in the model, the effects of taxation becomes virtually zero. All of the restaurant equations and all of the barber/beauty equations show zero effects of taxation on employment. Hotels show no effect of taxation in two out of the three tests performed. There does seem to be a robust negative effect of payroll taxation on employment. This may reflect the fact that very large hotels may be too large to escape enforcement of labor standards in some cities. In those locations, big hotels may not be able to avoid having to pay taxes on their workers. In contrast, hotels can more easily hide their other taxable liabilities, such as receipts. Plus, the other establishments, restaurants and hotel/barber shops being smaller can more easily evade labor inspection in the first place. As a result, hotels show no adverse effects on employment for non-payroll taxation and for taxation as a whole – and the other two industries show no adverse effects of taxation period. Overall, an advocate of cutting taxes to create jobs would find little support from these numbers.

O'Connor, taxation and employment

O'Connor argued that if there were to be a widespread refusal to pay taxes, the state would lose the ability to reproduce capitalism. The conservative counterargument to this is that taxation draws money out of the private sector that would otherwise be used to create jobs. By this logic, the tax revolt that O'Connor fears would actually be beneficial because it would shift resources from a profligate government to a wealth-creating private sector.

The analysis presented here strongly supports O'Connor and casts doubt on the neoliberal "Tea Party" position. There were few theoretical reasons to expect that tax reduction would increase job growth in the private sector. Worse, even among Brazilian small firms, some of the most economically vulnerable enterprises imaginable, facing a regime of high nominal taxation, tax burdens had no empirical correlation with employment. Absence of geographical competition between firms with differing tax rates, inability to substitute firm output with alternative untaxed products and competitive advantage being determined by non-tax-related costs all reduce the elasticity of employment to taxation. These were absolutely relevant to the Brazilian hotels, restaurants and barber shops in this analysis – and would apply to other firms in the Third World and the developed world as well. The Brazilian firms had an additional protection from taxation in that evasion of taxes was relatively easy. This condition is also fairly widespread in the Third World, although it is less relevant to more developed settings.

Overall, the chapters thus far have shown that many government programs in Brazil produced substantial employment gains. Airports, roads, water, sewage systems and vocational education all increased jobs and reduced poverty. In contrast, tax reduction produced no significant increases in employment. The combined picture supports the O'Connorian position that state expenditures help to reproduce capitalism, and that reducing state resources threatens employment and economic growth.

However, not all determinants of employment in hotels, restaurants and barber/beauty shops were the direct result of government spending. There were subtle economic, social and environmental factors that also played a significant role. Government could have effected these economic, social and environmental factors, but their effect on these parameters would have been weak and indirect. We now turn away from O'Connorian models to different and fairly unusual determinants of job creation. The next analysis looks at real estate markets – and the unexpected relationships between employment and the structure of urban space.

8
How Rent and Urban Verticalization Can Reduce Employment

The literature on economic development in Latin America pays very little attention to urban space and rent. Urban geographers often focus on general questions of urbanism and the spatial distribution of economic activities within and across cities – and pay less attention to whether the structure of cities produces overall economic growth per se. This paper argues that development economists and urban geographers have more to say to each other than might be otherwise supposed – and that the exact form of urbanization has non-trivial effects on poverty in the Third World that have been missed.

In particular, urban structure, shapes the overall amount of commercial space available to producers and with it, levels of rent. As urbanization occurs, cities verticalize. Verticalization changes the supply of buildings, altering the availability of commercial space, and raising the cost of rent. This puts a rent squeeze on small entrepreneurs. These higher rents can reduce employment notably in space-sensitive labor intense industries that are important sources of jobs for the poor. Rent effects can put a drag on the otherwise positive relationship between urbanization and economic growth. Under such conditions, considerations of state policy that affect the availability of commercial space might be important – particularly policies involving downtown development or rent control. This argument is illustrated by materials on Brazilian restaurants and barber shops between 1940 and 1980 where the relationship between rent and employment was particularly pronounced.

Sergipe as a lead sector in residual employment in barber/beauty

The present argument had its origin in the observation that Sergipe, a Northeastern state that is the smallest state in Brazil, led Brazil in residual barber/beauty employment, notably in the 1940–80 period. In 1940, it had the second highest residual barber/beauty employment of all the non-Amazonian states. For every other year from 1950 to 1980, Sergipe led Brazil outright. This is a remarkable performance for an otherwise obscure state with no obvious unusual economic advantages.

This finding precedes the great Cardoso explosion in vocational education – and cannot be explained by SENAC dynamics. Wages, taxes and costs of material were typical of those in the Brazilian Northeast, where many other states had low residuals. There were no special corporatist organizations of barbers or beauticians that allowed for the pooling of social capital for mutual defense. There were no unusual ethnic ties among barbers.

In fact, the first response of Sergipano academics of their state's strong performance in barber/beauty was skepticism and surprise. The numbers were solid (and were reconfirmed for 2000 in an intuitive manner by the author doing block listings). The skepticism of the Sergipano academics came from the fact that Sergipe had rarely excelled on any other indicator of economic performance. The literature on the economic history of Sergipe paints a picture of backward uncompetitive agriculture, a small and fragile industrial sector and a capital city that survives narrowly on central-place functions. (Wynne 1973, Almeida 1991, França 1999)[1] Nothing I found disconfirmed that picture.

The one distinctive feature of Sergipe – was that Sergipe had low rent. Rent data comes from the same source from which the employment estimates are derived: the 1940–80 Brazilian Service Censuses. These censuses contain data on every commercial cost paid by the service firms in the census. All of the Sergipean cost profiles were typical of the Brazilian Northeast – except rent. In 1940, Sergipe had the 6th lowest rent of any non-Amazonian state in Brazil. In 1950, it was the 2nd lowest, and 1960 the 3rd lowest. In 1970, 1975 and 1980, Sergipe had the absolute lowest rents for barbers and beauticians in non-Amazonian Brazil.

This led to an investigation in Brazil as a whole on the determinants and effects of rent in Brazil as a whole. The traditional literature on urbanization in Latin America was not helpful.

Traditional dualistic accounts of urbanization and economic development

The pre-existing literature on urbanization and economic development essentially ignores questions of the causes and effects of rent. There is a massive literature on Third World cities – but most of this does not discuss the relationship between urban structure and national rates of employment or economic growth per se. The literature that addresses this narrow question is smaller and generally focuses on urban dualism, the coexistence of a wealthy urban center with a periphery that is desperately poor. (Berry 1981, Roberts 1978, Sassen 2000)

There is some consensus as to what causes this dualism. The economic growth, and wealth are caused by

1) *the concentration of administrative functions in cities.* (Berry and Kasarda 1977, Santos 1993)
2) *the concentration of transportation facilities in cities.* (Stinchcombe 1968, Estall and Buchanan 1964) and
3) *the concentration of information and technology in cities.* (Santos 1993, Castells 1991, Sassen 2000)

There is also some agreement about what creates the large poverty populations in Third World cities. Low urban incomes and extensive slums are a product of

1) *globalization* (Santos 2001, Robinson 2004)
2) *extensive rural-urban inmigration* (ECLA 1962, Roberts 1978, Singer 1973)
3) *limited educational attainment within the poverty population* (ECLA 1962, Campino et al. 1985, IPEA 2000)
4) *disarticulation within the primary sector* (Roberts 1978, Barnet and Muller 1974)
5) *hypertrophy of the secondary sector* (Berry and Kasarda 1977, Singer 1973, Portes et al. 1989)
6) *weak public services and government regulation* (Berry 1981, Cardoso and Ribeiro 1996)
7) *political processes* (Portes and Walton 1971, Perlman 1976)

Dualistic treatments of Third World urbanism make a number of legitimate and useful claims. However, two mild critiques can be put forward. The first is that traditional analyses of Third World dualism put excessive emphasis on the creation rather than the destruction of jobs. Positive accounts emphasize urbanism's role in the development of advanced technological sectors; more critical accounts emphasize how urbanism produces low quality peripheral employment such as sweatshops and self-employed street vending. There is less explicit attention to how urban development might eliminate jobs altogether – rather than merely create unremunerative jobs.

Secondly, little attention is given to the actual role of buildings and commercial space in the study of city life and employment. While urbanization involves many considerations, one of the most obvious is that cities increase the number of large, tall buildings. The substitution of large collectively-used structures for simple single family dwellings has many consequences, including the increased monopoly control of structures and access to space.

Urbanization, space and economic growth

The significance of commercial space. Little attention has been paid to access to commercial space as a factor in economic growth. Space is a form of capital when implicated in the production process. (Harvey 1982, França 1999) Not all producers have equal access to space – and not all producers can find space of the quality and quantity that they need. Large capitalist firms usually have easy access to space, although this process may be politically mediated. (Harvey 1982) Middle sized firms may lack political influence, but can generally purchase whatever space they need on the open market. Microentrepreneurs in contrast may not have the financial assets to pay commercial rent. Such marginal businesses may be forced to choose between working in the residence of the primary entrepreneur or not having a location at all.

Working in a home puts substantial restrictions on a small firm. There are obvious limits on firm growth due to limits on the machinery, supplies and staff that can fit into a small urban dwelling. Most importantly, domestic location restricts one's access to potential markets. Locating in a commercial center, or in a district that contains other firms working in one's particular sector, may be one of the few ways of attracting customers. The marketing question is less of an issue for firms that sub-contract work from larger producers. Such enterprises can make themselves known by one-on-one contacts with potential outsourcers. Such contact is especially easy when the microentrepreneur is a former worker for the large firm in question, or knows people who can make the appropriate introductions. Work from one or two institutional clients can be more than sufficient to keep a smaller firm working at full capacity.

The marketing problem becomes more severe if the firm must sell to the general public or to a large number of dispersed clients. Here, location in a residential neighborhood can isolate the firm from the places where customers go to seek the kinds of service offered by the company. Many services must compete on convenience as well as price and quality. Central location can produce access to a broad array of consumers coming from all over a region; location in a remote district may reduce one's potential market to the small population of residents in the one's own neighborhood.

This was made quite clear in my fieldwork among Sergipano barbers and beauticians. I interviewed a number of barbers and beauticians who worked in both commercial premises and private homes. I only encountered two examples of successful beauticians who worked out of their own homes. Nearly all of the successes that I met worked in commercial premises with good street traffic. The street did not necessarily have to be downtown. One success was on the main street of a *favela* (slum) on the main bus route to the center city. Another success was on a busy commercial street in a densely settled working class residential district. In contrast, I encountered significant numbers of marginal and failing barber/beauticians working out of their homes. The ones who lived in remote areas were particularly likely to have left the sector. Obviously these stories have multiple causes. Lack of success lowers the ability to

Figure 8.1   Cost Components of Selected Brazilian Industries 1940–1980

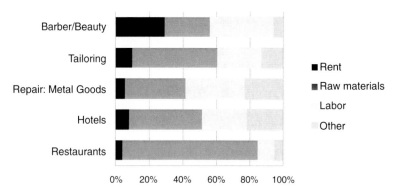

pay rent, which further lowers success. However, access to space was a make or break point for most of the barber/beauticians.

Why were barbers and beauticians so sensitive to the question of rent and the availability of space? The issue is that barbers and beauticians have very few other costs – so rent looms large in their total budgets.

Data on the cost structure of Brazilian firms comes from the Brazilian Economic Censuses. These censuses exist for industry (manufacture), agriculture, commerce (retail and wholesale trade) and the services. These censuses show the actual costs paid by firms in the industries that were covered. These are remarkable data for social scientists – and are generally underused, both in Brazil and by foreign students of Brazil.

The Service Census shows the cost structure of barber/beauty shops and a number of other types of service establishments. Rent represented three times as large a share of total costs in barber/beauty than it did in even the second most rent industry sector in the table. Rent represented 29 percent of the total costs of barber/beauty shops, as opposed to 10 percent of the costs of tailor shops, 8 percent of the costs of hotels, 6 percent of the costs of repair shops and 4 percent of the costs of restaurants.

The centrality of rent for barbers and beauticians came from the relative unimportance of other factors of production. Restaurants were heavily driven by materials costs. Eighty-one percent of the expenses of restaurants went to food. In a profound sense, a restaurant is merely another form of grocery store, where the food is consumed on the premises rather than taken home. Materials also represent 44 percent of the costs of hotels. This is because the purchase of the actual premises of the hotel tends to be a one-time major capital expenditure. Once the basic hotel is obtained – the primary variable expenses are the food and alcohol that is served in the hotel restaurants and bars. This is particularly the case in nations other than the United States, such as Brazil, where breakfast is automatically included in the daily rate. Repair shops spend 40 percent of their expenses on raw materials, and tailors spend 52 percent of their expenses on the same. The importance of parts and cloth to these producers is obvious.

The second major expense is labor. Barber and beauty shop work is labor intense, so it is not surprising that labor represents a large percentage of total outflows. Thirty-nine percent of all barber/beauty expenses go to personnel. In restaurants, this figure is a mere 10 percent. Even if a restaurant employs French chefs and sommeliers – the cost of purchasing prime ingredients for haute cuisine more than matches the additional expense of hiring skilled labor. Hotels spend 27 percent of their budgets on labor, a number identical to what is spent by tailors. Repair shops spend 39 percent of their expenses on labor, which reflects the artisanal nature of some repair work.

Outside of rent and labor, there are not very many other expenses in a barber/beauty shop. Other expenses (taxes, advertising, insurance, legal etc.) only represent 5 percent of the expenses of barber/beauty shops. This number is 5 percent for restaurants, 22 percent for hotels (fees to travel agents and marketing being an issue here), 25 percent for repair shops (capital goods being important in this case) and 13 percent for tailoring.

Thus, even though rent was the second most important factor of production in barber/beauty shops, the absence of either material or other expenses increased the saliency of the costs of commercial space. Furthermore, barbers and beauticians need access to locations with high customer access, making it difficult for them if they have to accept cheaper locations out of the main flow of commercial foot traffic.

So barbers and beauticians are space-sensitive. What then are the rent dynamics that determine employment in space-sensitive industries?

Determinants of rent

There are at least four factors that determine rents. The first two involve supply and demand. The greater the supply of rental space, the lower the price of that rental space will be. The greater the demand for rental space, the higher the price of that rental space will be. The supply of space is determined by the number of available buildings. The more buildings, the more locations a potential renter can consider for locating his firm.[2] Demand is determined by economic development. The greater the level of economic activity, the more firms that will exist that are competing for the supply of commercial space.

> H_1: *Rents will be negatively correlated with the number of buildings in a region.*
>
> H_2: *Rents will be positively correlated with economic development.*

A third consideration is the verticalization of buildings. Large multi-user structures will have higher rents than smaller single occupant facilities. Verticalization reflects the concentration of real estate value in a small number of select locations. If everyone needs to locate downtown, and there is a limited amount of land area downtown, developers will build increasingly dense multi-user structures to accommodate as many tenants as possible; the higher rent paid by these tenants will reflect the desirability of their central location.

However, the verticalization of buildings is also associated with the development of a landlord class that can exert monopoly power by controlling access to building space. In a city with large numbers of simple single-user structures, there is typically broadly dispersed control over the ownership of these structures. Individual home ownership or store ownership is possible because the cost of each structure is low. Furthermore, small scale makes self-construction of new facilities a practical alternative for residents or business people of modest means.

In contrast, few individual residents or business people could construct a 40 story condominium tower, or a downtown office skyscraper. The increasing scale of buildings concentrates the space used by large numbers of tenants under the control of a small number of owners and developers. Some of this comes from the fact that one building can now represent the homes or workspaces of hundreds of renters. Some of this comes from the fact that reducing the viability of small projects represents a form of restriction of market entry and promotes the ownership of multiple buildings by the same small group of real estate investors. This increases the concentrated control by real estate interests of the supply of commercial space and in both senses of the word, creates monopoly rents.

H3: *Rents will be positively correlated with the degree of verticalization of buildings in a region.*

The present discussion has focused on market factors. However, social and non-economic factors play a significant role in rent determination as well. The most important sociological determinant of rent is the intervention of the state in the real estate market. Many forms of political action shape urban dynamics, such as the planning of downtown development projects, the creation of zoning laws, the construction of public housing, the development of public markets, the state financing of residential and commercial construction, and the promotion or discouragement of real estate investment as a whole by the regulation of interest rates by public monetary authorities. All of these considerations introduce institutional and social factors into the setting of market rents and property values.

The most important of these state interventions is rent control. Rent control puts an obvious limitation on the price of space and facilitates the economic survival of rent sensitive enterprises. Generally as urbanization increases, increasing economic activity and verticalization will raise rents significantly, by increasing both the demand for and the monopoly control of space. If the state chooses to implement rent control, it can preserve employment in those sectors that might otherwise be eliminated by increases in the cost of commercial space.

H4: *Rent control will lower rents even in the face of market factors that would have produced rent increases.*

Analysis

The above hypotheses are tested with data on employment in Brazilian barber/beauty shops between 1940 and 1980. The rent data are those reported by the Brazilian Service Census, corrected for regional price differentials and divided by receipts to remove the effect of scale. The receipts denominator has a double advantage. The first is that it removes the effect of scale from the analysis, *without using employment* per se. This reduces the danger that any negative result would be an artifact of employment appearing on both sides of a regression equation. Secondly, because both rent and receipts are measured in the same metric, local nominal currency, dividing one by the other eliminates all variations that would be due to currency fluctuations – a major consideration in an economy with the massive price instability of Brazil.

To test the effect of the number and shape of buildings, we use material from the 1970 Brazilian Predial Census. This is another relatively unusual census – a census of all of the buildings available in Brazil![3] Most nations have a household census, which collects data on household units, and includes data on the physical structures in which they live. However, household censuses limit themselves to residential structures and do not include government offices, churches, or more importantly, commercial buildings. The predial census includes all of these. The census also includes information on the number of floors as well as the number of buildings. While number of floors is not the same as square footage, it does provide a proxy for the concept of usable space. The ratio of floors to buildings gives an index of verticalization – which is hypothesized to have important effects on rent.

Regression analyses were performed adding rent to the core models of Chapter 2. The results overwhelmingly confirmed the importance of rent for barber/beauty shops. Rent had a very strong negative relationship to employment. The coefficient was statistically significant and the new equation had a much higher goodness of fit than did the original rent-less core equation. More specific information about the equation can be found in the Appendix *Details of Statistical Results*.

We now test hypotheses H_1 through H_3 by looking at the determinants of rent. For the 19 non-Amazonian states in 1970 for which data were available, we calculated Pearson correlations for the relationship between economic development, the actual structure of the buildings within a state, and the rent paid by barbers within that state as a percentage of their receipts. As before, the actual Pearson coefficients can be found in the Appendix *Details of Statistical Results*. All of the correlations were significant, large and in the direction predicted by the hypotheses. Actually, the correlations were very high. A correlation of 0.50 is considered to be a very strong relationship. Five out of eight of the correlations are correlated with an absolute value of 0.70 or higher. Two are between 0.50 and 0.70; the weakest is at 0.46.

Essentially rent was strongly related to all three measures of economic development – infant mortality, urbanization and female labor force participation. Essentially economic development increases the demand for commercial space, as increasing rates of economic activity require the increased use of space for economic purposes. Increased demand for space increased the price of obtaining that space.

Just as demand for space raised rents, the supply of space reduced rents. The number of buildings per capita showed a very strong negative correlation with rent. The more buildings there were in a state, net of the population, the lower was the commercial rent. There was a similar relation between the number of floors of commercial space per capita and commercial rent: the more floors, the lower the rent. The two correlations were nearly identical – which suggests the obvious high correlation between the number of buildings and the number of floors in a state.

Verticalization – the ratio of floors to buildings – also increases rent. Verticalization represents the concentration of usable space into a small number of large structures – which facilitates the monopolistic control of space by landlords. The correlation of rent with verticalization was very strong – well over 0.70. Rent also correlated with the verticalization of new construction – although not as much as with total verticalization.

The presence of new construction is also positively associated with high rent. This was the highest correlation observed in the dataset. There are many interpretations possible for this finding. This could reflect the destruction of older small structures and their replacement with larger newer structures. This could be another indicator of verticalization. My own best guess is that this represents the effect of rent control. Older buildings were subject to stringent policies of rent control. New buildings were unaffected by these laws, leaving the landlord free to set the rent at whatever level he or she liked. Thus, the new construction measure is quite possibly reflects the balance of controlled and uncontrolled rents with uncontrolled rents being higher.

The effect of rent control on rents and therefore on employment may have been more important than writers on Brazil acknowledge. To consider this, let us review the history of rent control in Brazil in greater detail.

The presence and extent of rent control[4]

Rent control was first implemented in Brazil in the Decreto N. 24150 of April 20, 1934. This was one of the pro-working-class policies of Getulio Vargas, the left-wing general who governed Brazil from 1930 to 1945 and then again from 1951 to 1954. Vargas instituted a number of populist policies introducing the secret ballot, providing the vote to women, instituting a national social security program, and passing generous worker protection laws. (Burns 1993) In 1934, he sponsored nationwide rent control legislation of a remarkably rigorous nature. The primary targets of this policy were residential tenants; however the legal regime for commercial tenants was practically as generous. All leases were now required to have a minimum length of at least five years. When these leases lapsed, they were to be renewed at their old rate in nominal currency.

If the landlord wanted a rate increase, he had to go to court and show that the prevailing market rate was higher than that in the lease. Note that even if judges were uniformly sympathetic to landlords in these hearings, the Brazilian justice system is notoriously slow. The delays associated with obtaining a clearance from a judge would have added significant time to the application of the old lease rates beyond the nominal period of five years.

The landlord could avoid the hearing by one of three methods. He could have a signed offer from a third party for the property; he could revert use of the property back to members of his own family; as a last resort, he could destroy the property and build a new one which would be free from the terms of the old lease. The first two options were only partially useful. The landlord could not relet the property to anyone in the same line of work as the original tenant, meaning for example that a restaurant would have to be converted into a non-restaurant facility if it were to be relet to a third party. Even these conditions were not enough to guarantee a rate increase. The tenant could appeal that the new lease was out of line with current market conditions. The tenant could demand to be indemnified for the cost of moving and the tenant could demand penalties for a host of procedural irregularities. To provide disincentives for third parties to agree to accept higher rents, the law allowed that the third parties, as well as the landlord, could be subject to substantial penalties if the tenant suffered any financial losses due to irregularities in the releasing process.

Under occasional conditions, a lease could be renegotiated under a three year rather than a five year time frame. Hyperinflation was one such qualifying condition. However, even a three year lag allows for dramatic lowering of the value of a nominal rent, when prices are rising at the extreme rates that were typical of Brazil during the worst of its bouts with inflation.

Subsequent changes in the law made leases more rigid in the face of inflation rather than more flexible. In 1975, the Salário Mínimo was banned as being the basis for monetary corrections in rent negotiations. Since the Salário Mínimo was used as the basis for all sorts of other inflation-based adjustments, the removal of this factor made rents relatively more rigid. In 1979, a law was passed banning midlease changes of rent in any form. Very limited inflation-based adjustments were made possible, but the primary forms of the 1934 law were fully maintained. The leasers had to agree to the change – otherwise no rent changes were possible. In the event of no agreement, the landlord had to wait until the end of a five year period and then commence a process of judicial review. Even with consent, adjustments could only be made on an annual level. Annual adjustments, even if agreed upon, would have been an inadequate basis for change in a period where prices were octupling every five years.

The only relief for landlords was that in 1979, there was a one-time-only updating of rent rates to reflect monetary adjustments that had occurred between the inception of the lease and 1979. There was no other mass adjustment during this period, and while the mechanisms for rent setting have changed somewhat subsequently, no other mass adjustment has occurred up to the present day.[5]

The probable effect of rent control on rents

Brazil both urbanized and underwent significant inflation between 1940 and 1980. Given the results of the correlation analysis, one would expect that real rents in Brazil would have risen between 1940 and 1980.

Figures 8.2 and 8.3 show the trends in Brazil from 1940 to 1980 in urbanization, rents and inflation. All figures are ecological means, in which each state is given an equal weight, regardless of

Figure 8.2   Trends in Rent and Urbanization in Brazil 1940–1980 (1980 = 100)

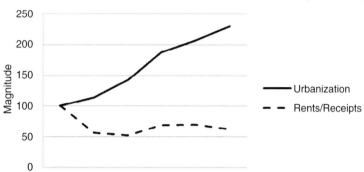

Figure 8.3   Trends in Rent and Inflation in Brazil 1940–1980 (1940 = 100)

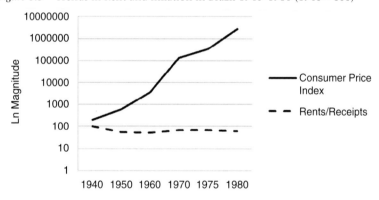

population. The urbanization and rent data come from the censuses. The price measure is the index of prices of consumer goods in Rio de Janeiro.

The key findings of these graphs is that rents as a percent of receipts were more or less stable in Brazil from 1940 to 1980 – with a tendency if anything to go down. In contrast, both urbanization and inflation increased enormously. Urbanization increased in every decade. In 1940, the average state in Brazil was 26 percent urban; in 1980, the average state was 61 percent urban. The increase in inflation was even more dramatic. Figure 8.3 requires the use of a logarithmic scale just to keep the inflation curve on the page. The price index rose from 100 in 1940 to 2,739,616 in 1980. Prices quintupled in the 1940s, septupled in the 1950s, increased by over thirtyfold in the 1960s, nearly tripled again between 1970 and 1975, and octupled between 1975 and 1980.

Inflation is a very powerful reducer of factor costs in an environment where there are institutional barriers to rapid price adjustments. Seidman (1994) has shown that Brazil experienced a parallel phenomenon with labor costs, where rapid inflation combined with slow, awkward adjustments in salary rates, led to the substantial lowering of worker's real wages, along with substantial windfall profits for management. The data presented here suggest similar processes were occurring in the real estate market. The existence of rent control froze rents at rates far below market levels and insulated small producers from the adverse consequences of urbanization and verticalization. New highly productive firms could find expensive space in freshly constructed, modern facilities. However, older producers were sheltered from the price changes occurring in the property market, and were experienced a significant substantive reduction in their factor costs. As we have seen from the statistical analysis, some of these savings were translated into increased employment.

Conclusion

This chapter provides both theoretical arguments and empirical materials that suggest that the sociology of development needs to begin to reconsider spatial factors in its analysis. Attention to legitimate concerns about international finance, local ownership and state policy must not lose sight of the fact that the determinants of many of forms of employment are based on simple costs and on the availability of factors of production. While rent may not play as much of a role as financial capital or labor, it is nevertheless an important factor of production. The dynamics that shape the offer of space are profoundly sociological and are integrally related to social structure, political dynamics and the changing constellations of class.

Rent was an important predictor of employment in restaurants and barber/beauty. Employment in both sectors was probably increased by the rent control that existed in Brazil during this period.

Does this mean that modern Third World governments should institute universal rent control as a tool for raising employment? Expanding this analysis to an entire economy requires considering other factors that could not be incorporated into an analysis of barbers. Some sectors are not particularly affected by rent dynamics at all. We present no data on hotels because hotels do not rent space. Production facilities with fixed locations, such as coal mines, would not likely to be affected by rent dynamics. The list of rent-immune sectors is probably long.

More importantly, a key source of employment in most Third World economies is civil construction. Building new housing is an important component of economic growth – and one that is easily as neglected in the study of economic development as are hotels, restaurants and barber/beauty shops. Rent and rent controls are likely to have profound effects on the dynamics of new housing starts and employment in the building trades. The full impact of these mechanisms would need to be considered making any dramatic changes in national rental laws.

However, what can be said is that urban planners and municipal authorities need to think about access to commercial space for small and marginal enterprises. One of the advantages of old un-redeveloped Third World center cities is that they are virtual rabbit warrens of small-scale enterprise. Cheap older buildings help to support a rich population of minor enterprises – such as photographers, internet cafes, key shops, and photocopy stores. When these old centers are redeveloped, the spaces for small marginal businesses often disappear. The beautiful new skyscrapers have a gigantic empty atrium where there once were 40 offices for struggling petty bourgeoisie. The urban economy may benefit from the highly productive, high value added, financial or corporate offices that exist in the upper stories of the new skyscrapers. But what has been gained in the production of elite office space has been lost in the unemployment of a host of microbusinesses who needed access to center city traffic.

There ought to be a way to zone and design Third World center cities to make adequate space for both types of users. Urban architecture is not irrelevant to the creation of employment in the service sector. If downtown development exclusively considers the creation of glamorous high rent projects – and leaves no space for the low rent user – the jobs that are created in one highly visible sector may be wiped out in a sector that no one is watching.

9
Frontier Development as Job Creation – With Social Costs

Brazil, like every other land-based nation in the Western Hemisphere, has a frontier. It is not unreasonable to posit that the presence of a frontier has some effect on economic growth. Frontiers provide land, which is a form of capital. They provide mineral extractive sources that can be developed. They stimulate migration. This development is not cost free. The damage done by frontier openings to the environment and to indigenous populations is well known and of concern. However, the opening up of interior lands has some effect on economic growth, although the size of this effect has never been precisely estimated. If the effects of opening the frontier were small, it would make the ecological damage associated with this process indefensible. If the benefits of opening the frontier were substantial, this could pose significant moral and policy questions about the trade-offs between the elimination of poverty and the preservation of the environment.

Why might frontiers stimulate economic development? The case of the Brazilian Center-West provides one set of answers. The southern Amazonian frontier turned into an agricultural powerhouse. The Center-West became a center for large capital intensive high efficiency soybean farms, making Brazil the number one exporter of soy products to the world. The Center-West would also become the dominant producer in Brazil of cattle, cotton, sorghum and rice. (Pereira 1995, IBGE 2004a, 2004b)

Furthermore, the migration stimulated by the opening of frontiers stimulated an expansion in housing, infrastructure creation, retail trade and services. Any increase in population will stimulate in industries designed to serve a general population. The new population will require houses, roads, stores, schools, churches and hospitals, infrastructure that needs to be built only once – but which nevertheless produces a substantial spike in civil construction. The increase in employment in retail trade, education , religion and medicine will be less dramatic at the beginning, but more enduring in the long run as the population will continue to require these services on a permanent basis. Thus there is a non-trivial multiplier effect associated with the opening of frontiers, as the demand for labor increases in a wide variety of sectors independent of the primary crop, mineral or industry that stimulated the outward expansion in the first place.

As a result, frontier expansion can produce economic growth in a number of unexpected sectors; in some cases, that growth can be greater than the growth produced by policies explicitly associated with the sector itself. We will argue that this is exactly what happened in Mato Grosso – in an industry rarely considered in Amazonian discussions – the hotel industry. Between 1940 and 1980 Mato Grosso, rose to a dominant position in the Brazilian hotel and restaurant trade in Brazil. This rise occurred despite the presence of governmental policies oriented towards developing hotels in competing regions.

Terminological note: When this chapter refers to Mato Grosso, it refers to the area that now comprises both the states of Mato Grosso and Mato Grosso do Sul. In 1979, the former state of Mato Grosso was divided into the two states that exist today. Since this chapter involves 1940–79 when the state was undivided, we use the historical terminology and boundaries.

Mato Grosso as a leader in hotel and restaurant employment

When this study was commenced, it was expected that Rio de Janeiro would lead Brazil in residual hotel and restaurant employment, due to its scenic advantages, its role as a cultural center and its long tradition of world class hotels. It was also expected that in the 1970s Bahia would replace Rio as the highest residual due to the urban renewal of Salvador in the 1960s and 1970s and the substitution of Salvador for Rio as the number one tourist destination in Brazil. (EMBRATUR 2000)

Table 9.1 shows that this is not what occurred. Rio was only fourth highest in hotels in 1940, and at some points had the lowest residuals in Brazil. Only Rio's restaurants showed the expected high residuals. Bahia did show the upward curve that was expected, although its revival began earlier than expected in 1960.

The biggest surprise was Mato Grosso. Mato Grosso started poorly as expected, but its residuals rose rapidly. After 1960, it was the dominant

Table 9.1   Rankings in Residual Hotel and Restaurant Employment for Selected Brazilian States: 1940–1980

	Rio De Janeiro		Bahia		Mato Grosso	
	Hotel	Restaurant	Hotel	Restaurant	Hotel	Restaurant
1940	4th Highest	Highest	5th Lowest	2nd Lowest	4th Lowest	6th Lowest
1950	5th Highest	Highest	5th Lowest	5th Lowest	4th Lowest	2nd Lowest
1960	Lowest	7th Lowest	2nd Highest	5th Lowest	3rd Highest	6th Lowest
1970	2nd Lowest	4th Highest	4th Highest	5th Lowest	**HIGHEST**	**HIGHEST**
1975	9th Lowest	2nd Highest	4th Highest	7th Highest	**HIGHEST**	**HIGHEST**
1980	8th Highest	2nd Highest	7th Highest	Highest	**HIGHEST**	4th Highest

force in Brazil in hotels. After 1960, it was also the dominant force in Brazil in restaurants, although it began to fade slightly in 1980.

The Mato Grosso hotel and restaurant renaissance was based on the government opening up of the Amazonian frontier. In an attempt to promote agricultural development, and populate geopolitically sensitive areas near Brazil's borders, the military government of the 1960s and 70s invested extensively in the economic development of the Amazon. Many of the effects of the opening of the frontier were pathological: deforestation, social dislocation, and violent conflicts over land tenure. (Martins 1980)

However, despite this turmoil, westward expansion turned out to be far more successful than its architects had ever imagined could be possible. One of the immediate effects was to promote substantial immigration into the west. This was particularly the case in Mato Grosso. Many of these migrants came from the far south of Brazil; their chosen destination was the far north of Mato Grosso. As such a steady stream of travelers crossed the state of Mato Grosso. A number of small cheap hotels and restaurants arose along the border to take care of the needs of these workers in transit. When they arrived in the north of Mato Grosso, they encountered another set of cheap hotels and restaurants, oriented less towards providing services to people in transport and more towards the provision of migrants with leisure time activities. These eastern and far northern hotels and restaurants were located in areas of relatively negligible economic development. The introduction of a population of travelers and high-spending workers into these impoverished settings produced a surge in hotel and restaurant employment in excess of what would be expected from the local market. This produced a core of primitive hotel capitalists that could then be the seed for future development in the sector.

Brazilian frontier policy and the big push west

So what accounts for the resurgence of hotel and restaurant employment in Mato Grosso? The key issue was the flood of inmigration that entered the state in the 1960s and 1970s. The 1960s saw the beginnings of the great push west that was to revolutionize the spatial distribution of Brazilian population and economic activity. Prior to 1960, Brazil was a littoral society, not unlike an Atlantic Chile with most of the population centers being located on the coast.

Before the 1960s the sheer isolation of Mato Grosso kept it relatively depopulated and economically marginal. Distance from markets kept agriculture relatively primitive – even by Brazilian colonial standards. Agriculture was generally of a subsistence nature, with small-scale cattle ranching near Cuiabá and Rondonopolis. (Pereira 1995) The one exception to this was mate, which had profitable outlets to by river to Paraguay and Argentina. However, mate declined in the twentieth century as better located farms in Parana came to dominate the market. (Rodrigues 1984)

By 1940, only the far south of the state had any connection to the rest of Brazil by railroad. The capital, Cuiabá, not only lacked rail connections, but lacked even a bridge over the Cuiabá river, leaving it separated from two-thirds of the state that it governed. (Abreu 2001) However, in the 1940s, the Vargas government began to take an interest in Mato Grosso, as rubber became an increasingly important military supply. The federal government sponsored an agricultural colony in Dourados in the far south of the state; substantial resources were put into Dourados even though the early returns were not encouraging. After the construction of a railroad spur, the colony took off. (Abreu 2001, Povoas 1996) Dourados is now the technological center of a thriving export-oriented agricultural belt located in the far south of Mato Grosso do Sul.

The linkage of southern Mato Grosso to the south of Brazil by rail combined with the success of the Dourados colony, to encourage the migration of gauchos from Parana and Rio Grande do Sul into the south of Mato Grosso. This process was intensified by a transition away from labor to capital in southern Brazilian agricultural technology. Both mechanization of crops as a whole and the shutting down of coffee farmlands produced a stream of agricultural workers – some of them in possession of capital. They came to the southern half of Mato Grosso, generally near Dourados or Campo Grande. When their enterprises succeeded, this encouraged other gaucho migrants as well as further investments in lands in more northerly parts of the state. (Mueller 1981)

In the 1950s, the federal government sponsored two major road building projects in the Amazon – the Belem-Brasilia road and the Cuiabá-Santarem road. (Abreu 2001) These two roads combined with pre-existing river transport to provide the first time ever north-south transversal of the Amazon. Settlement began to occur on these roads as migrants from Mato Grosso do Sul moved north to the Amazon looking for further economic opportunities. (Mueller 1981) Some of this migration was state sponsored and took the form of relatively unsuccessful publicly financed colonization projects. (Castro et al. 1994) Some of the rest was spontaneous, producing either relatively marginal subsistence agriculture, or small-scale individual mining operations. (Martins 1980, Interview with João Carlos Barrozo 1982)

The speed of Amazonian development was intensified dramatically by the military government after 1964. The Brazilian government had been promoting westward expansion since the Vargas era; the decision to build Brasilia and the Cuiaba-Santarem highway was made in the 1950s by the Kubitschek administration. However, after the Revolution of 1964, the government of Brazil began to give special priority to the settlement of the Amazon as a strategy for national development. (Mueller 1981)

Besides road building, the primary government tool for settling the west was the use of tax incentives. (Mueller 1981) The original application of tax incentives of the Amazon was the 1957 creation of a tax-free custom-free zone in Manaus. Manaus was such a success that in 1962, the Quadros government extended the use of tax incentives to the Amazon in general.

In 1966, the military government intensified this process. Two new organs of Amazonian development were created: SUDAM and the Banco de Amazonia. Between them, SUDAM and the Banco de Amazonia administered a vast array of economic incentive programs, which generally combined subsidized credit with generous deductions in income taxes. By investing in the Amazon, a corporation or individual could get 50 percent of their income tax reduced. Furthermore, credit packages required that investors provide only 25 percent of the total investment in a project, in return for ownership of 100 percent of the equity. With only 25 percent of their own money at stake, many investors felt that they had nothing to lose. There was a huge response to these early projects; SUDAM financed over 180 projects worth over $317 million US dollars, the majority being agricultural or ranching projects. (Mueller 1981)

The settlement of these new *latifundia* led to substantial deforestation, social dislocation and overt conflict. The big land owners had to clear their land at once to show their investment was productive and thus qualified for a tax deduction. Substantial numbers of migrant workers were hired to cut down broad swathes of forest, and put cattle on the cleared land that remained. However, because the viability of these areas as cattle ranches was often tenuous, the post-deforestation investment in ranching was usually minimal. (GPC 1980)

A further issue was the creation of substantial social conflict over the control of land. Much of the land that was distributed by SUDAM was in fact occupied. Questionable means were frequently used to clear SUDAM projects of pre-existing landholders. (Abreu 2001, Martins 1980) Almeida (1989) shows that over 4000 families were involved in land disputes in Mato Grosso in the middle 1970s. Nearly 2000 of these families were involved in conflicts in which violence was used. There is little doubt that the government opening of the north of Mato Grosso was profoundly violent and socially disruptive.

The great migration

The opening of the Amazonian Frontier produced substantial migration into Mato Grosso. Figure 9.2 shows the number and origin of migrants to Mato Grosso in both 1970 and 1980. Between 1960 and 1970, over 433,000 people migrated to Mato Grosso; over 486,000 more entered the state between 1970 and 1980. The 1960–70 migrants represented an increase of 48 percent over the 1960 population; the 1970–80 migrants represented an increase of 30 percent over the 1970 population. This was thus a very substantial flow of population.

The origins of these migrants differed between the two decades. These origins matter, because travelers from different states would have taken different routes to Mato Grosso, and the impact of their travels on the economy of the state would have varied.

In the 1960s, nearly half of the migrants to Mato Grosso came from São Paulo. In the next decade, the absolute volume of Paulista migration into Mato Grosso would fall by nearly half. In 1960, the second largest source of migrants was the Northeast. The Northeastern States produced just over 15 percent of Mato Grosso immigrants. However, by 1980, the absolute flow of nordestino migration would drop to less than half of its original amount. There were comparable declines in the absolute volume and relative share of migrants coming from Minas Gerais, Rio de Janeiro and Espirito Santo.

This loss of migrants from the east was more than compensated for by a dramatic increase in migrants coming from the far South of Brazil. The number of migrants from Parana rose from less than 50,000 in 1960–70 to almost 200,000 in 1970–80. The number of migrants from Santa Catarina and Rio Grande do Sul rose from less than 8,000 in 1960–70 to over 40,000 in 1970–80. There were minor increases as well in the migrants coming from Goiás and the Distrito Federal and from other Amazonian States.

Destinations changed as well during these two periods. Migration in the 1960s was heavily oriented to the southern half of the state, notably around the newly developing agroexport sectors near Campo Grande and Douradoes. The 1970s saw the true opening of the northern frontier, with migrants moving all the way to the Amazon – particularly to the far Northeastern and north central parts of the state.

The changes in both origins and destinations produced very different patterns of migration for the two decades. This is because migrants coming from different states entered Mato Grosso in different geo-

Figure 9.1   Entrance Points for Migrants to Mato Grosso 1970 and 1980

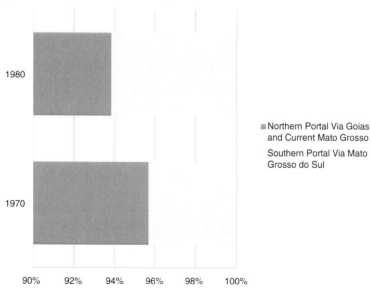

graphical locations. Migrants from Minas Gerais, Goiás, Rio de Janeiro and the Northeastern States, would have entered Mato Grosso via the border with Goiás. The Goiás border covers the Northeast of the state, and primary road connecting the states enters Mato Grosso roughly on a level with Cuiabá. From this northern point, the flows would have dispersed, with some migrants going north into the Amazon, some going west to Cuiabá and some going south to Rondonópolis and Campo Grande. We refer to this point of entry as the Northern Portal.

Migrants from São Paulo, and the far Southern states would have used a Southern Portal. They would have entered the state at practically the southeastern corner of the state, where Mato Grosso meets Paraná. While some migration would have continued west to Campo Grande and Dourados, most would have traversed the entire length of the state going to the new opportunities in the Amazon.

Figure 9.1 shows the relative share of migrants using the Southern and Northern Portals. In these calculations, migrants were assumed to enter from the Southern Portal if they came from Parana, São Paulo, Santa Catarina or Mato Grosso do Sul. Migrants were assumed to enter from the Northern Portal if they came from Goias, Distrito Federal, Minas Gerais, Rio de Janeiro, Espirito Santo or a Northeastern State. Figure 9.1 shows that in 1960–70, migration was roughly evenly divided between the two portals, with 40 percent using the Northern Portal and slightly 60 percent using the Southern Portal. Use of the Northern Portal dropped off with the decline of migration from Minas Gerais and the Northeastern states. Increased migration from Goiás and the Distrito Federal did not compensate for this loss. In contrast, there was a dramatic increase in the migration coming through the Southern Portal, notably from the rise in migrants coming from Parana, Santa Catarina and Rio Grande do Sul. These increases were so substantial as to more than compensate for the decline in migrants coming from São Paulo.

The result of this was a new concentrated stream of migrants entering the state from the southeastern corner and traversing the entire length of the state. This represented a substantial new flow of travelers; this flow of travel would be the basis of the renaissance of Mato Grosso hotels.

How hotels fit in

The substantial migration that both Amazonian and non-Amazonian development provided was the key to the rise of hotel and restaurant generation in Mato Grosso. The hotels and restaurants served three functions. Firstly, they provided road service to migrants passing through the eastern half of Mato Grosso on the way to destinations deeper into the state. Travelers needed places to eat and sleep.

Documentation of the dramatic effect of migration on the hotel economy of Mato Grosso can be found in the 1980 *Diagnostico Socioeconômico do Estado de Mato Grosso*. *When* the Mato Grosso hotel boom was at its peak, the state of Mato Grosso commissioned economic planners to visit every municipality in the state commenting on the potential for economic development. The results of their work were published in the "Socioeconomic Diagnostic of the State of Mato Grosso" which discussed the hotel industry on a town by town basis along with the state of the other sectors of the economy.

In their analysis of Garças, on the far eastern border of the state, they noted the existence of whole hotel towns, whose economic subsistence seemed to depend entirely on providing travel services to migrants. They made similar observations about Rondonopolis and Jaciara in the center of the state. Rondonopolis was the center of a new and dynamic soybean economy with service employment in its own right. Even allowing for soybeans, they attributed the thriving hotel economy of the region to the substantial through traffic associated with recent migration. (GPC 1980)

Secondly, the hotels and restaurants provided services linked to the temporary travel required to set up new businesses in the expanding areas. New entrepreneurs had to visit their new estates, set up and arrange for the appropriate clearing of land, and make the appropriate legal arrangements. These new upper class visitors would have had to make use of the typical facilities used by businessmen on a business trip.

Thirdly, the hotel and restaurant sector would have provided entertainment services to both permanent and temporary residents seeking to enjoy their newly acquired wealth. With few other entertainment options available, a hotel or restaurant with beer or music would have been a significant attraction to the new local labor force.

It is possible that prostitution may have contributed to the demand for hotels as well. The economic analysts of the *Diagnostico Socioeconômico* do not discuss prostitution per se, and all observations on this point are necessarily speculative. However, consider that on the Mato Grosso frontier, many of the elements for the development of a sex industry were present. There was a substantial influx of young unattached males. These males had access to – by their standards – significant disposable income. There was substantial proletarianization of the local female population, through the land loss occurring among the local indigenous and non-indigenous population. Local women were being deprived of their livelihood be it through subsistence agriculture, hunting and gathering or small-scale mineral operations. Traditional Indian communities were undergoing severe and possibly catastrophic cultural change – undercutting the moral authority of traditional leaders – and the capacity of local communities to provide social regulation. All of this would seem to be a tailor-made formula for the development of prostitution.

The historical record is silent on this aspect of the development of Mato Grossense hotels. However, it is not at all silent on the role of migration. Contemporary observers concurred with much of the previous analysis. The State Economic Reports on the Development Potential of Municipalities noted the dependence of hotel business on road trade from migrants. They noted that these establishments catered to a popular rather than a middle class clientele – and that hotels often showed up in areas of social tension, and agrarian disputes. (GPC 1980)

Statistical support

The regional distribution of hotel employment supports this argument. Table 9.2 lists the mesoregions of Mato Grosso in order of relative per capita employment in hotel and restaurants, along with an indicator of immigration – population growth – and geographical location.

The relationship between population growth and hotel employment is weak. The northernmost area of the state led the state in hotel employment – and had rates of population growth that dwarfed those in the rest of the state. However, beyond that, there is little relation between population growth and hotel employment elsewhere in the state.

This weak relation stems from that hotel employment being more likely to occur in the areas through which migrants *passed through*, rather than at their final destinations. As such, it was heavily concentrated on the eastern border of the state, and was particularly heavy in portals leading into Mato Grosso elsewhere.

After Northern Mato Grosso, the second heaviest center of hotel and restaurant employment was Paranaiba, on the eastern edge of present day Mato Grosso do Sul. This was the main entry point for migrants from Minas Gerais. It was also a through point for migrants from the Rio Grande do Sul and Parana to pass through on the way north to Amazon.

The third largest concentration was in Tres Lagoas. This too is on the eastern edge of the state, and is the portal from São Paulo. The next three largest centers are also on the eastern border of the state, and between all of them the eastern frontier makes up one large hotel belt. Other locations

Table 9.2   Selected Characteristics of Mesoregions in Mato Grosso 1980

Mesoregion	Hotel-Restaurant Employment P.C.1980	Population Growth Rate 1970–80	Geographical Location
North Mato Grosso	0.0111	3.62	Far North
Paranaiba	0.0106	0.18	Eastern Edge of MS – Portal from Minas Gerais
Tres Lagoas	0.0104	0.09	Eastern Edge of MS South of Paranaiba – Portal from São Paulo
Alto Taquari	0.0100	0.35	North of MS Incl. East Edge – Links Paranaiba and TL to Norte MT
Garças	0.0094	0.05	Eastern Edge of Current MT – North of Alto Taquari Links AT to Norte MT
Dourados	0.0089	0.21	Far South of MS Incl. East Edge – Portal to Parana
Pantanais	*0.0087*	*–0.03*	*Far SW of MS – Pantanal*
Bodoquena	0.0086	0.21	Center West of MS
Rondonopolis	0.0086	0.22	Center South of Current MT
Cuiaba	0.0085	0.86	Center of Current MT
Alto Guapore-Jauru	*0.0084*	*0.90*	*SW Corner Current MT – Pantanal*
Alto Paraguai	0.0078	0.79	West of Cuiaba
Campo Grande	0.0069	0.84	Center of MS
Municipio of Santo Antonio deLeverger	0.0045	–0.017	Location of Aguas Quentes

MT = Mato Grosso   MS = Mato Grosso do Sul

had far fewer hotels and restaurants, even if they were economically dynamic. Note for example that Campo Grande, the rapidly growing commercial central city for the south of the state, and Cuiabá, the capital of the state all had fairly mediocre rates of hotel and restaurant employment.

Alternative specifications

Of course, this is not the only potential explanation of high residuals in Mato Grosso. Skeptical readers might argue that the findings in Table 9.2 are the result of any of the following:

1) FEDERAL POLICIES FOR THE PROMOTION OF TOURISM. It could have been that the official national policies of EMBRATUR for the stimulation of hotel and employment provided a distinctive advantage to Mato Grosso.
2) STATE POLICIES FOR THE PROMOTION OF TOURISM. It could have been that the Mato Grossense government itself took a leading role in the promotion of tourism – and that its successful actions paid off for the state.
3) THE RISE OF ECOTOURISM. Currently, ecotourism is a dominant factor in the travel business in the west. Mato Grosso is the home of the Pantanal – a famous ecologically important marshland. The focused development of this area could have accounted for the Matogrossense advantage.
4) ENTREPRENEURIAL EXCELLENCE IN MATO GROSSO HOTELS. The Mato Grossense hotel community may have had a set of businessmen with unusual skills and a capacity for delivering a high quality product. Superior business practices and superior hotels might have produced a Mato Grossense competitive advantage.

The rest of the chapter will show that these four explanations are inconsistent with the data.

Alternative 1: Federal Tourism Development Policy. The development of tourism during this period was the official responsibility of EMBRATUR. Brazil has had a history since the 1930s of having some form of official government planning and regulation of tourism. However, until 1971, most of these organizations produced written plans but had minimal effects on actual policy. (Cruz 2001) In 1967, EMBRATUR was founded and given a more active role in the state promotion of tourism. (Ferraz 1977) A rigorous program of state ratings and inspections of tourist facilities was developed. Substantial funds were committed to hotel development, notably with the creation of the investment program, FUNGETUR in 1971. (Cruz 2001) Throughout the 1970s, there was aggressive public investment in hotels using a combination of tax subsidies, loans and grants. In principle, if Mato Grosso had benefited disproportionately from such federal monies, this could explain the high employment in hotels and restaurants.

Figure 9.2   Hotel Rooms with EMBRATUR Financing per Capita 1973–1980

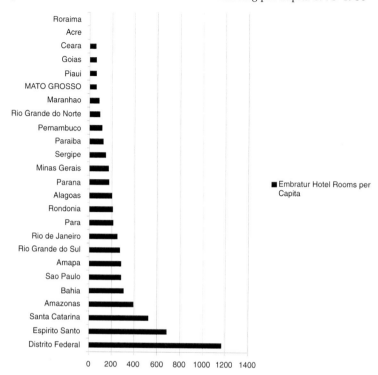

Figure 9.2 shows the regional distribution of EMBRATUR hotel invest-ments from 1973 to 1980. The material comes from the EMBRATUR yearbooks.[1] In terms of the gross number of hotel rooms financed, the five top states were São Paulo, Bahia, Rio de Janeiro, Minas Gerais and Rio Grande do Sul. Hotel investment was concentrated in the major centers of prosperity and population. In this regard, Mato Grosso received only 154 rooms, a total lower than that of only four other states.

However, what is significant is hotel room investment per capita – since obviously larger states will receive larger shares of investment. However, even on this measure, Mato Grosso performed relatively poorly. Mato Grosso ranked sixth from the bottom in per capita federal invest-ment in hotel rooms. It was outranked not only by the great centers of population and industry, but by nearly every coastal state in Brazil except Ceara. Some other factor was causing employment in Mato Grosso to be high.

Alternative 2: Tourism Development by the Mato Grosso State Government.
It was originally expected when this project began that high residuals
would be associated with some sort of provincial state-based rational
economic planning, analogous to the state-led development celebrated in
the work of Celso Furtado (1968) and Peter Evans (1979). In Mato Grosso
this turned out not to be the case. The state of Mato Grosso did have a
tourism policy, but it was small. The actual number of hotel and tourism
development projects that were taken on before the 1990s was very limited.
Furthermore, these projects were not located near the regions of high
residuals in employment.

The original state sponsored hotel development in Mato Grosso was
sponsored by Governor Julio Muller in the late 1930s and 1940s. He
arranged for one hotel to be built in the downtown area of Cuiabá, the
capital city. This was to be the last public investment in any urban hotel
for the remaining 40 years. The other more enduring investment was
a small hotel to be built at Aguas Quentes – a thermal springs to the
southeast of Cuiabá. (Povoas 1996) The springs themselves are relatively dramatic and feature a thermal pool within ten yards of a beautiful waterfall with cold water. Both in terms of scenic beauty and the
high quality of the baths, Aguas Quentes was an obvious candidate for
development. The springs were in a remote depopulated area with no
paved roads linking them to any major cities. Reflecting this, the original hotel at Aguas Quentes was extremely small, more like a forest
lodge than a serious resort. (Povoas 1996)

After the initial construction of Aguas Quentes, there was no further
tourist policy until the 1970s. The economic development agency for
the state, CODEMAT (Companhia de Desenvolvimento do Mato Grosso)
concentrated its efforts on road building, energy projects and agricultural
colonies, most of these in the Amazonian north of the state. Policy for
the center and south of the state emphasized the construction of silos
and refrigerated warehouses to facilitate the transport of grain and meat
products to market. (Abreu 2001)

In the 1970s, hotel development returned to Mato Grosso. The
primary economic development plan for Brazil was the 1971 *Primeiro
Plano Nacional de Desenvolvimento* with the Matogrossense implementation being known as the *Plano Fragelli*. The *Plano Fragelli* emphasized road
building, energy projects and agriculture but it did have a small tourism
component – the reconstruction of the hotel at Aguas Quentes. The
economic significance of this investment was minimal. Aguas Quentes
received 1,680 thousand cruzeiros, representing less than one-third of
1 percent of the development budget. (Abreu 2001)

That said, tourism however was now a small part of the planning process. In 1974, an official state agency for the development of tourism was created, DETURS. However, the performance of DETURS was not strong. In 1975, the first year of this agency, some 74 percent of its budget was put into a project for a zoo. The zoo was never built – or ever referred to again despite a one year expenditure of 15 times the amount allotted to Aguas Quentes. (Annual Messages 1975–80)[2] Of the remaining money, after Aguas Quentes, the rest went to tourist information booths and the promotion of cultural events. (Annual Message 1975)

The "zoo" aside, Aguas Quentes continued to be the dominant project of the state tourism agency. A mixed private/public corporation was established to build and run the hotel. Most of the costs were borne by the state of Mato Grosso.[3] The forest around the springs was incorporated into a state wildlife refuge. A new and larger hotel was built. The road to Aguas Quentes from Cuiabá was paved. (Annual Messages 1975–80)

Tourist development outside of Aguas Quentes was modest. Some work was done developing the Chapada de Guimaraes, a *cerrado* with spectacular waterfalls. There was an inventory of tourist sites and some organizational development. (Annual Messages 1976–80)

Obviously, the evaluation of the role of the Mato Grosso government in producing jobs in hotels and restaurants depends on an assessment of the impact of Aguas Quentes. Table 9.2 shows the ratio of hotel employment to population in each of the mesoregions of Mato Grosso has a special line for the *município* of Santo Antonio de Leverger, the location of Aguas Quentes. Note that Santo Antonio de Leverger has the *lowest* rate of hotel employment of any area in Mato Grosso. This finding is not surprising, given the relative isolation of Aguas Quentes The suggests that factors other than Aguas Quentes and official Mato Grosso tourist policies caused Mato Grosso's hotel success.

Alternative 3: Ecotourism. Contemporary readers might be likely to associate hotel employment with the presence of ecotourism in the Pantanal. The Pantanal is a famous wetland in the west of Mato Grosso characterized by extraordinary biodiversity and enormous populations of beautiful tropical birds. Today it is one of the leading destinations for ecotourism in Brazil rivaling the Amazon and Foz de Iguaçu. (Mato Grosso – Turismo Puro, 1995)

Nature-based tourism would in principle produce high residuals from the model used in this analysis. Locations of natural beauty are generally found in remote depopulated areas. This could produce concentrations of tourist employment in areas where there was little demand from the local population, and thus produce high residual employment.

Undoubtedly, ecotourism in the Pantanal contributes to Matogrossense employment residuals in the present day. However, it is unlikely to have caused such residuals in the 1960s and 70s. Abreu (2001) has done an exhaustive review of the history of the development of the Pantanal. Until the 1990s there was very public investment in the Pantanal at all – touristic or non-touristic. The relatively minor allocation of funds that this area received was oriented towards farming and ranching. The current ecotourism movement in the Pantanal was created by a federal sustainable development initiative that began in the mid-1990s. (Abreu 2001)

However, in principle, such ecotourism could have had its roots in private sector initiatives that received no government funding. The table on hotel employment (Table 9.2) by mesoregions belies such a claim. The text in italics shows the mesoregions of Mato Grosso that contain the Pantanal. Levels of hotel employment in the Pantanal were modest. The Pantanal in the area that is now Mato Grosso do Sul (Pantanais) ranks 7th out of 13 mesoregions in hotel employment. The Pantanal in the area that is in the current state of Mato Grosso (Alto Guapare) ranks 11th out of 13 in hotel employment. The centers of hotel development were in regions not currently known for ecotourism at all.

Alternative 4: Entrepreneurial Excellence in Mato Grosso Hotels. In theory, it is possible that Mato Grosso had a long standing tradition of artisanal excellence in the hotel trade. Local informants were skeptical of such a claim. I discussed these residuals with several professionals familiar with Mato Grossense travel. A travel agent in Rio de Janeiro, speaking in 2002, noted that he got more complaints about hotel quality in contemporary Mato Grosso than he did from most other Brazilian bookings. He knew of no evidence that hotel quality had been better in any earlier period.

An informant familiar with hotels in Mato Grosso do Sul in the 1970s reports that the hotels in that state were rudimentary. Most of the facilities in Campo Grande, the largest city, were small working class bed and breakfasts. These catered to a popular constituency and were extremely modest. The best hotel near the informant's rural home had seven rooms, no air conditioning, and a shower that sprayed all over the toilet and sink. It was considered to be prestigious because it had individual bathrooms in every room.

These qualitative impressions are matched by the more systematic observations made by contemporary observers. The "Socioeconomic Diagnostic of the State of Mato Grosso" of 1980 discussed the hotel industry in every *município* in the state along with the health of the other sectors of the economy. Nearly everywhere they went, the inspectors criticized the quality of both hotels and restaurants vigorously. They had good things to say about hotels in Cuiabá, Barra de Garças, and São Felix de Aragauia. (They particularly liked the floating hotels in the latter location.) They accepted as tolerable the hotels in Poxoreo and Alta Araguia – acknowledging that these are lower income properties, catering to the popular classes.

In virtually every other location in the state, their critiques of the quality of the hotels were scathing. Most cities were described as having hotels that were "precarious", "unacceptable", or "extremely weak". Their complaints were repetitive and intense. (GPC 1980) Remember that these economists had to *stay* in the hotels that they were writing about, while they were collecting the data on other sectors. As a result, these writers had to experience any discomforts that existed, personally.

Even promoters of the Mato Grosso economy were hard pressed to defend the quality of Mato Grosso hotels. Lenine Povoas, a prominent politician and historian of Mato Grosso, wrote a "marketing" book in 1977, extolling investment opportunities in her state. Her *Mato Grosso: uma Convite a Fortuna* (Mato Grosso: An Invitation to Good Fortune) is an exhaustive review of the commercial potential of Mato Grosso – with glowing descriptions of Matogrossense agriculture, mining, industry and infrastructure. When the time comes to discuss tourism, the tone changes from promotional to restrained. She says her hotels are "comparable in quality with what could be found in São Paulo or Rio de Janeiro", faint praise given that both cities have both good and bad hotels. She points out that some Mato Grosso hotels have air conditioning. She says nothing about the quality of Matogrossense restaurants, and explicitly acknowledges that the hotels in Mato Grosso could not support a major influx of tourists. She concludes by making a plea to out-of-states to provide investment in this area. (Povoas 1977, pp. 29–37, espec. p. 31) If there had been a well known artisanal tradition of inn-keeping in Mato Grosso, there is no reference to this either in the Povoas promotion or any other writing this author has seen on Mato Grosso hotels.

Conclusion

So what does this analysis about Mato Grosso hotels and restaurants say about the relationship between the state and economic development?

Mato Grosso led the nation in residual employment in hotels and restaurants. This prime position was not the result of entrepreneurial excellence among Mato Grosso hoteliers. Nor was it the result of Peter Evans-style state promotion of tourism, hotels or restaurants. However, the state was in fact, critical to the development of Matogrossense hotels. The opening of the Amazonian frontier was a state regulated and mediated action. One effect of the opening of the frontier was the stimulation of large-scale migration into Mato Grosso. This migration stimulated the rise of the hotel and restaurant industry by creating substantial demands for travel services.

What general lessons can be learned from this seemingly obscure and idiosyncratic case?

1) States create economic growth by sponsoring migration. In this case, economic growth was stimulated by providing temporary accommodation to migrants. However, migration creates a demand for more permanent accommodation as well. Whenever people move from region to region, they create a need for housing, infrastructure and services in the new location to which they have moved. New roads, new schools and new cities have to be built. This produces both a one-time increase in construction employment, and a more lasting increase in permanent services employment.

2) Brazil's push to the west was an important stimulus to growth – at least as important as the development of such public investments as PETROBRAS and state supported steel. In the economic history of North American nations such as the United States and Canada, it is taken for granted that the opening of the West was a key component in those nations economic development. South American nations have frontiers of equal importance. Many of the divergences between Latin American nations in their rate of growth may come from differential state policies as to the timing and effectiveness with which their frontiers were opened.

3) Not all state policies that effect employment are explicitly designed to effect job in that sector. The opening of the West had a far greater effect on hotel and restaurant employment than did any of the explicit policies of EMBRATUR or the Mato Grosso government to expand tourism in Brazil. State policies have both intended and unintended effects – and the accidental consequences of policies not intended to affect employment at all can result in having effects far more profound than the obvious actions of promotors of service employment per se.

10
When Does Not Being Green Reduce Employment?

(with David Watkins)

In the chapter on PRODETUR and the construction of infrastructure, we found ecological projects had no effect on tourism employment. However, this does not mean that ecological considerations are completely irrelevant to the economy. Green development can promote economic growth – while unsustainable development can have deleterious long-term economic consequences. (Bunker 1990, Field 2001)

A full discussion of environmental economics is beyond the scope of the present book here. Even a full discussion of tourism and the environment is beyond the scope of the present chapter since a thorough treatment would require considering the complexities surrounding ecotourism. (Honey 1999, Higham 2007)

However, it is not unreasonable to claim that tourism benefits from a clean and beautiful environment. Tourists want nice landscapes, perfect beaches, exotic animals, beautiful mountains and verdant forests; they do not want factory smokestacks, chemical smells, and contaminated water. Since tourism does provide employment, it represents one sector of the economy which benefits from preserving nature.

Thus it comes as no surprise that ecological programs have been integrated into Brazilian state managers' strategies for the development of tourism. The most obvious example of this is the promotion of the Amazon and the Pantanal for ecotourism. However, the Northeast has seen its share of "green" development – with the nature preserves of PRODETUR being noticeable examples.

However, in the Northeast, tourism faces a very real ecological threat, the destruction of beaches by heavy industry, and by residential development. (Ruschmann 1997) A literature already exists on the adverse relationship between residential development and the preservation of the beaches. Cassia Cruz has documented the substantial degradation of the sand dunes of the beaches of Natal as a result of overbuilding and overuse. (Cruz 2000) Similar processes are occurring in Bahia. (Oliveira 2007) Many of PRODETUR's ecological reserves were immediately threatened by real estate booms and road building next to these newly created desirable areas. (Perazza and Tuazon 2006)

However, as serious as the problem of residential development is, the biggest threat to Brazilian beaches comes from heavy industry. Aracaju's most important beach, Atalaia, is near an enormous butane refinery. At Fortaleza's Iracema beach, swimming is impossible. The pollution comes from a combination of sewage and industrial outflow. Visitors to Fortaleza's main hotels must travel to a distant district, the Praia de Futuro, in order to swim. This trip takes them both through Fortaleza's seaside industrial district and a densely populated slum.

Cities are complex places with complex economies. Although state managers are motivated to move toward environmentally sustainable development projects such as ecotourism, local economies still rely on heavy industry. The pollution these industrial activities generate may threaten the tourism sector and the environmental stability on which it depends.

In this chapter, we investigate the relationship between pollution and employment in the hospitality sector. In order to do so, we add a measure of industrial pollution to the core models of Chapter 2.

Ultimately we find industrial pollution does not affect employment in the restaurant sector, which tends to depend more on the patronage of the local population than on tourist demand. Pollution does significantly diminish employment in hotels, where revenues rely on visitors from outside the local economy.

Technical section: How to measure pollution

Measuring pollution is a non-trivially difficult problem. No social science has a standard indicator of pollution that is useful for most purposes. We developed our own index by adapting a pollution measure designed by the World Bank. Non-technical readers who are not concerned about the minutiae of how such indices are constructed should feel free to skip to the next section. However, because the measure that is used here is new, and could be of use to other researchers, the methodological specifications are discussed here.

The World Bank developed the Industrial Pollution Projection System as a measure of the total pollution produced by individual nations. (Hettige et al. 1995, Mani and Wheeler 1998) It is constructed using sectoral composition data for the national economy and previous World Bank measurements of the air and water pollution output of economic sectors. (Hettige et al. 1995) Using these data, sectoral pollution can be calculated for a nation or region by multiplying each sector's contribution to GDP by a coefficient representing estimated pollution per dollar of GDP. The Mani-Wheeler index is a simplification of this principle.

Mani and Wheeler argue that the great majority of industrial effluence is due to a small group of industries. Thus it is possible to adequately measure the total pollution produced by the economy by calculating the total produced by the dirtiest sectors. These sectors are:

a) the chemical industry,
b) the paper industry,
c) metallurgy and
d) non-metallic mineral refining.

Simplifying the index eliminated the distortions associated with the inclusion of the irrelevant clean sectors. This index made possible a multitude of important analyses on the longitudinal changes in the volume of pollution and the correlation between ecological damage and the processes of economic development. (Mani and Wheeler 1998, Hettige et al. 2000, Mani and Ja 2006)

The Mani-Wheeler index in its pure form is a useful tool for international analyses. For most studies of within-nation differences in pollution, and in particular for such studies in the Brazilian context, the measure can be further improved. Many nations produce oil. A study of Brazil, and especially of Northeastern tourism, cannot ignore the prominent oil refining industry. Similar issues would exist in the United States, Canada or Mexico. In the original World Bank estimates found in Hettige et al. (1995), oil refining was one of the most polluting sectors of the economy. Mani and Wheeler excluded it from their index not due to irrelevance, but because changes in the price of oil destabilized the measure. Having a measure of pollution that gyrates depending on oil markets is obviously methodologically undesirable. That said, the energy sector is one of the most components of the Northeastern economy. Oil production and refining is particularly concentrated in important centers of tourism with Rio de Janeiro and Bahia being particularly important cases. Excluding energy production and petroleum would ignore the effect of refinery pollution on tourism which is one of the central goals of this analysis.

To eliminate the legitimate problem of price volatility, we calculate the Mani-Wheeler index using measures of sectoral employment rather than GDP. This change insulates the index from changes in relative prices and thus renders the index more suitable for analyzing the energy sector. Our index of industrial pollution is therefore the portion of total employment in Mani and Wheeler's four pollutant sectors plus the oil and coal refining industry. Data on the sectoral composition of employment are found in the demographic censuses of 1991 and 2000.

This modification carries with it a minor methodological cost. Employment is being used as a proxy for production which in turn is being used as a proxy for toxic outputs. If there are enormous differences in capital labor ratios in different periods or among different regions, then measures of labor alone will not measure total production and will thus misestimate pollution. Fortunately, this problem is relatively minor. Nearly all petroleum production and refining is extremely capital intensive. Empirical inspection of longitudinal and cross-sectional differences in capital labor ratios in energy production showed relatively minor differences during this period. Given that the alternative measure, GNP was affected by prices which were not at all stable during this period, the employment-based measure used here has substantially greater validity and reliability.

An additional plus is that the analysis requires data on pollution for Census microregions. Employment data are readily available at this level of aggregation, while GNP by industry statistics are only available at the national level. This makes the index presented here superior for regional analyses and opens up Mani-Wheeler type analyses for discussions of pollution within as well as between national economies.

Results

The general finding is that pollution reduced employment for hotels but not for restaurants. These conclusions apply to all of Brazil. The analysis is similar to that of those in Chapters 2 and 3 that looked at every microregion of Brazil in 1991 and 2000 as opposed to that in Chapter 4 which refer exclusively to the Brazilian Northeast.

In the statistical analysis, we took the core equations of Chapter 2 for the 1991–2000 period and added the data on participation in industrial pollution.[1] The actual numerical coefficients, significance tests and goodness of fit statistics for these equations can be found in the Appendix *Details of Statistical Results*. The goodness of fit of these models was similar to that of the core equations – with acceptable goodness of fit for hotels and excellent goodness of fit in the other two sectors.

For hotels, the most important finding is that pollution had a negative effect on employment in hotels. The effect was statistically significant and similar in size to the year effect. The impact of industrial pollution is about 70 percent of the effect of having a UNESCO site of cultural importance in the microregion. In other words, higher levels of industrial pollution lowered employment in hotels to an extent equal to 70 percent of the positive effect of having a colonial city, such as Ouro Preto, in the microregion. This is an extremely substantial effect.

The other variables in the model behave as they did in Chapter 2.

The pollution effect was much more modest in the restaurant sector; the Mani-Wheeler index was not statistically significant when regressed on restaurant employment. Because the effect was statistically insignificant and practically zero, whether it was positive or negative is inconsequential. The effect of pollution was smaller than all other variables in the model.

That differing results were found for hotel and restaurant employment does not disconfirm the general thesis that pollution lowers employment in tourism. In fact, this disparity parallels the effect of PRODETUR on tourism employment. PRODETUR also affected hotels but not restaurants. The explanation is the same for either variable. The level of employment in hotels is determined by tourism, while restaurant employment is determined more narrowly by the purchasing power of the local population. The market for restaurants is the resident population of the microregion. Support for this view can be found in the fact that microregional income correlated more strongly with restaurant employment than hotel employment.[2] Because visitors are more important for hotels than for restaurants, PRODETUR and pollution have more impact on this sector.

Can pollution cause people to live in one region instead of another? Probably not. The population resides in the area for reasons that are fixed and rigid. Residents have jobs or family ties that bind them to a specific place. Rio de Janeiro residents have professional or familial reasons for being in Rio de Janeiro just as São Paulo residents have similar attachments to São Paulo. The local level of pollution is a minor factor in determining where people live relative to other economic or personal considerations. Migrants are more likely to consider environmental quality than those already settled, but pollution is a secondary concern even when choosing where to relocate for a long period. (Hunter et al. 2003)

In contrast, pollution can have a substantial impact on where one goes to vacation. In general, a tourist lacks strong ties to any specific destination. He or she may choose from among many options, considering the attractions of disparate competing regions. Tourists routinely reject places that are dirty or unappealing in favor of a place that is more satisfactory.

Ecotourists in particular travel to enjoy clean and natural local environments. Thus, the ecological effect is more important in hotels because tourists consider the quality of the environment before choosing their options for leisure. Survey research by the Association of British Travel Agents found that 83 percent of British respondents believe dirty beaches or unclean water matter "a great deal" in choosing or recommending destinations; 45 percent of respondents consider air pollution of equal importance. When surveyed, German and American respondents indicated similar, if slightly less pronounced, preferences. (Goodwin and Francis 2003)

This analysis suggests difficult choices for public policy. On one hand, preserving the environment is important in its own right, and more so when policies promote tourism as a development strategy. Tourism creates jobs and attracts foreign capital. Tourism is substantially more labor intense than most other sectors, especially the most pollutant industries, and thus tourism has a unique potential to dent urban unemployment. Economic activities based on tourist demand are also much less land and capital intense than heavy industry. (Mani and Wheeler 1998) This means the barriers to entry can be extremely low for small businesses. Brazilian beaches have substantial amounts of small-scale enterprise. Not only do bars and restaurants cluster along the streetside, but ambulatory merchants walk up and down the beach itself. Artist's fairs (some of which can be quite large) cluster in locations with particularly heavy street traffic. So the employment associated with beaches can be quite substantial.

On the other hand, pollutant industries create jobs too. The oil, chemical, metallurgical, mineral, and paper industries cannot reasonably be abandoned as they support the technological development of the economy. In this regard, the energy sector in particular is extremely strategic in the modern world as sources of non-renewable energy are dwindling but necessary. Retaining advanced technology in heavy industry is important for competing in the international economy; the Brazilian technological advantage in the global market for steel is well known.

Policy must balance tourism with other social ends. This does not mean tourist considerations should always be thrown by the wayside when potential conflicts emerge. Tourism employs many, is ecologically sustainable, and is socially and economically beneficial to the residents of the region where it takes place. The labor intensity of tourism is an essential consideration – it makes tourism an important weapon in the war against disarticulation.

11
Palliative Development and the Great Theories of Development

This book has emphasized the key role of the state in producing economic development in the Third World.

States in the Global South need to build physical infrastructure, develop human infrastructure, and do so in a way that does not compromise their financial sovereignty and lead to dependency on international creditors.

The State also needs to re-prioritize Palliative Development along with Transformational Development – by stimulating small labor intensive enterprises that provide services and employment to the local population. Such development strategies are very inexpensive and avoid debt and dependency on international creditors. Such a strategy provides many of the demand-increasing benefits of import substitution, without the distortions of traditional inward-looking IS policies.

This chapter completes the analysis by considering the larger theoretical impact of our findings. We discuss how the present arguments interface with the classic arguments of development sociology and heterodox development economics. Most of this non-neoclassical literature has emphasized the inherent limits of neoliberalism, the specifications of the successful creation of a developmentalist state, and the role of trade and globalization in promoting growth, or increasing the capacity of nations in the global South to survive in the face of global competition. We concur with most of the well-known institutionalist writers in this tradition. However, the present findings suggest interesting tweaks and modifications of their arguments. The larger claims of the sociological/

heterodox positions are generally supported – but alternative methods are suggested for achieving the institutionalists' desired ends.

A complete review of the entire history of the debate on the developmentalist state would be tedious – and would be generally unnecessary for most readers of this volume. However, many of the great sociological and heterodox writers have made particularly strong and interesting claims; the present work in many cases speaks to these claims. In this discussion, we link particular authors to a handful of primary ideas that they have made particularly emphatically – or which represent their fundamental response to the question of the state and development. In most cases, other authors have had those ideas and the authors under discussion have had other ideas. However, the shorthand of "one writer – one idea" allows for the easy identification of critical concepts in a form that facilitate exposition and are recognizable to followers of the traditional debates.

Two relatively obvious arguments are made first before moving to positions that are more subtle.

James O'Connor: States produce development by constructing infrastructure

The O'Connorian analysis is clearly supported by our general analyses of infrastructure provision and by our more detailed analysis of the beneficial effects of expanding airports. This argument has been made emphatically by Aschauer (2000) who argues that public capital provides significantly greater returns to growth than does private capital. His measure of public capital generally is dominated by infrastructural investment. The argument also parallels John Kasarda's advocacy of the importance of airports. (Irwin and Kasarda 1991, Kasarda and Sullivan 2006) Joseph Stiglitz (1996, 2006) has also emphatically emphasized the importance of infrastructure provision. Sunkel (1993) also forcefully advocated the construction of infrastructure as a strategy for developing the locally-owned and controlled natural resources of the global south.

Albert Fishlow: Avoid debt

Albert Fishlow argued in 1990 argued that a wide variety of state development regimes can produce growth – so long as those development programs avoid foreign indebtedness. This argument seems prescient in the light of the traumatic experience of the 1990s and the first decade of the 2000s, in which debt-induced financial crises constrained both growth and human development throughout most of the global South.

The dangers of indebtedness are now widely acknowledged by such many authors as Griffith-Jones and Sunkel (1986), Cardoso (2009), Amsden (2001), and Chossudovsky (1997), just to name a few.

This book has largely emphasized the advantages of cheap development – state interventions into the economy that do not cost very much money. Vocational education, water systems, road building, tourism promotion – none of these are terribly expensive policies. Naturally for any given development strategy, there are more expensive and less expensive options. The chapter on debt showed that even with the relatively inexpensive programs advocated here, Brazil chose higher cost rather than lower cost options that unnecessarily increased its foreign loan obligations. However, with care and attention, development choices can be made that choose cheaper rather than more expensive strategies, and carefully monitor the administration of these programs in the interest of efficiency. Such budgetary discipline can vastly increase the strategic choices open to otherwise financially fragile nations.

Let us move now to a set of less obvious implications of the present analysis.

Osvaldo Sunkel: Import substitution fails to raise popular standards of living which in turn dooms levels of education and domestic savings

Sunkel (1993) was one of the first post-CEPAL institutionalists to reject the traditional model of import substitution. Sunkel argued that most Third World economies cannot "seal off" the financial leakages associated with imports, because they have to buy petroleum and in many cases, food. As such, without strong exports, they face perpetual balance of payments problems which leave them vulnerable to foreign indebtedness. Sunkel was a forceful advocate of East Asian style export-led development which would give them access to the larger and wealthier markets of the developed world. Most present day economists concur with this analysis and so do I.

Sunkel goes on to argue that debt would lead to a reduction in the welfare state – that would lead to disarticulated growth and widespread poverty. This poverty *in and of itself* would be enough to stifle the autonomous technological development of import-substituting economies. Widespread poverty would reduce domestic savings – as the poor are forced to devote all of their resources to meeting short-term pressing needs. Poverty would also reduce education – due to increased use of juvenile and adolescent labor, and lower parental capacity to monitor children's school attendance and study habits. Such reduced educational attainment would have spillover effects on worker productivity levels and would inhibit the capacity of countries to obtain technological competitiveness in the global marketplace.

This is an extremely important argument. It is one worth repeating time and time again to those writers who deny the relationship between inequality and development.

Import substitution clearly fails as a strategy for producing egalitarian un-disarticulated development. However, export-led industrialization does not have much of a better record in dramatically reducing social inequality. There are plenty of exporters with low levels of educational attainment and savings.

East Asia attains its high levels of domestic savings and education through vehicles independent of export-led industrialization. Such strategies as paying workers low base wages and high annual bonuses encourage savings as workers ration the use of their bonuses over the course of a year. Cultures that emphasize education – and strong state enforcement of educational attendance are helpful as well.

However – Sunkel's point that egalitarian development promotes both education and savings is an important point. The present book suggests that egalitarian development is not going to be the product of either import-substitution or export-led industrialization per se. It comes from a commitment by the government to produce egalitarian labor-intense development. The palliative programs suggested here all increase employment for the poor at little cost. More so, they can be implemented under *either* an import substitution or export-led industrial regime. What matters is the commitment to palliative development – a question which is independent of the strategy of transformative development.

Ha-Joon Chang: Protect infant industry from imports

Although Ha-Joon Chang (2003, 2008) is broadly supportive of the general lineages of East Asian developmentalist states, he is particularly well known for his opposition to free trade. In this respect, he takes the strong position about the defense of infant industries associated with Friedrich List (1983), Alexander Hamilton (1790) and more recently, Eric Reinert (2007).

Despite the impressive evidence in Chang and Reinert for the presence of restriction of strategic imports on the part of nearly every known successful economic developer, the role of tariff protection in promoting development has recently been severely challenged. Jeffrey Williamson has shown for the 1870–1950 period that different regions of the world vary in the extent to which tariff protection positively or negatively correlates with development. Worse – Latin America was historically associated with the highest level of protective tariffs in known history, and yet has had a mediocre record of economic growth.

Obviously, much of the basis of Chang's logic depends on whether there is any infant industry which tariffs can protect. Many exogenous considerations reduced the Latin American manufacturing base including low levels of education, small domestic markets due to income inequality, and a politically connected agrarian class more interested in promoting export agriculture and purchasing foreign luxury goods than they were in developing their own manufactures; all of these could have reduced the relevance of tariff control as a developmental strategy.

Chang's argument is far more relevant to transformative development than it is to the palliative arguments that are made here. That said, an important component of his argument is the creation of a protected market for a nation's own domestically produced goods and services. Many of the labor intense personal services are inherently protected from the danger of being supplanted by foreign competition. An external competitor can flood one's retail market with cheap imported manufactures; it can flood the service sector with services that can be provided offshore. It cannot flood the service sector with services that have to be provided locally. Barbers, beauticians, domestic servants, security guards, taxi drivers, construction workers, and hotel and restaurant employees – all of these are provided by local labor and the proceeds go into the local economy. Few of these are transformative industries – but they do provide palliative employment.[1]

A cognate point can be made about tourism. Sunkel (1993) emphasizes the importance of developing a country's own native resources. Geography and place are resources that nations absolutely control. There is a standard literature in tourism studies about how tourism promotes development and assists in generating valuable foreign exchange. (Sinclair 1998, Tisdell and Kartik 1998) However, much progressive academics may dislike the artificiality and inauthenticity of tourism, the arguments that tourism is labor intensive, promotes a favorable balance of payments – and can be sustainable if done right, are arguments that need to be taken seriously. Support for local services provides a non-transformative version of the some of the benefits traditionally associated with import restriction.

Cardoso and Faletto: A class alliance of the middle class and the working class is a fundamental precondition for egalitarian development

Cardoso and Faletto (1979) are less concerned about the rate of development per se than the class composition of ruling alliances within developing nations and how this effects the form of development – enclave vs. dispersed, inegalitarian or egalitarian, authoritarian or democratic. They associate egalitarian development with the rise of left wing pro-labor regimes such as those of Peron and Vargas, and the syndicalist and welfare-state policies that were implemented by these leaders. Alternative class coalitions lead to latifundism, commodity-based rather than manufacturing-based development, or industrialization under conditions of extreme disarticulation. The first two concentrate wealth in the hands of the elite. The third permits the transfer of wealth to the middle class but does not create a prosperous working class.

We do not doubt that the impact of working class/middle class alliances has been substantial, and that the populist regimes produced by such coalitions have produced significant institutional gains for workers. However, the labor laws and welfare state provisions of Latin America have been no silver bullet. Few of these laws pertain to workers in the informal sector, which represents an enormous percentage of the lower classes. Syndical legislation has been of tremendous benefit to a portion of the working class – workers working in large unionized firms, and workers in enterprises that are too big to escape policing. They have been particularly helpful to workers working in multinational corporations and parastatals. However, the institutions of the great populist regimes have failed to do much for the unorganized poor.

Palliative development policy represents an alternative that can help reach these unorganized workers. The difference in income between unemployment and working in the labor intense sector is substantial. Furthermore, palliative development does not require any particular class coalition as a precondition for political support or implementation. There is little about providing vocational education, building sewers, or promoting tourism that would be objectionable even to a far right government. Palliative development policies can represent a "consensus" policy that rises above the ebb or flow of class coalitions, national party politics, or the comings and goings of democratic governance. It provides a method for making development more egalitarian that rises above the macropolitical concerns that are the main preoccupation of Cardoso and Faletto.

Ben Fine: Macrocapital always dominates developmentalist states

Cardoso: State-led development is invariably captured by private interests

Ben Fine and Fernando Henrique Cardoso are on opposite ends of the political spectrum – but converge significantly on the likelihood and undesirability of state development programmes being captured by large private capitalist interests.

Ben Fine is primarily known for his extensive and scathing reviews of economic literature. (Fine 2003, 2006, Jomo and Fine 2006) His assaults on the internal contradictions and lack of empirical foundation of modern neoclassical development economics are welcome, and cogent. However, Ben Fine is no friend of traditional development statists either. He is relatively silent on the question of whether East Asia industrial policies were successful or not – although his attacks on neoliberalism might suggest some approval of statism. His most explicit statement on the state and development is his 2006 essay on "The Developmental State and the Political Economy of Development" in Jomo and Fine. Here his focus is not on whether tariffs or development banking works – but whether autonomous development states exist at all. His claim – note the contrast to Weiss below – is that such states are almost wholly subservient to national macrocapital. Furthermore, as semi-peripheral states, their increased wealth further bolsters the strength of local economic elites and makes the state even more of a captive instrument of the haute bourgeoisie.

Fernando Henrique Cardoso, a center-right social democrat, and as President of Brazil, implementer of significant semi-neoliberal economic reforms, has a long standing record of agreeing with Fine's position. His early work on the class structure of the Brazilian State emphasized "rings of influence" where individual networks of economic elites allied with networks of politicians and bureaucrats to pursue particularistic factional gains. Cardoso's argument that the multiplicity and power of such rings prevented the Brazilian state from either governing in the interest of the nation or the capitalist class as a whole. He repeated this claim in his analysis of the state and development in his early Senatorial career, in his post-presidential autobiography, and in his theory piece in *Studies in Comparative International Development* where he attempted to reconcile his past and current thinking with world-systems theory. (Cardoso 1991, 2006, 2009)

"Capture of the state by capitalist interests" is a less important issue among the small firms that are the basis of palliative employment. Hotels, restaurants and barber/beauty shops are a non-factor in national politics. Hotel associations can be meaningful in municipal politics – notably in questions of downtown development. Trade associations in restaurants and barber/beauty are often active in working with state vocational educational programs – where they have significant (and useful) input into the content and organization of training courses. However, such interests have little influence on fundamental questions of development policy. They are frequently ignored when their agendas run counter to larger better organized factions, such as construction lobbies. Furthermore, the broadly dispersed nature of restaurants and beauty shops – and even for that matter hotels – prevent make it hard for any conceivable policy to significantly damage the many for the benefit of the few.[2]

This is not to say that all palliative development is free from Fine/Cardoso style instrumentalist concerns. The capture of both national and local governments by construction interests is well known. Some of the distortions this has produced, such as the perennial wastage of funds on water-rechanneling projects in the Northeast, or bus monopolies in major cities are well known. However, highly dispersed industries with extensive self-employment and easy entry are less subject to such distortions than are sectors with greater capacity for cartelization and rent-seeking oligopoly.

Peter Evans and Linda Weiss: Successful state-led development requires consultation and integration with knowledgeable capitalists

Peter Evans in his *Embedded Autonomy* (1995) and Linda Weiss in her *Myth of the Powerless State* (1998) make similar arguments that successful state-led development requires capitalists to be active in political consultation and to have a real voice in public decisions. Otherwise, state bureaucrats run the risk of making decisions that are not technically well informed. This is a decided contrast with the arguments of Fine and Cardoso – and is reasonable so long as the capitalists are not so powerful that autonomous decision-making by the state is lost forever. This is the essence of Peter Evans's balanced advocacy of embeddedness and autonomy.

Evans and Weiss are probably correct 90 percent of the time. There are however, rare occasions, where the state intentionally takes on "crazy" initiatives that fly in the face of capitalist advice – and these lucky adventures work out well. This is particularly the case when the state is promoting projects that would compete with pre-existing enterprises. Established barbers and beauticians universally opposed the flooding of the Sergipe hair care market with more graduates of vocational courses in professional hairdressing than the market could possibly stand. The state intentionally created cutthroat competition between established and neophyte barbers and beauticians. In the end, employment in the sector was significantly increased, because supporters of the neophytes invested extra money into the sector to insure that the new firms would survive.

The state of Rio Grande do Norte used state monies to build the most successful resort location in Brazilian history – the now famous Parque das Dunas near Natal. Virtually no local businessmen wanted to invest in the project; Brazilian hotel investors in other states shunned the development as being unworkable. The initial state-financed hotel was a smash success, and since then Rio Grande do Norte has been one of the prime tourism investment locations in Brazil.

The importance of capitalist consultation is similar to any other argument that takes the form of "One should always listen to Expert X". One *should* always listen to Expert X – except in the cases where Expert X is wrong.

Krugman: Modern development states are failing only by adding more capital and not by increasing the productivity of capital

Krugman has been one of the few institutionalist-friendly economists who has been roundly skeptical of the accomplishments of the East Asian developmental state. He argued that Dennison-style decompositions of East Asian growth into increases in capital stocks, labor stocks and productivity change show high increases in capital and labor stocks and no significant productivity change. He argues from this that East Asian development is not transformative, that the long-term prospects for East Asia are not good and that therefore the state and development literature is chasing a chimera. (Krugman 1994, 1999) This position gained significant attention in the aftermath of the Asian financial crisis of 1997.

This position was roundly attacked by Stiglitz (1996) on the grounds that a) decompositions of growth into increases in factor stocks versus the productivity of those stocks are methodologically unreliable and b) Krugman had vastly underestimated the fundamental role of government financed infrastructure in making the East Asian economies possible.

A work of empirical research on Brazil can obviously not comment on the historical components of East Asian growth. However, the findings on infrastructure for Brazil broadly support the arguments made by Stiglitz on this issue. Building infrastructure does contribute to the stock of capital, a point made conspicuously by Aschauer (2000). Both Aschauer and myself would argue that some spillover does occur to the productivity of private capital. An obvious example from this study is the airports in Northeastern Brazil valorized fruit farms all over the Northeast which could now export their fruit to foreign markets and obtain a higher international price for their merchandise.

However, Krugman's argument that states increase development by increasing the stocks of capital and labor in an economy is not a null position. The over-training of barbers and beauticians in Sergipe stimulated more capital to be put into the Sergipe beauty sector; employment was increased by an increase in capital stock, rather than capital productivity. So do states increase growth by increasing capital stocks or by increasing capital productivity? Yes and yes.

Alice Amsden: States stimulate growth by using information transfer to create superfirms with proprietary technology

Most of Alice Amsden's earlier writings involve the traditional developmental state arguments about market failure and governments picking and supporting winners. Her break away from this mold came in 2001 in *Rise of the Rest*. Here, she laid out an alternative theory of state-led development that emphasized the role of government in producing technology transfer to increase the rate of engineering learning within firms. Amsden argued that countries become dominant by having monopoly technology and such technologies are embedded in particular high performing firms rather than in the labor market as a whole. States produce growth by helping such firms obtain the scientific and production skills they need. In this respect, Amsden is somewhat of the Sanjaya Lall of the state and development literature.

We believe Amsden is 100 percent correct about the role of technology transfer in transformative development. In this regard, the *Rise of the Rest* is a classic statement. However, skill works somewhat differently in palliative development. The skills are dispersed among a broad set of individuals – and the challenge of expanding the sector is passing those skills on to a larger set. As such, labor markets and firm-general education are more relevant than would be the case for building a technological super-firm.

Consider two highly marketable palliative skills, cooking and hair-dressing. Now also consider two different levels of skill in these areas – a level of skill consistent with maintaining a viable firm of average profitability, and the level of skill consistent with creating a landmark firm with a reputation for distinction and unique products. The skills of fixing hair and cooking are spread throughout the population – hair-dressing within a large stock of barber/beauticians, and cooking within the population of virtually everyone who cooks (as far as understanding basics and home recipes) and in a smaller stock of professional cooks (as far as understanding cooking in volume as required by a restaurant). These skills are held by many workers in many firms, plus a large number of former workers who are not currently employed. Training opportun-ities are not scarce – and such skills can easily passed on by schools. Extra-ordinary skill requires training by a master – just as is the case in any artistic profession. However, in any nation, there exists a pre-existing stock of people who understand local preferences in hairstyles very well, or who truly understand the local cuisine. Amsden-like international competency transfer may be necessary to train a local cook in French or Italian or Chinese cuisine. However, the mastery of the local cuisine is readily available – and can be provided by individual apprenticeships negotiated through labor markets.

Sunkel's argument that disarticulating the economy increases general education levels and with it general skill levels is highly relevant to this discussion. While the slow increase in human capital that would come from upwardly mobile poor people sending their children to school is not as fast or efficient as the far more focused methodologies advo-cated by Amsden, it does represent "an extra bet" that someone some-where in the economy can generate a new technology that may be of use. Railroads emerged as an accidental by-product of having to move coal out of mines. Coca Cola was a by-product of an independent phar-macist trying and failing to make a headache remedy. Generalized edu-cation does promote generalized innovation; a very small number of these innovations will produce unexpected monopolies.

Bruce Cumings, Robert Wade and Dani Rodrik: States need to develop the technocratic capacity to choose the right products and the right firms that warrant public support

The classic expositions of Cumings (1984), and Wade (1990) emphasized the social considerations that allowed state administrators to have the competence to wisely choose what products needed to be supported at what time, what firms would best for manufacturing those products, and when the time has come to shift either product mixes or firms. The state is under the obligation to pick winners. Although there have been many specifications of what would be ideal rules for how deciding how firms and industries should be chosen, Rodrik (2007) has developed a simple specification that seems fairly robust: the state should make its best judgment but then provide subsidies for only a limited period. If the firm or industry cannot attain global competitiveness, the state should move its public investments to another firm or sector.

From the standpoint of transformational development, Rodrik's rule is sensible. Infrastructure promotion and palliative development reduce much of the need for the state bureaucracy to have to be able to predict winning industries and firms. Infrastructure by its nature is flexible. It can be used by firms in a wide variety of industries and for a wide variety of purposes. Schooling, roads and airports support a broad spectrum of different types of economic activities. The analysis of airports showed that even when airports were expanded to promote tourism, firms in agriculture, industry and services all benefited from the additional transport capacity. One of the standard topes in traditional rural sociology is how the construction of a highway through a rural area leads to the creation of a wide variety of non-extractive activities, unrelated to the original intentional use of the highway. Although some rationing is necessary to determine where a particular piece of infrastructure will be placed, there is far less necessity for builders of infrastructure to develop a fine-grained industrial composition strategy.

Furthermore, palliative development tends to involve the promotion of many small firms rather than one or two large ones. This lack of concentration reduces the market distortions that come from creation artificial monopolies – one of the reasons that Rodrik recommends that industrial subsidies be of limited duration. Furthermore, working with a large population of relatively frail firms rather than a small number of secure protected ones, insures that there will be a natural division into winners and losers based on market competition. Palliative development requires fewer "underwriting" skills from the state bureaucracy. The state merely selects a labor intensive sector and chooses to support it with infrastructure – rather than having to select which individual firms represent the best chance to become a world class competitor. As such, palliative development is within the range of feasibility for state bureaucracies of limited technical competence; the Cumings-Wade model makes far more demands on the human capital of state planners themselves.

Joseph Stiglitz: The grand synthesis

The dominant model from which the book is derived is James O'Connor. However, most development readers will notice substantial similarities between the thinking here and the writings of Joseph Stiglitz. His 1996 analysis of the East Asian crisis was that

1) Egalitarianism helps to promote growth by promoting literacy and reducing fertility.
2) Infrastructure is critical to growth.
3) Higher education and government support of science is critical to growth.
4) There is no one silver bullet that produces growth. Both strategies that we would call transformational, such as compensating for market imperfections in the supply of information, and palliative, such as ensuring guaranteeing basic standards of living, are beneficial to development.

We agree entirely.

12
Development Strategies in a Post-Debt World

Much of the writing about the Third World state in the 1980s and 1990s was about the inability of governments to do their job due to the immense problems associated with international debt. Debt changes the repertoire of what types of policies are available to states who wish to be effective. The debt crisis of the mid-1980s smashed the paradigm of state-led heavy industrialization by wrecking the viability of import substitution, closed border modernization schemes and the state bankrolling of long-term capital intensive heavy industry. Fifty years of thinking on the state and economic development had to be thrown out – and new models had to be developed.

Fortunately, a fundamental and positive change is now at hand. Third World nations are *coming out of debt* – a development that would have been seen as being inconceivable in the 1990s. South Korea has paid off its debts. Thailand and Brazil have accumulated enough foreign cash reserves to pay off their entire foreign loan obligations. Argentina has repaid all of its debt to the International Monetary Fund. While not every nation has been able to clean up its balance sheet, the number of countries that are becoming debt free is steadily increasing.

The circumstances that allowed much of the Third World to escape the debt trap are as unexpected as the circumstances that created the Third World debt crisis in the first place. In the 1970s, no one anticipated that the major banks would undercut the standards of their own risk assessment operations and would overcommit funds to the point of non-sustainability.

In the 1990s, no one anticipated that Hugo Chavez would refinance a proportion of Argentina's debt. No one anticipated that commodity booms in Asia would vastly increase the export earnings of Asian and Latin American agriculture.

178

In particular, no one anticipated the dramatic decline of the dollar. Since nearly all of the debts were dollar-denominated, the fall of the US currency vastly reduced the real burdens of the loan obligations the Third World was carrying. No one could anticipate that an American president would self-destructively destroy his own currency by cutting his own nation's taxes, increasing his own nation's domestic expenditures and then commencing on a series of colossally expensive foreign wars. George W. Bush, to the surprise of everyone, has become the unintentional savior of the Third World. The Third World debt had been denominated in dollars – making the strength of the dollar a key determinant of the payability or unpayability of international debt. Bush's crony capitalism, foreign policy extravagances and budgetary profligacy effectively gutted the dollar, the monetary pillar of the American imperium. This has been a major factor in bringing financial independence back to the Third World – and reviving the hopes of nationalist state-led development.

The balance sheets of governments are now being restored. The restoration is not perfect; many of them will be left with significant burdens of indebtedness to nations other than the US or to investors in their own country. But most countries are more financially independent than has been the case in the last 40 years.

Thus the upcoming decade represents an era where Latin American states have choices – real choices. What should be done with this new opportunity is an open and fascinating question. The most interesting alternatives are being discussed by the left. Should Latin America use its control of its natural resources to bargain aggressively with the core economies – and reduce its exposure to penetration from multinational capital? Should Latin America try to create a smaller version of East Asian developmentalist states? Should participatory budgeting and the political mobilization of local electorates be used to produce an *economia solidária* and reduce the capture of public economic policy by local and international special interests? Or – if you are a conservative – is this the hour to do away with the bloated government bureaucracies that produced the debt crisis in the first place and produce economies that are streamlined and nimble with the government facilitating integration into a larger world with its capital stocks and markets?

Our position

We believe that the road to economic development in the post-debt future will involve lots of government interventions involving small low-likelihood-of-failure reforms rather than single grand interventions that can succeed or fail dramatically. These reforms are likely to be routine, rather than dramatic. This boringness is a source of strength rather than a weakness. Their very normalcy and seeming triviality reduces the risk of opposition from national or transnational elites, eliminates them as grounds of contention and helps to insure that they will be allowed to succeed without being undercut by special interests.

Small invisible reforms have a further advantage: small means cheap – and cheap means multiple. Low cost programs are useful in helping to avoid future debt dependency. Government programs that can be financed by local resources are government programs that do not mortgage the nation's future to external special interests in the future.

However, a more important consideration is that small programs allow the funding of many, many initiatives rather than one big publicity grabbing campaign. All programs have intrinsic weaknesses and all programs have capacities to fail. A nation that diversifies its state interventions into a diversified portfolio of hundreds of different independent programs increases the likelihood that some of these programs will succeed – and even that a small number will succeed spectacularly. If programs are cheap, the benefits of one big success that majorly advances the prospects of a region and allows for imitation in other regions – more than compensates for an army of other programs that did little but cost little as well. When programs are cheap and uncontroversial, a nation can afford to have many of them fail as long as their failure does not produce financial ruin or permanently antagonize powerful enemies. The benefits from the small number that succeed will more than cover for whatever number of programs do little.

In this regard, Brazil might be regarded as a model of what a successful post-debt development plan might look like. Brazil has carefully avoided the antagonistic public relations of a Venezuela or a Bolivia – while maintaining significant capacity to use diplomacy to do hardball negotiating with foreign powers on individual issues of critical importance to its economy. For example, Brazil was able to use within-Washington lobbying and the threat of WTO sanctions to successfully overturn the Bush administration's limits on the importation of Brazilian steel – while maintaining collegial relationships with the United States.

Brazil's economic development policy can be easily seen as a diversified portfolio of routine projects – many of which have paid off. Modest investments in the state agricultural research agency, EMBRAPA, have produced proprietary technology in the cultivation of soybeans. Brazilian agro-investors have used these technologies to make Brazil one of the world's leading exporters of soybeans. The success of Brazil's far-seeing early investments in ethanol and alternative energy are well known. Public investment in PETROBRAS, the state oil firm, have been only a small component of overall economic development strategy; yet this has paid off in the discovery of deep sea gas fields that will be an important component of Brazilian growth for years to come. Support for agri-business, alternative energy and petroleum development have come from Brazil's own home-trained corps of engineers developed at Brazil's own state and federal university systems; although Brazilian public institutions of higher education may be inferior to those in the United States and Europe, they are strong compared to many such institutions in Latin America.

The previous summary just illustrates the most famous success story of a long list of small-scale development projects. An examination of the portfolio of the Brazilian national or regional development banks will show small-scale investments in just about every industry possibly imaginable. This is not to speak of investments in all types of infra-structure, both physical and social, and support for the work of other government agencies.

One of the best illustrations of Brazil's "smallball" diversified approach is, fittingly, the work of SEBRAE, Brazil's agency for the promotion of small business. SEBRAE is highly decentralized – with individual state SEBRAEs generating customized plans to meet the needs of their own economies. That said, most state SEBRAEs run a huge array of dif-ferent programs – almost all of which are routine, uncontroversial, and inexpensive. SEBRAE administers microcredit programs,[1] business education programs, export promotion programs, technical consultation programs where SEBRAE subsidizes the costs of an skilled engineer or businessman providing direct assistance to a microfirm, arts festivals, trade shows, public television programs on how to run a business, entre-preneurship contests for teenagers, publication of an enormous series of pamphlets explaining the concrete requirements of administering specific types of business, organization of purchasing cooperatives, organization of marketing cooperatives, organization of congresses where small busi-nesses can share technical skills, negotiation of public spaces where small businesses have access to subsidized retail space, and the list goes on and on. Even if most of these programs were failures, probably enough of them to succeed to justify SEBRAE's extremely modest overall expenses.

This is not to say Brazil desists from "change the world through revo-lutionary vision" approaches. Porto Alegre's open budgeting and par-ticipatory democracy are well known – and these innovations are being introduced in cities throughout the nation. Brazil is an enthusiastic supporter of the *economia solidária* and commits significant public monies to support this cause. Brazil certainly provides diplomatic support to such populist regimes as Venezuela and Ecuador who are explicitly challenging American and European dominance head on. That said, Brazil is careful about hedging the glamorous with the boring – and covering the confrontational with the small scale, the uncontroversial and the relatively unlikely to fail.

Brazil does not have the option of becoming a traditional developmentalist state. The Taiwan and Singapore roads are closed to it. The globalization of the 1990s has allowed for substantial multinational penetration of Brazil's primary industrial, commercial and financial establishments. Brazil's major banks are now by and large, foreign owned, as is its steel industry, its automobile industry, its beverage industry as well as others. Renationalization might be possible – but Taiwan and Singapore never had to "regain" their enterprises from foreign hands. The East Asian developmentalist states essentially began with their productive capacities under the ownership of nationals, making regulation by law and local administrative fiat a practical alternative. American and European governments were not going to come to the aid of Taiwanese or Singaporean capitalists to the same extent that they would if the Brazilian government were to nationalize American or European-owned assets.

The ravages of the 1990s (and the electoral considerations surrounding the return to democracy in the 1980s) have also compromised the capacity of the Brazilian state to completely exclude private interests from using state resources on their own behalf. Corruption remains a pervasive problem in Brazil. Scandals routinely occur at state, federal and local levels and *desvio* or the dissipation of public funds is a routine feature of public projects.

The non-independence of public organs has been intensified by the rise of crime in Brazil and the development of the *poder parallelo* or parallel power – the effective creation of "brown zones" of lawlessness within Brazilian cities which are effectively run by narcotraffickers. Narcotraffickers both endorse politicians for political office and in some cases, run for office themselves. (Political participation is motivated in part by the Brazilian law that makes elected representatives immune from prosecution as long as they continue to hold public office.) With policemen, judges, district attorneys and now elected representatives under the control of drug gangs, the Brazilian state is open as never before to capture by private sectional interests. And this is to say nothing of more benign forms of capitalist participation in electoral politics, where local economic interests who work for the re-election of a candidate expect some sort of gratitude after the candidate is returned to office.

The preceding argument does not imply that the Brazilian state cannot or does not stand up to individual capitalists. Barbara Geddes (1996) has made compelling, sophisticated arguments about how Brazil is structured as a mixture of autonomous and non-autonomous public organs, with high levels of technocratic performance being possible in the autonomous units. However, there are enough channels for sectional interests to capture portions of the Brazilian state to pre-empt a traditional East Asian style developmental strategy where a state with embedded autonomy dictates development policy to a set of capitalists who have few choices but to follow the Minister of Industry's bidding.

These considerations have implications for those who believe that any kind of profound democratic transition in Brazil would lead to a marked increase in economic development or increase in overall prosperity. Participatory budgeting and other populist methods of increasing the transparency of government are powerful tools in the elimination and reduction of corruption. As such, Porto Alegre style super-democratic municipal governance has much to recommend it, because it helps to reduce the loss of public monies that leak out to inappropriate sources and insures that the substantial amount of money Brazil collects in taxes really does go to publicly shared economic and social goals. This is an extremely non-trivial benefit.

However, let us assume that there are no internal dynamics within participatory budgeting that might lead to its own decline. Let us assume, contrary to the experience of workers' councils in China or Yugoslavia, that workers' willingness to devote large amounts of time to municipal governance will not decline. Further assume there is no problem with the succession of generations of voters, and that no new voters will enter the scene whom take democratic powers for granted and are uninterested in the minutiae of public administration. Assume as well that participatory processes are not captured by any activists with political ambitions who hope to transform popular mobilization into a device for furthering their electoral careers. Also assume that the process is not captured by technocrats who figure out how to shield municipal decision-making from supposedly "unwise" decisions by uninformed voters whose short-term preferences would be disastrous from some scientifically conceived "long-term good". Assuming there is no Michellian bourgeoisification of popular mobilization that reintroduces the iron law of oligarchy (and special interest representation) to participatory leftist politics. On top of these, assume that there is no economic crisis or political crisis that would make the current administration seem ineffective – and make voters want to jettison participatory budgeting as part of a campaign to "flush the incompetent old guard out and bring in real reform". Thus in this scenario, the mechanisms of popular representation would remain un-cooptable and representatives of the left would remain un-corruptable.

Participatory budgeting and populist democracy would *still* have a hard time transforming itself into a mechanism for deep-seated progressive state-led economic development. The significant decisions concerning economic development are generally made at the executive (or in the case of contentious disputes, judicial) level and not by the passage of legislative acts. The relative invisibility of executive administrators and judges buys them substantial leverage to distance themselves from popular directives and make governmental decisions based on criteria that are meaningful for their office. These decisions may be technocratic. They might also be instrumentalist as representatives of capitalist class fractions use the social network, ideological and economic resources at their disposal to capture particularly salient components of public policy.

The viability of popular democracy as a tool for creating "a new" economic development depends on the same types of factors promoting state autonomy that are germane to determining the viability of an East Asian developmentalist state. Participatory budgeting and other forms of hyper-democratic governance may be useful in promoting a transfer of income between social classes – and may be a political tool to help struggle for a meaningful welfare state. However, the effects on economic development itself, with its concomitant reduction in the extent of poverty, are likely to be fairly modest.

A similar level of caution may need to be applied to the developmental consequences of the "progressive *rentier*" strategies put forward in Venezuela and Bolivia. Under Chavez or Morales, the state uses its control of local natural resources to drive hard bargains with international capital. The proceeds from this bargaining are used to fund progressive social programs for the reduction of levels of social inequality and poverty.

This is an attractive strategy – but it is limited to the nations that have oil. Natural resource endowments are an unstable support for a welfare state. The traditional argument against commodity-based development strategies that global commodity prices fluctuate dangerously. This might make it unwise to use soybeans or meat as a basis for a progressive *rentier* state in Uruguay or copper as a basis for a progressive *rentier* state in Chile. Petroleum is a reasonable exception to this rule. The price of oil has always been high – and will continue to be high for the foreseeable future.

A further issue is that natural resource endowments tend to be regionally concentrated – and are an open invitation to subnational disputes between regions with and without the valuable commodity. Nigeria had its Biafran war where Hausa and Yoruba crushed the Ibo who controlled Nigeria's oil territories. Chile had its civil war between copper and non-copper regions. Such regional rivalries create ample opportunities for international capital to participate in strategies of "divide and conquer" and re-establish the control of critical resources by comprador elites. This is a greater issue for Bolivia than for Venezuela, since in Bolivia, the gas states are controlled by non-Indians who are hostile to the progressive *rentier* ambitions of the Morales government.

There is nothing intrinsically wrong with negotiating the best price for the natural resources one has, and using those proceeds to fund economic development. Brazil does exactly that with the proceeds from PETROBRAS – and will continue to do so as its new deep sea gas fields come on line. However, even if the strategy works to perfection, one needs to have some idea of what one intends to do with the proceeds from oil, that can promote a more diversified and robust economic development for the future. This means paying as much attention to the reinvestment process as it does to the process of hardball negotiating with the developed nations.

This returns diversified small projects to the center of attention as a strategy for state promotion of economic development. Because such investments are relatively inexpensive, they can succeed whether or not the larger national strategies they are linked to prosper or fail. They run relatively little risk of loss, can be run under a wide variety of political regimes, and incur relatively few social costs in the form of rancorous social disputes or the creation of international tensions.

However, it is one thing to run a programme of diversified small investments – and another thing to run such a programme effectively or well. What does the present book tell us about how to organize such a program of routine pro-development state interventions?

The lessons of this book

1) *Effective state development projects can be cheap.* The projects in this book that were shown to work were relatively inexpensive compared to the normal "heavy industry start-ups" that feature in most discussions of the state and economic growth. Correcting for

capital market failures by starting heavy industries can be a costly proposition. In contrast, of the various effective projects that were discussed in the book, only the airports could really be considered to be expensive. Sewers, local roads, vocational education programs or creating spaces for small entrepreneurs are relatively low cost propositions. Furthermore, the chapter on development budgets showed that it is sometimes possible to reduce the cost of big ticket projects by intelligent rationing of sub-projects for maximum impact. The entire PRODETUR initiative could have had its costs reduced by half with only a moderate reduction in its overall benefits. Living on a budget does not mean being ineffective.

2) *Physical infrastructure matters. Airports really matter.* Roads, water projects, sewer projects, and bus stations all increased employment. Airports substantially increased employment – and increased overall GDP in every sector except heavy industry. What is particularly remarkable about airports is that they took effect *nearly immediately.* GDP rose markedly within one year of the completion of airport expansions. Most other development projects have far longer lags and do not create jobs nearly this rapidly.

   The private sector is not going to build airports, ports, highways or energy grids in the quantity needed to cover for population growth or develop new industries. Even if some infrastructure can be developed in the corporate sector, most of this will have to come from the state. Note that there is nothing wrong with recreational infrastructure. The parks and beach improvements constructed by PRODETUR created real jobs – and also significantly improved the quality of life of the citizens of the areas where such infrastructure was provided.

   That said, many nations are now facing serious infrastructure shortages. Brazil has recently experienced two shut-downs – an *apagão eléctrica* or multimonth power black out in 2002 and an *apagão aerea* or air traffic paralysis in 2006–7. Both of these threw the country into chaos. A modern economy can not survive with office buildings having to shut off their lights and computers at 4PM, or 60 percent of all flights being cancelled every day. Investing in infrastructure prevents such crises from happening – and gives a society the physical capacity to expand production.

3) *Development planners need to pay attention to the industries that provide the multiplier effect for growth as well as those with transformative technologies.* This book was about the development potential of labor intensive industries with low human capital requirements. Labor intensive

industries create jobs. Low educational requirements help in opening up these jobs to poverty populations. Traditional capital intensive industrialization has produced too much disarticulation and too many cases of growth with only limited poverty reduction. Disarticulation came about because planners did not pay enough attention to multiplier effects. They assumed that if new technologically advanced industries were brought to their country, that the spillover effects would automatically benefit poor people.

This argument was not necessarily wrong. However, a more sure-fire way to guarantee that disadvantaged populations benefit from development is to pay explicit attention to the industries that will produce spillover employment once base industries are implanted. This means consciously monitoring the industries that draw their stimulus from workers' wages; these generally are consumer products, retail trade, and personal services.

This book has shown that is NOT the case that all labor markets respond to exogenous changes in income with the same amount of employment in personal services. Government policy matters. Government policy needs to be adjusted to help consumer product industries, retail trade and personal services to guarantee that whatever stimulus occurs from base industry produces the largest multiplier effect possible.

4) *Tourism development is an anti-poverty program.* The importance of tourism follows from the previous discussion. Tourism is labor intensive, and has the moderate human capital requirements required to be accessible to poverty populations. Tourism is also a "multiplier" sector, because increases in personal income increase consumption overall, and recreational travel is a form of consumption.

The main body of the book did not always discuss tourism development explicitly. However many of the key findings concerned programs that were designed as tourism programs. PRODETUR in particular, was designed to increase the flow of tourists to the Brazilian Northeast; the construction of airports, sewer lines, roads and the reconstruction of historical downtowns were all undertaken with this goal in mind. These investments produced substantial economic benefits, including in sectors not directly linked to tourism per se.

Academics tend to not like tourism development, because they don't like the Westernized distorting gaze of the tourist; they certainly don't like the artificiality of pre-packaged experiences. However, the authenticity of the tourist experience has little to do with the development potential of tourism as a sector. Tourism work is clean, ecological, and as was shown in the wage figures in Chapter 1, tolerably well paid. Tourism may be inauthentic, but it does help to reduce poverty.

5) *Vocational education programs work – When outlets exist for students to open their own firms.* The job training programs of SENAC were shown to significantly increase employment – but only in those industries in which independent entrepreneurship is possible. Those programs worked well for barbers, beauticians and restaurant staff. They did little to increase hotel employment. Training costs are very low in the Third World, because new workers can be paid next to nothing. Thus capitalists train workers routinely and are not entirely dependent on the state for human capital provision. The primary benefit of vocational education programs was their capacity to empower workers to start their own firms with their newly acquired skills. Even under conditions where markets were being flooded with trainees – as occurred in our primary case study, Sergipe – enough of the new start-ups survive to produce a significant aggregate increase in employment. A further extension of this logic is that any program that supports new entrepreneurship helps to reduce poverty. Microfinance, industry cooperatives, incubators, or even the multi-stranded "everything but the kitchen sink" support for small business that can be found in a complex program such as Brazil's SEBRAE are all probably worth supporting.

6) *Social capital is Keynesian expansion – Making solidary economies a good idea.* One reason vocational education raised employment, is that the friends and families of newly trained students volunteered space, capital and purchases as a way to help people for whom they cared. Social network ties were essential to providing investment and consumption that otherwise would not have been provided; as a result, social capital worked like Keynesian government expansion in increasing demand, increasing capital and raising the velocity of the circulation of money. In this regard, any social program that gets people to help their friends and neighbors, is going to increase consumption and investment and ultimately increase the rate of economic activity.

This makes the *economia solidária* look like it has potential as a strategy for increasing economic growth. The *economia solidária* uses a) social network links in communities, b) city and regional pride, c) nationalism, and d) mobilization into social movements as a strategy for getting individuals to work together in projects of economic cooperation that will increase local employment at the expense of foreign imports. In principle, this idea would seem to be a logical extension of the lessons drawn from the findings on vocational education.

Some caution is certainly warranted. Some economic enterprises or industries are intrinsically not viable. Not every Third World slum dweller can count on selling an unlimited supply of artificial flowers to their neighbors. However, ties of solidarity can maximize the potential of undertakings that have some legitimate economic basis in the first place. The development of such social capital through the *economia solidária* should be encouraged.

7) *Leave room for the little guy – Create physical spaces for businesses that require low rent.* The analysis of barbers and restaurants showed that there are some industries that are sensitive to the cost of rent. When space becomes too expensive, these firms are pushed out of business and aggregate employment is reduced. One may not want to tailor the economic policy of a nation to catering to this rent-sensitive sector – but providing some access to cheap space can be a development tool. Downtown redevelopment plans, zoning codes, and landlord-tenant laws can be written with an eye to creating some space for rent-sensitive enterprises. Developers may prefer plans that exclusively make space for big spending tenants. However, an empty marble atrium provides jobs only for security guards and cleaners. Small businesses can be put far enough from deluxe sites to insure the exclusiveness of elite locations – but near enough to those settings to insure some job creation from passing traffic.

8) *Frontiers are economic resources. How they are managed can affect growth.* The opening up of the Amazon in Brazil may have had as profound an effect on national economic development as anything Getulio Vargas accomplished in the Estado Novo. Brazil is not unique in this regard. Most nations have frontiers. Space is a factor of production. The most elementary treatments of rural economics start with land being an asset and total production being determined by the amount of land put in cultivation. In this regard, space is no different than land or capital. Students of economic growth *either* deal with frontier development and ecological issues *or* deal with mainstream industrialization. These two strands of thought need synthesis. The relative magnitude of the growth coming from frontier development and the magnitude of growth coming from state-led industrialization is an open empirical question – and little evidence exists that would allow for an adjudication of the debate.

9) *Reduce pollution.* Pollution does produce negative externalities that adversely affect other industries. Dirty industries reduced hotel employment. Other forms of activity can hurt fishing or real estate. Not every industry can be made perfectly clean – but reducing pollution does produce positive spillovers.

10) *Cutting taxes does not create jobs but does raise vulnerability to indebtedness.* The analysis of the relationship between tax burdens and employment supported the literature in public finance that shows that tax cuts do not raise employment. The claims of business lobbyists to the opposite effect are not supported by either pre-existing empirical literature or by the findings presented here. Tax cuts however do gut the ability of the state to provide public goods such as infrastructure. They also increase the risk that vital state functions can only be provided if the state receives extra revenues through foreign loans. Debt financing can be toxic. Cutting taxes and incurring debt to please a set of lobbyists is a waste of state money – and is the triumph of private over public interests.

Rethinking state effectiveness

This book has been an attempt to rethink how states become effective at increasing employment. The methodology was elaborate. It was necessary to use mathematical methods to adjust for market factors to really identify what state programs made a difference. But once the diagnosis was clear, so was the story. And the story was that of James O'Connor in his *Fiscal Crisis of the State.*

States are critical to reproducing capitalism – which is a point that has been sadly forgotten in this era of anti-tax mobilization and popular distrust of the shibboleth of "Big Government". It is ironic that just as neoliberal models of economic growth have been increasingly discarded for the Third World, they are gaining greater and greater currency within the developed nations. Latin America, Asia and Africa suffered miserably from the "lost years" in which social and economic development were frozen as states in fiscal crisis lost the capacity to provide the basic services that were necessary to provide growth. Let us hope that that experience will not be repeated in the developed world.

Appendices

Data and sources

The data come from two types of sources: the Brazilian Service Censuses of 1940, 1950, 1960, 1970, 1975 and 1980, and the Brazilian Demographic Censuses of 1991 and 2000. These two types of data sources are somewhat non-parallel and mandate separate analyses for 1940–80, and 1991–2000. Each type of dataset has its particular strengths, and allowing different analyses to focus on different issues that could not be studied with the other type of data.

BRAZILIAN SERVICE CENSUSES 1940–80. These are incredibly informative data sources. Unlike normal censuses of individual people, they are censuses of firms designed to collect information on economic activity. They contain exhaustive information about nearly every service sector firm in Brazil – including employment, revenue, legal status, origins of receipts, and a detailed breakdown of costs. Such materials allow for incredibly detailed analyses of the determinants of the profitability and volume of activity of firms – analyses that are impossible to do with a traditional census of individuals. The quality of these surveys was very fine – except for the Amazonian states. The data is so sketchy for the Amazonian states that they are dropped from analyses for this period.

The high quality of the Service Censuses of 1940–80 in the non-Amazonian states came from several sources. Informality rates mid-century were substantially lower than they are in the present day. They were lower during the Brazilian economic miracle, and under the military regime. The more lenient administration of the democratic late 80s and 90s, combined with the greater economic insecurity that existed during this period both motivated and facilitated greater amounts of clandestine economic activity.

Earlier industrial censuses also had better coverage rates because census takers used block listing and direct observational techniques to attempt to locate every enterprise in their census district. During the military government, these investigators had significant legal authority to support them, facilitating cooperation with the census taker. In the 1980s, there began to be greater reliance on using pre-existing listings of firms registered to pay social security tax, rather than direct counts of all activity in a geographical area.[1] As non-registration rose, coverage and reliability fell. The author's own methodological investigations of the Service Censuses show data of high quality and reliability from 1940–80 – with a dramatic decline in coverage quality beginning in 1985 that never really recovers. These investigations led the author to drop the use of the 1985 Service Census and limit Service Census analyses to the pre-1985 period.

That said, the richness of these earlier sources makes them an inviting data source for those years for which they are available. These data exist for states only – with no disaggregations into smaller regions.

BRAZILIAN DEMOGRAPHIC CENSUSES 1991–2000. This is the best source of information for employment for recent periods. The Brazilian census's coverage of individuals is extremely comprehensive, allowing them to capture most workers in both formal and informal employment.

The demographic censuses have an additional advantage of being capable of being disaggregated to any geographical unit desired. Our analyses for this period use *microregions*, units about the size of a US county, which roughly reflect local labor markets. Regionally disaggregated data is extremely important for the analyses of this later period, because of the analysis of tourism programs such as PRODETUR, which focused on very particular locations such as specific towns or specific beaches.

The downside of using the demographic censuses is that there is no data on any employer attributes – and in particular there is no data on any employer costs. Thus, many of the attractive analyses for the earlier period simply cannot be replicated on contemporary data.

The 1991–2000 census uses all of the microregions in Brazil, including the Amazon. The increased social development of the Amazon, combined with significant improvement in local governance in these areas made post-1980 Censuses in this region relatively accurate.

There is one exclusion from the 1991–2000 analyses: Fernando da Noronha. This is the Brazilian equivalent of an Atlantic Galapagos. This is a small set of isolated islands in the mid-Atlantic – that have an extremely unique and beautiful eco-system. Like the Galapagos, the primary – and only – industry of the region is tourism. The local population is very small, and nearly everyone works taking care of the visitors who come to see the flora and fauna. As a result, Fernando da Noronha reports nearly 100 percent of its population working in hotels and restaurants making it an extreme outlier. Because the circumstances of Fernando da Noronha are completely atypical of those that characterize anywhere else in Brazil, the case was removed to prevent it from distorting the more important estimates of determinants of employment on the mainland.

EMPLOYMENT. The dependent variable in the analysis is the total number of people employed in each of the three industries as a percentage of population. This is a measure of aggregate employment. This comes from the service censuses in 1940–80 analyses, and the demographic censuses in 1991 and 2000 analyses.

PER CAPITA INCOME. Income data for microregions are available in the population census; they are measured in "minimum wages" as a unit, rather than currency. Brazil underwent significant hyperinflation during the 1990s; money prices not only changed significantly over time but vary dramatically by region with the Northeast having much lower prices than the rest of the country. Minimum wage rates are roughly designed to have comparable purchasing power from year to year and from region to region (although political processes concerning national wage bargaining provides some modest variability in the purchasing power of the minimum wage.)

INFANT MORTALITY. This is an alternative measure of income. Using an non-monetary measure of income is necessary in the 1940–80 analyses because the 1940 and 1950 censuses have no data on income per se. That said, the infant mortality rate is an excellent measure of economic well being. High infant mortality is generally the result of low calorie consumption per capita, low access to medical care and low access to public sanitation. (Weeks 1986) Populations with low calorie consumption per capita and low access to medical care, clean water and basic sewerage are unlikely to have the disposable income to support consumption on luxury services.

There is a second reason for including infant mortality. The period of analysis, 1940–2000, saw substantial monetary instability in Brazil including an extended period of hyperinflation and multiple currency transitions. Price indices are less reliable over long periods of time than short periods of time, and are less reliable in the presence of dramatic inflation or deflation than in stable conditions. Given Brazil's tumultuous history of prices, and the very long period of the analysis, there is reason to be skeptical of any price index, no matter how carefully constructed.[2] Since "minimum wages" are in essence raw wage data adjusted by a price index, some caution needs to be used with that measure. It was considered prudent to include a measure of income that was robust to questions of currency valuation. Infant mortality rates come from Brazilian national health statistics.

URBANIZATION. We measure urbanization as percentage of a state's residents who live in cities with populations exceeding 100,000. This is available from the Demographic Census.

UNESCO WORLD HERITAGE SITE. We list here all the Unesco designated single point locations in Brazil as of the year 2000. These include both points of natural interest, such as the waterfall Foz de Iguaçu, and historic locations such as baroque colonial cities. A full list of Unesco World Heritage sites can be found at http://whc.unesco. org. The UNESCO world heritage sites for Brazil were:

a) The baroque colonial town of Ouro Preto
b) The historic center of Olinda
c) The missions at São Miguel das Missões
d) The historic center of Salvador
e) The church of Bom Jesus do Congonhas
f) Foz de Iguaçu (one of the world's great waterfalls)
g) Brasilia
h) The historic center of São Luis
i) The baroque colonial town of Diamantina

We excluded UNESCO attractions that are in multiple microregions. The Amazon is an obvious tourist attraction in Brazil – but including it would make a quarter of the country a tourist site. Visitors to the Amazon go to a wide variety of places with some Amazonian regions receiving lots of tourists while others receive very few. The Amazon is not a UNESCO World Heritage site, but the Mata Atlantica (the Atlantic Rainforest) is. Because the visitors to the Mata are broadly dispersed, no one particular area would have received an intense concentration of tourists.[3]

UPSCALE BEACHES. This variable is essentially beach location multiplied by state income. A dummy variable was created for whether a microregion is on the coast with interior areas having a score of 0 and shoreline areas having a score of 1. This was multiplied by the per capita income of the entire state in which the micro-region is located. The income data come from the Demographic Censuses.

FEMALE LABOR FORCE PARTICIPATION. Female labor force participation data was obtained from the Demographic Census.

TIME. The measure of time is the year of the observation. This simple device actually provides a good approximation of the model that could be obtained from more formal population ecological estimating techniques. The traditional population ecology model requires the use of a logistic regression, since one wants to fit an S-shaped curve to capture both the period of early growth and the period of later overcrowding. However, Hannan and Freeman generally observe their findings on datasets containing a hundred years or more of observations – in which both the early and later phases are observable. We observed no industry that was in both the early and later phases during 1940–2000; industries were either in one phase or the other. As such a simple linear time term was included, with the coefficient being consistently positive for young industries and consistently negative for mature ones.

Details of statistical results

Chapter 2   Core regression equations

The dependent variable in each case is the number of workers employed in each industry as a percentage of the population.

First figures are coefficients. Figures in parentheses are z-statistics, a t-like statistic for PCSE regression. All coefficients are significant at 0.05 or less unless indicated otherwise.

1940–1980

In the 1940–80 equations, the unit of analysis is the non-Amazonian state. The observations are 1940, 1950, 1960, 1970, 1975 and 1980. To insure standard state boundaries across dates, Mato Grosso is always combined with Mato Grosso do Sul and Guanabara/the Distrito Federal of Rio de Janeiro is always combined with the state of Rio de Janeiro. N = 111.

Hotels: Infant Mortality –0.748 (–10.39); Urbanization 1.04 (16.0); Time –1.33 (–8.34); *Female Labor Force Participation (–1.57) ns*. R^2 = 0.58.

Restaurants: Infant Mortality –0.985 (–4.46); Urbanization 6.74 (8.03); *Female Labor Force Participation 4.42 (1.01) ns; Time 1.95 (0.85) ns*. R^2 = 0.84.

Barber/Beauty: Urbanization 1.82 (11.3); Time –1.33 (–8.20); *Infant Mortality –0.006 (–0.19) ns; Female Labor Force Participation –0.026 (–0.08) ns*. R^2 = 0.71.

1991–2000

In the 1991–2000 equations, the unit of analysis is the Census microregion, an area about the size of a US county. The observations are 1991 and 2000. N = 1014.

Hotels: Income 5.01E-04 (6.70); Urbanization 0.00156 (5.64); UNESCO Heritage Site 0.00134 (5.91); Upscale Beach 5.57E-04 (4.98); Time –2.88E-05 (–6.03); *Infant Mortality –4.73E-06 (–1.07) ns; Female Labor Force Participation 5.20E-04 (0.52) ns*. R^2 = 0.27.

Restaurants: Income 8.06E-04 (2.33); Infant Mortality –1.48E-05 (–2.32); Urbanization 0.00498 (5.37); UNESCO Heritage Site 0.00147 (2.48); Upscale Beach 7.88E-04 (6.51); Time 1.75E-04 (12.2); *Female Labor Force Participation –1.01E07 (–1.00) ns*. R^2 = 0.57.

Barber/Beauty: Income 5.52E-04 (4.67); Urbanization 0.00360 (8.99); Female Labor Force Participation 0.00253 (5.87); UNESCO Heritage Site 2.14E04 (6.86); Time –0.13E-05 (–6.94); *Infant Mortality 5.14E07 (0.49) ns; Upscale Beach –4.71E05 (1.71) ns. 0*. R^2 = 0.72.

Chapter 3   Pearson correlations of government subsidized hotel construction with residuals from the core models

FINOR analyses are of Northeastern Microregions. N = 186.

FINOR Hotels 1981–91 – Residual Hotel Employment 1991 –0.04
FINOR Rooms 1981–91 – Residual Hotel Employment 1991 –0.04
FINOR Hotels 1992–2000 – Residual Hotel Employment 2000 0.10
FINOR Rooms 1992–2000 – Residual Hotel Employment 2000 0.24
FINOR Hotels 1981–91 – Residual Hotel Employment 2000 –0.07
FINOR Rooms 1981–91 – Residual Hotel Employment 2000 –0.07

FINOR Hotels 1981–91 – Residual Restaurant Employment 1991 0.11
FINOR Rooms 1981–91 – Residual Restaurant Employment 1991 0.08
FINOR Hotels 1992–2000 – Residual Restaurant Employment 2000 –0.05
FINOR Rooms 1992–2000 – Residual Restaurant Employment 2000 –0.03
FINOR Hotels 1981–91 – Residual Restaurant Employment 2000 –0.07
FINOR Rooms 1981–91 – Residual Restaurant Employment 2000 –0.10

FUNGETUR/Other analyses are of all Brazilian states. N = 27.

FUNGETUR/Other Hotels 1981–91 – Residual Hotel Employment 1991 0.09
FUNGETUR/Other Rooms 1981–91 – Residual Hotel Employment 1991 0.05
FUNGETUR/Other Hotels 1992–2000 – Residual Hotel Employment 2000 0.02
FUNGETUR/Other Rooms 1992–2000 – Residual Hotel Employment 2000 0.10
FUNGETUR/Other Hotels 1981–91 – Residual Hotel Employment 2000 0.04
FUNGETUR/Other Rooms 1981–91 – Residual Hotel Employment 2000 0.00

FUNGETUR/Other Hotels 1981–91 – Residual Restaurant Employment 1991 0.54
FUNGETUR/Other Rooms 1981–91 – Residual Restaurant Employment 1991 0.57
FUNGETUR/Other Hotels 1992–2000 – Residual Restaurant Employment 2000 0.43
FUNGETUR/Other Rooms 1992–2000 – Residual Restaurant Employment 2000 0.08
FUNGETUR/Other Hotels 1981–91 – Residual Restaurant Employment 2000 –0.24
FUNGETUR/Other Rooms 1981–91 – Residual Restaurant Employment 2000 –0.01

Chapter 3   Pearson correlations of the presence of completed PRODETUR projects with residuals from the core models

The unit of analysis is the Census Microregion. Only Northeastern Brazilian Micro-regions are considered. N = 186.

Water – Completed Water Project by 2000 with Hotel Residuals 2000 0.32
Sewer – Completed Sewer Project by 2000 with Hotel Residuals 2000 0.46
Environment – Completed Environment Project by 2000 with Hotel Residuals 2000 –0.23
Road – Completed Road Project by 2000 with Hotel Residuals 2000 0.21
Terminal – Completed Terminal Project by 2000 with Hotel Residuals 2000 0.21
Urbanization – Completed Urbanization Project by 2000 with Hotel Residuals 2000 –0.195
Airport – Completed Airport Project by 2000 with Hotel Residuals 2000 0.32
Any – Any Completed Project by 2000 with Hotel Residuals 2000 0.13
Project Count – Number Completed Projects by 2000 with Hotel Residuals 2000 0.27

Water – Completed Water Project by 2000 with Restaurant Residuals 2000 0.15
Sewer – Completed Sewer Project by 2000 with Restaurant Residuals 2000 –0.01
Environment – Completed Environment Project by 2000 with Restaurant Residuals
2000 –0.08
Road – Completed Road Project by 2000 with Restaurant Residuals 2000 0.02
Terminal – Completed Terminal Project by 2000 with Restaurant Residuals 2000 –0.08
Urbanization – Completed Urbanization Project by 2000 with Restaurant Residuals
2000 –0.144
Airport – Completed Airport Project by 2000 with Restaurant Residuals 2000 0.03
Any – Any Completed Project by 2000 with Restaurant Residuals 2000 –0.05
Project Count – Number Completed Projects by 2000 with Restaurant Residuals
2000 –0.01

N = 186

Chapter 5   Core regression equations plus vocational training
Format same as in Chapter 2 equations.

All equations are for 1991–2000. The unit of analysis is the Census Microregion.
N = 1014.

*Short-term equations that only include job training activity in the year of
the observation and the previous year*

Hotels: Income 5.08E-04 (5.43); Urbanization 0.00155 (5.67); UNESCO Heritage
Site 0.00132 (6.24); Upscale Beach 5.73E-04 (4.85); Year –2.99E05 (–4.87); *Infant
Mortality –4.53E06 (–0.98) ns; Female Labor Force Participation 4.98 (0.51) ns;*
SENAC Training 2.96E-08 (0.68) ns. $R^2 = 0.275$.

Restaurants: Income 8.42E-04 (2.25); Urbanization 0.00497 (5.29); UNESCO
Heritage Site 0.00139 (2.23); Affluent Beach 8.03E-04 (6.44); Year 1.68E-04
(9.87); *Infant Mortality –1.33E-05 (–1.77) ns; Female Labor Force Participation
–9.58E-08 (–1.03) ns;* **SENAC Training 1.88E-07 (1.59) ns.** $R^2 = 0.568$.

Barber/Beauty: Income 5.73E-04 (5.92); Infant Mortality 1.26E-06 (2.07);
Urbanization 0.00354 (9.24); Female Labor Force Participation 0.00214 (7.88);
UNESCO Heritage Site 2.03E-04 (7.52); Upscale Beach –7.54E-05 (–2.23); Year
–1.58E-05 (–5.23); **SENAC Training 2.12E-07 (10.25)**.
$R^2 = 0.725$.

*Long-term equations that include job training activity in the decade
previous to the year of the observation*

Hotels: Income 4.99E-04 (5.33); Urbanization 0.00156 (5.63); UNESCO Heritage
Site 0.00134 (6.43); Upscale Beach 5.7E-04 (4.84); Year –2.85E05 (–5.08); *Infant
Mortality –4.8E-06 (0.3) ns; Female Labor Force Participation 5.35E-04 (0.55) ns;*
SENAC Training 1.07E-08 (0.21) ns. $R^2 = 0.274$.

Restaurants: Income 8.50E-04 (2.33); Urbanization 0.00499 (5.37); UNESCO
Heritage Site 0.00134 (2.20); Affluent Beach 8.11E-04 (6.36); Year 1.66E-04
(10.78);

SENAC Training 3.46E-07 (16.21); *Infant Mortality –1.22E-05 (–1.76) ns; Female Labor Force Participation –9.44E-08 (–1.02) ns.* R^2 = 0.569

Barber/Beauty: Income 5.56E-04 (5.63); Infant Mortality 1.73E-06 (2.34); Urbanization 0.00357 (9.46); Female Labor Force Participation 0.0022 (6.36); UNESCO Heritage Site 2.07E-04 (7.13); Upscale Beach –6.62 (2.33); Year –1.37E-05 (–4.98); **SENAC Training 2.01E-07 (5.81).** R^2 = 0.720.

Chapter 7   Core regression equations plus taxes divided by receipts

Format the same as Chapter 2.

All equations are for 1940–80. The unit of analysis is Brazilian non-Amazonian states. N = 111.

Hotels: Infant Mortality –0.830 (–12.11); Urbanization 1.15 (13.67); Female Labor Force Participation –1.29 (–2.18) Year –1.51 (–8.69); **Non-Payroll Taxes 22.7 (0.76) ns.** R^2 = 0.60.

Hotels: Infant Mortality –0.789 (–15.41); Urbanization 1.30 (4.84); Female Labor Force Participation –1.15 (–2.09); Year –1.00 (–3.57); **Payroll Taxes –76.0 (–3.59)** R^2 = 0.60.

Hotels: Infant Mortality –0.818 (–16.26); Urbanization 1.23 (23.38); Female Labor Force Participation –1.21 (–2.14); Year –1.31 (–5.45); **All Taxes –36.0 (–2.10).** R^2 = 0.60.

Restaurants: Infant Mortality –1.03 (–3.5); Urbanization 6.72 (7.00); *Female Labor Force Participation 4.58 (0.95) ns; Year 1.64 (0.66) ns; **Non-Payroll Taxes –268 (–0.19) ns.*** R^2 = 0.84.

Restaurants: Infant Mortality –0.898 (–3.02); Urbanization 6.85 (7.29); *Female Labor Force Participation 3.73 (0.79) ns; Year 0.0984 (0.03) ns; **Payroll Taxes –212 (–0.75) ns.*** R^2 = 0.84.

Restaurants: Infant Mortality –0.886 (–2.94); Urbanization 6.86 (7.36); *Female Labor Force Participation 3.63 (0.77) ns; Year 0.420 (0.14) ns; **All Taxes 187 (0.69 ns).*** R^2 = 0.84.

Barber/Beauty: Urbanization 1.96 (10.61); Year –1.61 (–8.07); **Non-Payroll Taxes –458 (–3.13)**; *Infant Mortality –0.365 (–1.19); Female Labor Force Participation –0.119 (–6.05).* R^2 = 0.72.

Barber/Beauty: Urbanization 1.81 (11.5); Year –1.33 (–8.34); *Infant Mortality –0.00463 (–0.15) ns; Female Labor Force Participation –0.0344 (–0.09 ns); **Payroll Taxes 0.651 (–0.07) ns.*** R^2 = 0.71.

Barber/Beauty: Urbanization 1.91 (9.52); Year –1.33 (–9.19); *Infant Mortality 0.00841 (0.19); Female Labor Force Participation –0.390 (–1.09); **All Taxes 1.13 (0.13) ns*** R^2 = 0.70.

Hotel: Infant Mortality –0.877 (–9.22); Urbanization 1.32 (7.92); Year –1.33 (–6.48); Material Costs 89.1 (2.53); *Female Labor Force Participation –1.05 (–1.23) ns;* **Non-Payroll Taxes 40.0 (1.3) ns**. R^2 = 0.62.

Hotel: Infant Mortality –0.828 (–10.53); Urbanization 1.52 (11.41); Year –0.898 (–3.29); Material Costs 96.2 (2.97); **Payroll Taxes –70.4 (–3.24)**; *Female Labor Force Participation –0.949 (–1.22) ns*. R^2 = 0.63.

Hotel: Infant Mortality –0.867 (–11.35); Urbanization 1.35 (8.80); Year –1.24 (–5.59); Material Costs 88.6 (2.57); *Female Labor Force Participation –1.06 (–1.36) ns;* **All Taxes –24.3 (–1.19) ns**. R^2 = 0.62.

Restaurants: Infant Mortality –1.18 (–3.68); Urbanization 6.76 (8.41); Materials Costs –564 (–2.65); *Female Labor Force Participation 4.53 (1.02) ns; Year 3.11 (1.42) ns;* **Non-Payroll Taxes 130 (0.11) ns**; R^2 = 0.84.

Restaurants: Infant Mortality –1.12 (–3.28); Urbanization 6.91 (9.71); Materials Costs –574 (–2.87); *Female Labor Force Participation 3.56 (0.95) ns; Year 1.40 (0.55) ns;* **Payroll Taxes 193 (0.98) ns**; R^2 = 0.85.

Restaurants: Infant Mortality –1.10 (–3.21); Urbanization 6.91 (9.77); Materials Costs –572 (–2.86); *Female Labor Force Participation 3.50 (0.94) ns; Year 1.66 (0.69) ns;* **All Taxes 177 (0.92) ns**; R^2 = 0.85.

Barber/Beauty: Infant Mortality –0.137 (–3.04) Urbanization 2.07 (15.6); Year –2.08 (–11.04); Rent –380 (–6.98) *Female Labor Force Participation 0.357 (1.27) ns;* **Non-Payroll Taxes –224 (–1.36) ns**. R^2 = 0.79.

Barber/Beauty: Infant Mortality –1.04 (–2.07); Urbanization 1.92 (18.4); Year –1.84 (–7.94); Rent –336 (–5.66*); Female Labor Force Participation –0.570 (–1.15) ns;* **Payroll Taxes 0.746 (–0.08) ns**. R^2 = 0.78.

Barber/Beauty: Infant Mortality –0.127 (–2.12); Urbanization 2.05 (15.58); Year –1.97 (–9.34); Rent –401 (–6.58); *Female Labor Force Participation –0.286 (–0.74);* **All Taxes 1.85 (–0.22) ns**. R^2 = 0.79.

Chapter 8   Core regression equations plus rent divided by receipts

Format Same as Chapter 2.

All equations are for 1940–80. The unit of analysis is Brazilian non-Amazonian states. N = 111.

Rarber/Beauty: –105 (–2.31); Urbanization 1.91 (18.4); Year –1.84 (–7.86); **Rent/Receipts –336 (–5.63)**; *Female Labor Force Participation 0.579 (1.67) ns*. R^2 = 0.78.

Chapter 8   Pearson correlations of the ratio of rent to receipts in barber/beauty to economic development and features of the stock of constructed buildings

The unit of analysis is the Brazilian non-Amazonian state. All data is for 1970. N = 19.

Rent-Urbanization 0.76
Rent-Infant Mortality –0.59
Rent-Female Labor Force Participation 0.55
Rent-Buildings Per Capita –0.76
Rent-Floors Per Capita –0.70
Rent-Building Verticalization (Floors per Building) 0.75
Rent-New Construction Per Capita 0.79
Rent-Verticalization of New Construction 0.46

Chapter 10   Core regression equations plus the modified Mani-Wheeler Index of Industrial Pollution

Format same as in Chapter 2.

Hotels: Income 4.76E-04 (4.21); Urbanization 0.00200 (5.55); UNESCO Heritage Site 0.00130 (5.75); Upscale Beach 5.65E-04 (5.28); Year –4.85E05 (–7.66); **Mani-Wheeler Pollution Index –0.0208 (–2.72)**; *Infant Mortality –6.17E-06 (–1.31) ns; Female Labor Force Participation 8.73E-04 (0.98) ns.* $R^2 = 0.286$

Restaurants: Income 8.06E-04 (2.33); Infant Mortality –1.49E-05 (–2.84); Urbanization 0.00501 (8.44); UNESCO Heritage Site 0.00147 (2.36); Affluent Beach 7.87E-04 (6.34); Year 1.74E-04 (6.95); *Female Labor Force Participation –1.01E-07 (–0.95) ns;* **Mani-Wheeler Pollution Index –0.00136 (–0.06) ns**. $R^2 = 0.566$

Notes

Chapter 1   Rethinking the State and Development: The Importance of Palliative Development

1   For contrasting cites of the earlier view that tourism fails to produce economic growth because profits are repatriated by multinational hotel owners see Zinder (1969) and Bryden (1973). Their position has been rightly criticized for under-estimating local participation in the tourism industry, missing key examples of governments regulating the outflow of tourism profits, and giving insufficient weight to the role of skilled entrepreneurship in determining the size of the multiplier. (Mullins 1999, Fainstein and Gladstone 1999)

Chapter 2   What Would Have Happened If the Government Had Done Nothing

1   Regression with panel corrected standard errors corrects for unspecified region specific and year specific omitted variables that can violate the assumption of independence of errors required for traditional ordinary least squares regression. On analyses that have more than two panels, a specification is used that also corrects for autocorrelation. For more on issues concerning the analysis of panel datasets see Beck and Katz 2011.
2   These may seem surprising to some readers who have seen equations with large numbers of variables used in other settings. Estimating an equation with 30 independent variables is not unlike looking at a dichotomous table with one dependent variable and 30 predictors. Each new variable requires a new "dimension" to the table, so this implies a 31 dimension table. To put one case in every cell, one would need a minimum of 2^{31} cases – or well over a billion cases. When there are not enough cases, many cells become zeros and the estimate becomes unreliable.

Chapter 3   O'Connorian Models of Development: How States Literally Build Economic Growth

1   Neither infrastructure nor direct state investment were particularly relevant to barber/beauty shops. Those programs were affected by other government policies discussed in later chapters.
2   Amsden (1989) and Szirmai (2005) summarize many of the key arguments.
3   Coca Cola has no real monopoly on the making of cola.
4   The general historical accounts of the history of FINOR, FUNGETUR and PRODETUR come from the following sources: Sudene and Banco do Nordeste (1986), Cruz (2000), Oliveira (2000), Ruschman (2002), Banco do Nordeste (2004), Pedroza and Friere (2005), Teles (2005), Perazza and Tuazon (2006).

5   These data do not speak to the argument that Northeastern tourism rose because a falling real restricted Brazilian's capacity to engage in foreign travel. However, national currency effects would be constant across all states and regions and have no effect on within-Brazil inter-regional effects. Thus the positive findings presented here are independent of currency effects and can not be "explained away" by exchange rates.

6   No attempt is made to count the number of projects within each type, or to count the amount of money invested. Counts of projects within type were often affected by arbitrary classification questions as to whether a set of works would count as one or as multiple projects. (Road projects were particularly subject to arbitrary definitions of "project borders"). Likewise measuring financial commitments runs into complexities based on differences between dates of disbursement of funds and dates of project completion.

7   There may have been a parallel effect on non-local tourism as workers in cities with new bus stations would have had greater capacity to visit beaches in microregions other than those where the bus terminal was located.

8   The present analysis can be thought of as a 50 percent sample with cross-cutting selection biases for positive and negative effects. The substantial coverage of the sampling frame and the mutually neutralizing effects of the selection biases are consistent with reliability in the test estimates.

Chapter 4   Major Infrastructure and the Larger Economy: The Central Importance of Airports

1   In statistical terms, growth rates were converted into their Z-scores.

Chapter 5   How Brazilian Vocational Education Reduces Poverty – Even If No One Wants to Hire the Trainees

1   Heckman Lalonde and Smith are well known critics of job training programs. They have strong concerns about whether American programs are funded at an adequate level to be effective. They do not share these reservations about the more generously funded programs in Europe. (Heckman et al. 1999)

2   See Heckman et al. (1999) for an extensive review of these. Within the hotel and restaurant sectors, nearly all the work uses measures individual success. See for example Ruschmann and Rejowski 1999.

3   The argument here would not hold if worker's productivity during training was zero or negative. Such a condition might apply for a trainee receiving classroom instruction but would rarely apply to a worker learning their trade on the shop floor. Even the most inexperienced novice can do something useful in a workplace, even if it is only to clean up, deliver objects or perform simple manual tasks. Learning on the shopfloor is one of the most basic and common forms of training.

4   Note the argument here refers narrowly to job training programs, and not about all education per se. Non-job-related education that provides fundamental firm general skills such as literacy and numeracy may have substantial effects on increasing economic growth. Likewise, educational improvements that improve

a nation's research capacities and its ability to produce technological innovations may be central for facilitating the transition from peripheral to core
status. As such, none of the present discussion should be viewed as con-
tradicting the claims of Krueger and Lindahl 2001, Glewwe 2002, or Behrman
1999 that show that at the national level education improves the productivity
of the factors of production and increases growth. Primary, secondary and
higher education perform different functions for the economy than does non-
school-based government job training.

5   A possible exception to this might be in the building trades, where workers
are expected to show up for work with their own tools.
6   SENAI is somewhat more expensive – being an industrial program that trains
on heavy machinery. (Campino et al. 1985)
7   Ivete Tiyomi Ida did an extensive series of evaluations of SENAI programs
that showed this result. See Ida (1987) for a typical example. On SENAC, see
SENAC (1986).
8   One of the more successful SENAC students that we interviewed in fact DID
run her business out of her driveway, under a covered portico.
9   There were too few cases to do an analysis for the earlier period.
10 All barber and beautician names in this chapter have been changed, and the
letters do not refer to letters in the informants' real names.

Chapter 6   Government Effectiveness in the Face of Debt

1   Bresser Pereira also argues that under conditions of debt, government programs have to be assessed for their overall effectiveness. In this he prefigures
the arguments of Dani Rodrik (2007), who argues that even the most interventionist states need to cut off the funding of state projects that fail to
become competitive before the middle term.
2   Even in the purchase of a bond, there are the questions of the future value of
the currency in which the bond is denominated, whether interest rates will
rise or fall and the liquidity of the bond should more attractive opportunities
emerge later.

Chapter 7   Why Reducing Taxes for Employers Does Not Raise Employment

1   Tax data are missing from the 1960 panel. The 1960 Census was generally
one of the least reliable and lowest quality censuses in Brazil. A ship carrying
most of the data and tapes for the Northeastern states was lost at sea, and the
Northeastern data had to be reconstructed on a very tenuous basis. (Edward
Telles, oral communication).

Chapter 8   How Rent and Urban Verticalization Can Reduce Employment

1   Since 1980, Sergipe has benefited enormously from newly discovered offshore oil and gas deposits which produced an energy boom. None of this

would have applied to the 1940–80 residuals which are the main focus of this chapter.

2 Note that a better statement of this position would be that rent is inversely correlated with the available floor-space rather than number of buildings. However, floor-space is contaminated with the effect of verticalization, which as we will see raises below, rather than lower rents. Preliminary empirical analysis used both building counts and floor counts to deal with this ambiguity and finds similar results for the two measures with slightly better fit for the building-based specification.

3 IBGE, the Brazilian Census Authority, was in the 1960s and 1970s, one of the most creative and innovative census agencies in Latin America. The Westernization of Brazilian Censuses was in some ways as regrettable as the Westernization of Brazilian music, representing the loss of incredible self-taught innovation and talent in favor of a standardized less interesting globalized product.

4 All of the legal material in this section is drawn from Almeida 1982 and Dos Santos 1995.

5 The loophole that landlords could destroy a building and replace it with a new structure became very important. This explains the extremely low rate of historical preservation in Brazil and the enormous preponderance of 60s–90s era modern buildings even in urban neighborhoods of earlier vintage.

Chapter 9   Frontier Development as Job Creation – With Social Costs

1 Figure 9.2 does not include data from 1978; however parallel tables on construction starts show 1978 was similar to other years.

2 We leave to the reader's imagination the interpretation of a project that spends a lot of money very, very quickly and then disappears from the public record – with nothing to show for the expenditure.

3 However, once developed, the resort was transferred into private hands. Copies of the transfer documents are posted prominently in the foyer of one of the principal buildings of the hotel.

Chapter 10   When Does Not Being Green Reduce Employment?

1 There were too few cases to do an analysis for the earlier period.

2 Pearson coefficients are 0.67 and 0.29 respectively. Both correlations are significant with a p value of less than 0.001; N = 1014.

Chapter 11   Palliative Development, and the Great Theories of the State and Economic Growth

1 Some readers may be skeptical of this claim because of arguments concerning the "McDonaldization" of the world – and that hotels and restaurants in the global south are being dominated by American and European chains. (Ritzer 2008) Levels of foreign penetration of the hotel and restaurant sector are often

exaggerated. One can find McDonalds, or a Starbucks in many Third World cities. However, even the most casual walk down any street will show the clear majority of bar and restaurants to be local with names that an American or Briton would not recognize. Foreign hotels can often be found in business centers; however, nationals often dominate the hotel sector in tourist areas frequented by nationals, on inter-regional highways, near bus stations, and in the bed and breakfast sector. In Aracaju, Sergipe where I did my fieldwork, foreign chains represented fewer than 2 percent of the restaurants – and fewer than 10 percent of the hotels. The ratios were not all that different in Rio de Janeiro.

2 The closest thing I found to a successful policy ring in hotels was an alliance of some hotel owners with political interests in Cuiabá. Even if this produced advantageous bookings of state business, and the allocations of some prime locations to this inner circle, hotel ownership in Cuiabá was still broadly dispersed, and overall levels of employment and prosperity in the sector were high.

Chapter 12   Development Strategies in a Post-Debt World

1 SEBRAE's microcredit programs are generally administered in coordination with a local development bank.

Appendices

1 Currently, most industrial enterprise samples are drawn from RAIS, the official compilation of legally registered firms. Informality makes this a very dubious sampling base – except for analyses which can legitimately be limited to a sample of very large firms.

2 The author has experimented with the effects of price indices constructed using different methodologies. The effects of using alternative metrics can be noticeable, although no changes materially alter the substantive conclusions reported in this book. (The year term included in the equations neutralizes some of these adverse effects.)

3 An obvious exclusion from the UNESCO list is the city of Rio de Janeiro. Alternate equations that treat Rio de Janeiro as if it were a UNESCO World Heritage site behave similarly to the models presented here.

Bibliography

Abreu, Marcelo de Paiva. 1989. *Ordem do Progresso – Cem Anos de Política Economia Republicana 1889-1989*. São Paulo, Editora Campus.

Abreu, Silvana de. 2001. *Planejamento Governmental: A SUDECO no Espaco Matogrossense: Contexto, Propositos e Contradicoes*. Dissertation thesis, Geography, Universidade de São Paulo.

Adelman, Irma. 2000. "Fallacies in Development Theory and Their Implications for Policy". Pp. 103-148 in Gerald Meier and Joseph Stiglitz (eds) *Frontiers of Development Economics*. New York, Oxford.

Ahmad, Ehtisham and Nicholas Stern. 1989. "Taxation for Developing Countries". Pp. 1006-1092 in Hollis Cherery and T.N. Srinivasan (eds) *Handbook of Development Economics*. New York, North Holland.

Alexim, Joao Carlos. 1993. "Training Programs for Small Firms: An Overview". Pp. 69-80 in Brigitte Spath (ed.) *Small Firms and Development in Latin America: Role of Institutional Environment, Human Resources and Industrial Relations*. Geneva, International Institute for Labor Studies.

Almeida, Alfredo Wagner Berno de. 1989. *Conflito e Poder: Os Conflitos Agrários na Amazôna Segundo os Movimentos Caponeses, as Instituções Religiosos e O Estado 1969-89*. n.p.

Almeida, Amador Paes de. 1982. *Locação Comercial*. 3rd Edition. São Paulo, Saraiva.

Almeida, Maria da Gloria Santana de. 1991. "Atividades Productivas". Pp. 61-126 in Diana Diniz et al. *Textos Para a Historia de Sergipe*. Aracaju, Universidade Federal de Sergipe.

Amed, Fernando Jose. 2000. *Historia dos Tributos no Brasil*. São Paulo, SINAS-FRESP.

Ammana, Paul and Gustav Schacter. 1985. "Some Statistical Interpretations of Vocational Education in Brazil". Pp. 85-112 in Schacter, Gustav (ed.) *Vocational Education in Brazil: Aspects of Economic Policy and Planning*. Boston, Northeastern.

Amsden, Alice. 1985. "State and Taiwan's Economic Development". Pp. 78-106 in Peter Evans et al. (eds) *Bringing the State Back In*. New York, Cambridge.

——. 1989 *Asia's Next Giant: South Korea and Late Industrialization*. New York, Oxford.

——. 2001. *Best of the Rest: Challenges to the West From the Late Industrializing Economies*. New York, Oxford.

——. 2007. *Escape From Empire: Developing World's Journey Through Heaven and Hell*. Cambridge, MIT.

Andersen, Arthur. 1976. *Basic Business and Tax Structure in Brazil*. Chicago, Arthur Anderson & Co.

Annual Message. 1974-2000. *Mensagem Apresentada a Assembleia Leislative Pelo Governador do Estado de Mato Grosso*. Archivos do Estado do Mato Grosso.

Artus, Jacques. 1972. "Econometric Analysis of International Travel". *IMF Staff Papers* 19: 579-614.

Aschauer, D. 2000. "Public Capital and Economic Growth: Issues of Quantity, Finance and Efficiency". *Economic Development and Cultural Change* 48: 391-406.

Auerbach, Alan. 1985. "Theory of Excess Burden and Optimal Taxation". Pp. 61–127 in Alan Auerbach and Martin Feldstein (eds) *Handbook of Public Economics*. New York, North-Holland.

Azeredo, B. 1993. *O Sistema Previdenciário Brasileiro: Diagnóstico e Perspetivas de Mudanças*. Rio de Janeiro, Centro de Estudos de Políticas Públicas.

Bacha Edmar, Milton da Mata and Rui Lyrio Modensi. 1972. *Encargos Trabalhistas e Absorcao de Mão-de-Obra: uma Interpretação do Problema e Seu Debate*. Rio de Janeiro, IPEA.

Baer, Werner. 2004. *Economia Brasileira*. São Paulo, Nobel.

Bailly, Antoine, William Coffey, Jean H.P. Paelinck and Mario Polese. 1992. *Spatial Econometrics of Services*. Avebury, Aldershot.

Banco do Nordeste. 1974. *Realizações em Credito Industrial e Serviços Basicos*. Fortaleza, Banco do Nordeste.

——. 2004. *Relatório Final de Projeto. Programa de Desenvolvimento do Turismo do Nordeste. Prodetur/NE I*. Fortaleza, Banco do Nordeste.

Barnet, Richard and Ronald Muller. 1974. *Global Reach: Power of Multinational Corporations*. New York, Simon and Schuster.

Barros, Ricardo Paes de and Rosane Silva Pinto de Mendonça. 1996. "Flexibilidade do Mercado do Trabalho no Brasil: Uma Avaliação Empírica". Pp. 157–202 in José Márcio Camargo (ed.). *Flexibilidade do Mercado de Trabalho No Brasil*. Rio de Janeiro, Fundação Getulio Vargas.

Bartik, Timothy. 2001. *Jobs for the Poor: Can Labor Demand Policies Help?* New York, Russell Sage.

Baumol, William. 2006. *Microeconomics: Principles and Policy*. Mason, Ohio, Thomson.

Beck, Nathaniel and Jonathan Katz. 2011. "Modelling Dynamics in Time-Series-Cross-Section Political Economy Data". *Annual Review of Political Science* 14: 331–352.

Becker, Gary. 1964. *Human Capital: A Theoretical and Empirical Analysis With Special Reference to Education*. New York, National Bureau of Economic Research.

——. 1981. *Treatise on the Family*. Cambridge, Harvard.

Behrman, Jere. 1999. "Labor Markets in Developing Countries. Pp. 2859–2939 in *Handbook of Labor Economics*. Orley Ashenfelter and David Card (eds). Amsterdam, Elsevier.

Berry, Brian. 1981. *Comparative Urbanization: Divergent Paths in the Twentieth Century*. New York, Saint Martins.

Berry, Brian and John Kasarda. 1977. *Contemporary Urban Ecology*. New York, Macmillan.

Bird, Richard. 1992. *Tax Policy and Economic Development*. Baltimore, Johns Hopkins.

Blau, Peter and Otis Dudley Duncan. 1967. *American Occupational Structure*. New York, Wiley and Sons.

Block, Fred. 1987. *Revising State Theory: Essays in Politics and Postindustrialism*. Philadelphia, Temple.

Bresser Pereira, Luiz Carlos. 1992. *Crise do Estado: Ensaios Sobre a Economia Brasileira*. São Paulo, Nobel.

Brittain, John. 1972. *Payroll Tax for Social Security*. Washington, Brookings.

Brown, Alison. 2006. *Contested Space: Street Trading, Public Space and Livelihoods in Developing Cities*. Rugby, U.K., ITDG.

Browning, Harley and Joachim Singelmann. 1975 *Emergence of a Service Society: Demographic and Sociological Aspects of the Sectoral Transformation of the Labor*

Force in the USA. Report Prepared for the Manpower Administration, U.S. Department of Labor. Document PB-254 B52, U.S. Department of Commerce. Washington D.C., National Technical Information Service.

Bryden, John. 1973. *Tourism and Development: Case Study of the Commonwealth Caribbean*. New York, Cambridge.

Bunker, Stephen 1990. *Underdeveloping the Amazon: Extraction, Unequal Exchange and the Failure of the Modern State*. Chicago, Chicago.

Burgess, Robin and Nicholas Stern. 1993. "Taxation and Development". *Journal of Economic Literature* 31: 762–830.

Burns, Bradford. 1993. *History of Brazil*. Third Edition. New York, Columbia.

Cacciamali, Maria Cristina. 1983. *Setor Informal Urbano e Formas de Participação na Produção*. São Paulo, Instituto das Pesquisas Economicas.

Calmfors, Lars. 1994. "Active Labor Market Policy and Unemployment: A Framework for the Analysis of Crucial Design Features". *OECD Economic Studies* 22: 7–47.

Camargo, José Márcio. 1996. "Flexibilidade e Produtividade do Mercado de Trabalho Brasileiro". Pp. 11–46 in José Márcio Camargo (ed.). *Flexibilidade do Mercado de Trabalho No Brasil*. Rio de Janeiro, Fundação Getulio Vargas.

Campanhole, Adriano and Hilton Lobo Campanhole. 1983. *Consolidação das Leis da Previdênica Social*. São Paulo, Atlas.

Campino, Antonio Carlos Coelho, Maria Cristina Cacciamsil and Otto Nogami. 1985. *Recursos e Desempenhos das Programas de Mão de Obra*. São Paulo, Nobel.

Cardoso, Adauto Lucio and Luis Cesar de Queiroz Ribeiro. 1996. *Dualização e Reestruturação Urbana: O Caso do Rio de Janeiro*. Rio de Janeiro, FASE.

Cardoso, Fernando Henrique. 1991. "Crisis of Development in Latin America". Pp. 132–143 in Fernando Henrique Cardoso et al. *Eight Essays on the Crisis of Development in Latin America*. Amsterdam, Center for Research and Documentation on Latin America.

——. 2006. *A Arte da Política: A Historia Que Eu Vivi*. Rio de Janeiro, Editora Civilisação Brasileira.

——. 2009. "New Paths: Globalization in Historical Perspective". *Studies in Comparative International Development* 44: 296–317.

Cardoso, Fernando Henrique and Enzio Faletto. 1979. *Dependency and Development in Latin America*. Berkeley, California.

Cardoso Jr., Jose Celso. 2001. "Crise e Desregulação do Trabalho no Brasil". Rio de Janeiro, *IPEA Texto para Discussão* #814.

Carroll, Glenn and Michael Hannan. 2000. *Demography of Corporations and Industries*. Princeton, Princeton.

Case, Karl. 2004. *Principles of Microeconomics*. Upper Saddle River, N.J. Prentice-Hall.

Castells, Manuel. 1991. *Informational City: Information Technology, Economic Restructuring and the Urban Regional Process*. New York, Oxford.

Castro, Sueli Pereira, João Carlos Barrozo, Marinete Covezzi, and Orieste Preti. 1994. *A Colonização Oficial em Mato Grosso – a Nata e a Borra de Sociedade*. Cuiabá, Universidade Federal de Mato Grosso.

Chang, Ha-Joon. 2003. *Kicking Away the Ladder: Development Strategy in Historical Perspective*. London, Anthem.

——. 2008. *Bad Samaritans: Myth of Free Trade and the Secret History of Capitalism*. New York, Bloomsbury.

Chibber, Vivek. 2006. *Locked in Place: State Building and Late Industrialization in India*. Princeton, Princeton.

Chossudovsky, Michel. 1997. *Globalization of Poverty: Impacts of IMF and World Bank Reforms*. Highland Park, New Jersey, Zed.

Clapham, J.H. 1930. *Economic Development of France and Germany*. New York, Cambridge.

Cross, John. 1998. *Informal Politics: Street Vendors and the State in Mexico City*. Palo Alto, Stanford.

Crouch, G., L. Schultz and P. Valerio. 1992. "Marketing International Tourism to Australia". *Tourism Management*.

Cruz, Rita de Cássia. 2000. *Política de Turismo e Território*. São Paulo: Contexto.

Cumings, Bruce. 1984. "Origins and Development of the Northeast Asian Political Economy". *International Organization* 38: 1–40.

Currie, Janet and Ann Harrison. 1997. "Sharing the Costs: Impact of Trade Reform on Capital and Labor in Morocco". *Journal of Labor Economics* 15: S44–S71.

Dal Ri, Neusa Maria. 1999. *Economia Solidária*. São Paulo, Arte e Ciencia.

Dal-Rosso, Sadi. 1978. *Growth of Capitalism and the Transformation of the Labor Force in Brazil*. Ph.D. Dissertation, Sociology, University of Texas at Austin.

Davidson, Carl and Steven Woodbury. 1993. "Displacement Effects of Reemployment Bonus Programs". *Journal of Labor Economics* 11: 575–605.

Dedecca, Claudio Salvadori. 1998. "Emprego e Qualificação no Brasil dos Anos 90". Pp. 269–94 in Marco Antonio de Oliveira (ed.) *Reforma do Estado e Politicas do Emprego no Brasil*. Campinas, Unicamp.

De Soto, Hernando. 1989. *Other Path: Invisible Revolution in the Third World*. New York, Harper and Row.

Despres, Leo A. 1991. *Manaus: Social Life and Work in Brazil's Free Trade Zone*. Albany, SUNY.

Dobbin, Frank. 1997. *Forging Industrial Policy: United States, Britain and France in the Railway Age*. New York, Cambridge.

Dos Santos, Anselmo Luis. 1996. "Encargos Sociais e Custo do Trabalho No Brasil", Pp. 221–252 in Carlos Alonso B. de Oliveira and Jorge Eduardo Levi Mattoso (eds) *Crise e Trabalho No Brasil*. São Paulo, Scritta.

Dos Santos, Pires. 1995. *Teoria da Pratica de Locação Imobilaria*. Rio de Janeiro, Foreasi.

Dritsakis, N and S. Athanasiadis. 2000. "Econometric Model of Tourist Demand: Case of Greece". *Journal of Hospitality and Leisure Marketing* 2.

Durand, Jose Carlos Garcia and Leoncio Martins Rodrigues. 1979. "Evolução das Empresas Observadas". Pp. 57–97 in Henrique Rattner et al. (eds) *Pequena e Media Empresa no Brasil 1963/76*. São Paulo, Simbolo.

Dweck, Ruth Helena. 1998. "Serviços de Higiene Pessoaal: A Beleza Como Variavel Econômica – Reflexo Sobre nos Mercados de Trabalho e de Bens e Serviços". Pp. 92–121 in Hildete Perreira de Melo e Alberto Di Sabbato (eds) *Servicos No Brasil: Estudo dos Casos*. Brasilia, MICT.

——. 1999. "A Beleza Como Variavel Economica – Reflexo Nos Mercados de Trabalho e de Bens e Serviços". IPEA Texto Para Discussão #618.

Dwyer, Larry, Peter Forsyth and Prasada Rao. 2000. "Price Competitiveness of Travel and Tourism: Comparison of 19 Destinations". *Tourism Management* 21–35.

Easterly, William and Luis Serven. 2003. *Limits of Stabilization: Infrastructure, Public Deficits and Growth in Latin America*. Washington D.C., World Bank.

Easterly, William and Sergio Rebeldo. 1993. "Fiscal Policy and Economic Growth: An Empirical Investigation". *Journal of Monetary Economics* 32: 417–456.

ECLA (United Nations Commission on Latin America). 1962. *Urbanization in Latin America*. Paris, UNESCO.

EMBRATUR. 2000. *Pontos Turísticos*. Brasilia, EMBRATUR.

Esfahani, Haideh and Mario Ramirez. 2003. "Institutions, Infrastructure and Economic Growth". *Journal of Development Economics* 70: 443–477.

Esping-Anderson, Gosta. 2000. "Who is Harmed By Labor Market Regulation? Quantitative Evidence". *Why Deregulate?* Gosta Esping-Anderson and Marino Regini (eds). New York, Oxford.

Estall, R.C. and R Ogilvie Buchanan. 1964. *Industrial Activity and Economic Geography*. London, Hutchinson.

Evans, Peter. 1979. *Dependent Development*. Princeton, Princeton.

——. 1995. *Embedded Autonomy: States and Industrial Transformation*. Princeton, Princeton.

Evans, Peter and Michael Timberlake. 1980. "Dependence, Inequality and the Growth of the Tertiary: A Comparative Analysis of Less Developed Countries". *American Sociological Review* 45: 531–552.

Fainstein, Susan and David Gladstone. 1999. "Evaluating Urban Tourism". Pp. 21–34 in Dennis Judd and Susan Fainstein. *Tourist City*. New Haven, Yale.

Fedderke, J.W., P. Perkins and J.M. Luiz. 2006. "Infrastructural Development and Long Term Economic Growth: South Africa 1875–2001". *World Development* 34: 1037–1059.

Fernald, John. 1999. "Roads to Prosperity: Assessing the Links Between Public Capital and Prosperity". *American Economic Review* 89: 619–638.

Fernandez, Roberto. 2006. "Networks, Race and Hiring". *American Sociological Review* 71: 42–71.

Ferranti, David, Guillermo Perry, Indermit Gill, Jose Guasch, Carolina Sanchez-Paramo, Norbert Schady and William Maloney. 2003. *Closing the Gap in Education and Technology*. Washington D.C., World Bank.

Ferraz, Joandre. 1977. *Legislação de Turismo: CNTur e Embratur*. São Paulo, Edições LTr.

Field, Barry. 2001. *Environmental Economics*. New York, McGraw-Hill.

FIESP. 1993. *Encargos Sociais*. São Paulo, FIESP.

Fine, Ben. 2003. "New Growth Theory". Pp. 201–218 in Ha-Joon Chang (ed.) *Rethinking Development Economics*. London, Anthem.

——. 2006. *Economic History and Theory: From Classical Political Theory to Economics Imperialism*. London, Routledge.

Fishlow, Albert. 1990. "Latin American State". *Journal of Economic Perspectives* 4: 61–74.

Fogaça, Azuete. 1998. "Educação e a Reestruturação Produtiva no Brasil". Pp. 295–327 in Marco Antonio de Oliveira (ed.) *Reforma do Estado e Politicas do Emprego no Brasil*. Campinas, Unicamp.

Fogel, Robert. 1964. *Railroads and Economic Growth: Essays in Economic History*. Baltimore, Johns Hopkins.

Font, Mauricio. 2003. *Transforming Brazil: Reform Era in Perspective*. New York, Rowman and Littlefield.

França, Vera Lucia Alves. 1999. *Aracaju: Estado e Metropolização*. Sao Cristovão Universidade Federal de Sergipe.

França Filho, Genauto Carvalho and Jean-Louis Laville. 2004. *Economia Solidária: um Abordagem Internaçional*. Porto Alegre, Universidade Federal de Rio Grande do Sul.

Franco, Luiz Antonio Carvalho and Sidnei Sauer Drona. 1984. *Breve História da Formação Profissional no Brasil*. São Paulo, Fundacao Senafor.

Frank, Andre Gunder. 1967. *Capitalism and Underdevelopment in Latin America*. New York, Monthly Review Press.

Frechtling, Douglas. 2001. *Forecasting Tourist Demand*. New York, Butterworth Heinemann.

Friere, Laura Lucia Ramos. 1995. "Turismo e Sua Importancia Para a Economia Do Nordeste". Pp. 177–240. *Banco do Nordeste: Diretrizes Para Um Plano De Açao Do Banco do Nordeste 1991–1995*. Volume 4. Fortaleza, Banco do Nordeste.

Fuhr, Harald. 1993. "Mobilizing Local Resources in Latin America: Decentralization, Institutional Reforms and Small Scale Enterprises". Pp. 49–66 in Brigitte Spath (ed.) *Small Firms and Development in Latin America: Role of Institutional Environment, Human Resources and Industrial Relations*. Geneva, International Institute for Labor Studies.

Furtado, Celso. 1968. *Teoria e Política do Desenvolvimento Econômico*. São Paulo, Editora Naçional.

——. 1983. *Accumulation and Development: Logic of Industrial Civilization*. New York, Saint Martins.

Gadrey, Jean. 1992. *L'Economie des Services*. Paris, La Découverte.

Galhardi, Regina and Nicholas Mangozho. 2003. "Statistics on Investment in Training: An Assessment of Data Available and Cross Country Comparability". Working Paper, International Labor Organization InFocus Programme on Skills, Knowledge and Employability, Geneva.

Gazeta Mercantil. 1997. *Analise Setorial: Aeroportos*. Volume 12 of *Panorama Setorial*. Recife, Gazeta Mercantil.

Geddes, Barbara. 1996. *Politician's Dilemma: Building State Capacity in Latin America*. Berkeley, California.

Gershenkron, Alexander. 1962. *Economic Backwardness in Historical Perspective*. London, Praeger.

Glewwe, Paul. 2002. "Schools and Skills in Developing Countries: Education Policies and Socioeconomic Outcomes". *Journal of Economic Literature* 40: 436–482.

Goodwin, Harold and Justin Francis. 2003. "Ethical and Responsible Tourism: Consumer Trends in the UK". *Journal of Vacation Marketing* 9: 271–284.

GPC. 1980. *Diagnostico Socioeconomico do Estado do Mato Grosso*. Cuiaba, Gabinete de Planejamento e Coordinação, Estado do Mato Grosso.

Granovetter, Mark. 1985. "Economic Action and Social Structure: Problem of Embeddedness". *American Journal of Sociology* 91: 485–510.

Gray, H. Peter. 1966. "Demand for International Travel by the United States and Canada". *International Economic Review* 7: 83–92.

Green, Howard, Colin Hunter and B. Moore. 1990. "Applications of the Delphi Technique in Tourism". *Annals of Tourism Research* 2: 270–279.

Gret, Marion and Yves Sintomer. 2005. *Porto Alegre Experiment: Learning Lessons for Better Democracy*. New Brunswick, New Jersey, Zed.

Griffith-Jones, Steffany and Osvaldo Sunkel. 1986. *Debt and Development Crises in Latin America: End of an Illusion*. Oxford, Clarendon.

Gruber, Jonathan. 1997. "Incidence of Payroll Taxation: Evidence From Chile". *Journal of Labor Economics* 15: S72–S101.

Hamermesh, Daniel. 1993. *Labor Demand*. Princeton, Princeton.

Hamilton, Alexander. 1790. *Report on Manufactures*. Pp. 70–163 in Henry Cabot Lodge (ed.) *Works of Alexander Hamilton*. New York, Putman.

Hannan, Michael and John Freeman. 1989. *Organizational Ecology*. Cambridge, Harvard.

Harberger, Arnold. 1974. *Taxation and Welfare*. Boston, Little and Brown.

Harrison, Ann and Edward Leamer. 1997. "Labor Markets in Developing Countries: An Agenda For Research". *Journal of Labor Economics* 15: S1–S19.

Hart, Robert. 1984. *Economics of Non-Wage Labor Costs*. Boston, Allen and Unwin.

Harvey, David. 1982. *Limits to Capital*. London, Verso.

Hawke, G.R. 1970. *Railways and Economic Growth in England and Wales 1840–1870*. Oxford, Oxford.

Hechter, Michael. 1975. *Internal Colonialism: Celtic Fringe in British National Development 1536–1966*. Berkeley, California.

Heckman, James, Robert Lalonde and Jeffrey Smith. 1999. "Economics and Econometrics of Active Labor Market Programs". Pp. 1865–2097 in Orley Ashenfelter and David Card (eds) *Handbook of Labor Economics*. Rotterdam, Elsevier.

Henshall, Janet and R.P. Momsen, Jr. 1974. *Geography of Brazilian Development*. London, Bell and Sons.

Hettige, Hemamala, Mathukumara Mani and David Wheeler. 2000. "Industrial Pollution in Economic Development: the Kuznets Curve Revisited". *Journal of Development Economics* 62: 445–476.

Hettige, Hemamala, Paul Martin, Manjula Singh and David Wheeler. 1995. "Industrial Pollution Projection System". Policy Research Working Paper 1431. World Bank. Policy Research Department. Environment, Infrastructure and Agriculture Division.

Hicks, John 1963. *Theory of Wages*. New York, Saint Martins.

Higham, James. 2007. *Critical Issues in Ecotourism: Understanding a Complex Tourism Phenomenon*. Burlington, Ma., Butterworth Heinemann.

Hirnaux, Nicolas. 1999. "Cancun Bliss". Pp. 124–42 in Dennis Judd and Susan Fainstein (eds). *Tourist City*. New Haven, Yale.

Hobsbawm, Eric. 1969. *Age of Revolution*. New York, Praeger.

Holtz-Eakin, Douglas. 1994. "Public Sector Capital and the Productivity Puzzle". *Review of Economics and Statistics* 76: 12–21.

Honey, Martha. 1999. *Ecotourism and Sustainable Development: Who Owns Paradise?* Washington D.C., Island.

Hoogvelt, Ankie. 1997. *Globalization and the Postcolonial World*. Baltimore, Johns Hopkins.

Horowitz, Morris. 1985. "Organization of the Brazilian System". Pp. 39–44 in Gustav Schacter (ed.) *Vocational Education in Brazil: Aspects of Economic Policy and Planning*. Proceedings of the Conference Held at Northeastern University, July 11–12, 1984. Boston, Northeastern.

Hoselitz, Bert. 1963. *Sociological Aspects of Economic Growth*. Glencoe, Free Press.

Hulten, Charles and Robert Schwab. 2000. "Does Infrastructure Investment Increase the Productivity of Manufacturing Industry in the U.S.?" Pp. 81–104 in L. Lau, *Econometrics and the Cost of Capital*. Cambridge, MIT.

Hunter, Lori, Michael White, Jani Little and Jeannette Sutton. 2003. "Environmental Hazards, Migration, and Race". *Population & Environment* 25: 23–39.

IBGE. 2004a. *Produção Agrícola Municipal: Culturas Temporárias e Permanentes.* Brasilia, Instituto Brasileira de Geografía e Estatística.

——. 2004b. *Produção da Pecuária Municipal.* Brasilia, Instituto Brasileira de Geografía e Estatística.

Ida, Ivete Tiyomi. 1987. *Estudo Analítico com Egressos do Treinamento de Soldador Oxiacetilênico e de Soldado Eclético.* São Paulo, SENAI-SP.

Illeris, Sven. 1996. *Service Economy: Geographical Approach.* New York, Wiley.

IPEA (Instituto das Pesquisas Econômicas Aplicadas). 2000. *Desigualidade e Pobreza no Brasil.* Brasilia, IPEA.

Irwin, Michael and John Kasarda. 1991. "Air Passenger Linkages and Employment Growth in US Metropolitan Areas". *American Sociological Review* 56: 524–537.

Johnson, Chalmers. 1982. *MITI and the Japanese Miracle: Growth of Industrial Policy 1925–75.* Stanford, Stanford.

Johnson, Peter and J. Ashworth. 1990. "Modelling Tourism Demand: A Summary Review". *Leisure Studies* 9: 145–160.

Jomo, K.S. and Ben Fine. 2006. *New Development Economics: After the Washington Consensus.* New Delhi, Tulika.

Kasarda, John and David Sullivan. 2006. "Air Cargo, Liberalization and Economic Development". *Annals of Air and Space Law* 31: 214–230.

Kehoe, Timothy and Jaime Serra-Puche. 1983. "Computational General Equilibrium Model With Endogenous Unemployment: Analysis of 1980 Fiscal Reform in Mexico". *Journal of Public Economics* 22: 1–26.

Kindleberger, Charles and Bruce Herrick. 1977. *Economic Development.* New York, McGraw-Hill.

Kinugasa, Tomoko and Andrew Mason. 2007. "Why Countries Become Wealthy: The Effects of Adult Longevity on Saving". *World Development* 35: 1–23.

Kliman, Mel. 1981. "Quantitative Analysis of Canadian Overseas Tourism". *Transportation Research* 15A: 487–497.

Kohli, Atul. 2004. *State-Directed Development: Political Power and Industrialization in the Global Periphery.* New York, Cambridge.

Kon, Anita. 1997. "Transformaçoes Ocupaçionais Na Nova Economia de Serviços". Pp. 489–507 in *II Encontro Naçional da Economia Política.* São Paulo, PUC-São Paulo.

Krueger, Alan and Mikhael Lindahl. 2001. "Education for Growth: Why and For Whom?" *Journal of Economic Literature* 39: 1101–1136.

Krugman, Paul. 1994. "Myth of Asia's Miracle". *Foreign Affairs* 73: 62–79.

——. 1999. *Return of Depression Era Economics.* London, Norton.

Kuznets, Simon. 1966. *Modern Economic Growth: Rate, Structure and Spread.* New Haven, Yale.

Lafer, Gordon. 2002. *Job Training Charade.* Ithaca, Cornell.

Lahóz, André and José Roberto Caetano. 2001. "O Imposto Que Esmaga". *Exame* 748. September 5: 40–53.

Lange, Matthew and Dietrich Rueschemeyer (eds). 2005. *States and Development: Historical Antecedents of Stagnation and Advance.* New York, Palgrave Macmillan.

List, Friedrich. 1983. *Natural System of Political Economy.* London, Cass.

Loeb, Peter. 1982. "International Travel to the United States: An Econometric Evaluation". *Annals of Tourism Research* 9: 7–20.

Londono, Juan. 1996. *Poverty, Inequality and Human Capital Development in Latin America 1950–2025.* Washington D.C., World Bank.

Lundberg, Donald, M. Krishnamoorthy and Mink Stavenga. 1995. *Tourism Economics.* New York, Wiley.

Lynch, Lisa. 1994. "Payoffs to Alternative Training Strategies at Work". Pp. 53–96 in Richard Freeman (ed.) *Working Under Different Rules.* New York, Russell Sage Foundation.

Mainwaring, Scott. 1999. *Rethinking Party Systems in the Third Wave of Democratization: Case of Brazil.* Palo Alto, Stanford.

Mani, Mathukumara and Shreyasi Ja. 2006. "Trade Liberalisation and the Environment in Vietnam". Policy Research Paper 3879. World Bank. Policy Research Department. Environment, Infrastructure and Agriculture Division.

Mani, Mathukumara and David Wheeler. 1998. "In Search of Pollution Havens? Dirty Industry in the World Economy, 1960–1995". *Journal of Environment and Development* 7: 215–247.

Markert, Werner. 1997. *Formação Profisonal no Brasil: Reflexões, Teoricas e Analises da Sua Praxis.* Rio de Janeiro, Ediçoes Paratedise.

Marshall, J. Neill and Peter Wood. 1995. *Services and Space: Key Aspects of Urban and Regional Development.* Harlow, U.K., Longman Scientific.

Martins, Jose de Souza. 1980. *Expropriação e Violencia (a Questao Política no Campo).* São Paulo, Hucitec.

Massey, Doreen. 1974. *Towards a Critique of Industrial Location Theory.* London, Centre for Environmental Studies.

Mato Grosso – Turismo Puro. 1995. Anonymous promotional pamphlet. N.p.

McClelland, David. 1966. "Does Education Accelerate Economic Growth?" *Economic Development and Cultural Change* 14.

Ministerio do Trabalho. Secretario de Mao-de-Obra. 1982. *Catalogo de Cursos de Formacao Profissional de SNFMO.* Brasilia.

———. 1987. *Política Nacional de Formacão Profissional. Conselho Federal de Mão de obra.* Brasilia, Ministério de Trabalho.

Mitra, Arindam, Asrtromene Varoudakis and Marie-Ange Veganzones-Varoudakis. 2002. "Productivity and Efficiency in Indian States Manufacturing: Role of Infrastructure". *Economic Development and Cultural Change* 50: 395–426.

Morrison, Christian and Xavier Oudin. 1984. *Microenterprises and the Institutional Framework in the Developing Countries.* Paris, OECD.

Muller, Walter and Markus Gangl. 2004. *Transitions From Education to Work in Europe.* New York, Oxford.

Mueller, Charles. 1981. "O Estado e A Expansaõ Recente Da Frontiera Agricola na Amazona Brasileira". Texto para Discussao 85. Fundacao da Universidade do Brasilia.

Mullins, Patrick. 1999. "International Tourism and the Cities of Southeast Asia". Pp. 245–60 in Dennis Judd and Susan Fainstein. *Tourist City.* New Haven, Yale.

Musgrave, Richard. 1959. *Theory of Public Finance: A Study in Public Economy.* New York, McGraw Hill.

Nascimento, Amauri Mascaro. 1975. *Salario no Direito do Trabalho.* São Paulo, LTr.

Nove, Alec. 1992. "Some Thoughts on Plan and Market". Pp. 39–52 in *State and Market in Development: Synergy or Rivalry.* Louis Putterman and Dietrich Rueschemeyer (eds). Boulder, Lynne Rienner.

O'Connor, James. 1973. *Fiscal Crisis of the State*. New York, Saint Martins.

Oliveira, Antonio Pereira. 2000. *Turismo e Desenvolvimento: Planejamento e Organização*. São Paulo: Atlas.

Oliveira, Clonilo Moreira Sindeaux de and Pedro Jorge Ramos Vianna. 2005. *Desenvolvimento Regional: 50 Anos do BNB*. Fortaleza, Banco do Nordeste.

Oliveira, Elton. 2007. 'Impatos Socioambientais e Econômicos do Turismo e suas Repurcussões no Desenvolvimento Local: o Caso do Município de Itacaré, Bahia". *Interações (Campo Grande)* 8. http://www.scielo.br/scielo.php?script= sci_arttext&pid=S1518-70122007000200006&lng=em&nrm=iso&tlng=em

Orr, Larry et al. 1994. *National Job Training Partnership Act Study: Impacts Benefits and Costs of Title II-A*. Bethesda, Maryland, Abt.

Papanek, Gustav. 1992. "Effect of Government Intervention on Growth and Equity: Lessons from Southern Asia". Pp. 131–170 in *State and Market in Development: Synergy or Rivalry*. Louis Putterman and Dietrich Rueschemeyer (eds). Boulder, Lynne Rienner.

Pastore, José. 1997. *Encargos Sociais*. São Paulo, LTr.

——. 1998. *O Desemprego Tem Cura?* São Paulo, Makron.

Pedroza, Alda Nogueira and Laura Lúcia Ramos Friere. 2005. "Atividade Turística no Nordeste". ETENE Working Paper. Fortaleza, Banco do Nordeste.

Perazza, Maria Claudia and Raul Tuazon. 2006. "Prodetur/NE-1: Resultados e Lições Aprendidas". Report Prepared for the Banco do Nordeste. Fortaleza, Banco do Nordeste.

Pereira, Alfredo. 2000. "Is All Public Capital Created Equal?" *Review of Economics and Statistics* 82: 513–518.

Pereira, Benedito Dias. 1995. *Industrialização da Agricultura de Mato Grosso*. Cuiaba, Universidade Federal de Mato Grosso.

Pereira de Melo, Hildete, Frederico Rocha, Galeno Ferraz, Alberto Di Sabbato and Ruth Dweck. 1998. "O Setor Servicos No Brasil: Uma Visao Global – 1985/95". IPEA Texto Para Discussao #549.

Perlman, Janice. 1976. *Myth of Marginality*. Berkeley, California.

Pochmann Marcio, 1999. *O Trabalho Sob Fogo Cruzado: Exclusão, Desemprego e Precarizacção no Final do Século*. São Paulo, Editora Contexto.

Portes, Alejandro, Manuel Castells and Lauren Benton. 1989. *Informal Economy: Studies in Advanced and Less Developed Nations*. Baltimore, Johns Hopkins.

Portes, Alejandro and John Walton. 1976. *Urban Latin America: The Political Conditions From Above and Below*. Austin, Texas.

Potter, George. 2000. *Deeper Than Debt: Economic Globalization and the Poor*. Sterling, Virginia, Kumarian.

Povoas, *Lenine*. 1977. *Mato Grosso: uma Convite a Fortuna*. Rio de Janeiro, Guavira.

——. 1996. *Historia Geral de Mato Grosso de Proclamação aos Dias Atuais*. Cuiabá, Lenine Povoas.

Rabushka, Alvin and Bruce Bartlett. 1985. *Tax Policy and Economic Growth in Developing Nations*. Washington, USAID Bureau for Program and Policy Coordination, Office of Economic Affairs.

Rakowski, Cathy. 1994. *Contrapunto: Informal Sector Debate in Latin America*. Albany, SUNY.

Reed, M.C. (ed.). 1969. *Railways in the Victorian Economy: Studies in Finance and Development*. Newton Abbott, Devon, David and Charles.

Reinert, Erik. 2007. *How Rich Countries Got Rich and Why Poor Countries Stay Poor*. New York, Public Affairs.

Rios-Neto, Eduardo and Ana Maria Oliveira. 2000. "Politíticas Voltadas a Pobreza: o Caso de Formação Profissional". Pp. 589–614 in Ricardo Henriques (ed.) *Desigualdade e Pobreza no Brasil*. Rio de Janeiro, IPEA.

Ritchie, Bruce and Crouch G. 2003. *Competitive Destination: Sustainable Tourism Perspective*. Wallingford, U.K. CAB.

Ritzer, George. 2008. *McDonaldization of Society*. Thousand Oaks, California. Pine Forge Press.

Roberts, Bryan. 1978. *Cities of Peasants: Political Economy of Urbanization in the Third World*. Beverly Hills, Sage.

Robinson, William. 2004. *Theory of Global Capitalism*. Baltimore, Johns Hopkins.

Rodrigues, J. Barbosa. 1984. *Historia de Mato Grosso do Sul*. São Paulo, Escritor.

Rodrik, Dani. 2007. *One Economics: Many Recipes. Globalization, Institutions and Economic Growth*. Princeton, Princeton.

Rosenstein-Rodan, Paul Narcyz. 1943. "Problems of Industrialization of East and South-East Europe". *Economic Journal* 201–211.

Rostow, Walter. 1960. *States of Economic Growth*. New York, Cambridge.

Ruschmann, Doris. 1997. *Turismo e Desenvolvimento Sustanável: a Proteção de Meia Ambiente*. Campinas, Papirus.

——. 2002. *Turismo no Brasil: Analíse e Tendências* Baueri. Brazil, Manole.

Ruschmann, Doris Van de Meene and Miriam Rejowski. 1999. "Condicoes e Perspetivas do Mercado do Trabalho No Setor do Turismo". Pp. 149–182 in EMBATUR. *Estudos do Turismo Brasileiro*. Brasilia, EMBRATUR.

Ryan, Paul. 2001. "School to Work Transition: Cross-national Perspective". *Journal of Economic Literature* 39: 34–92.

Sanchez-Robles, Blanca. 1998. "Infrastructure Investment and Growth: Some Empirical Evidence". *Contemporary Economic Policy* 16: 98–108.

Sanders, Thomas. 1985. "Brazil's Microbusiness Law". *USFI Reports* 26: 1–6.

Santos, Milton. 1993. *Urbanização Brasileira*. São Paulo, Hucitec.

——. 2001. *Por Uma Outra Globalização*. São Paulo, Record.

Santos, Roberto. 1973. *Leis Sociais e Custo da Mão-de-Obra No Brasil*. São Paulo, LTr.

Sassen, Saskia. 2000. *Cities in a World Economy*. Thousand Oaks, California, Pine Forge.

Schmitz, Hubert. 1982. *Manufacturing in the Backyard: Case Studies on Accumulation and Employment in Small-Scale Brazilian Industry*. Allenheld, New Jersey, Osmun.

Schwartzman, Simon. 1992. *Space for Science: Development of the Scientific Community in Brazil*. College Park, Pa., Pennsylvania State.

SEBRAE. 2004. *Fatores Condicionantes e Taxa de Mortalidade de Empresas no Brasil*. www.sebrae.com.br/br/mortalidade_empresas/

SEBRAE-SP. 2005. *Sobrevivência e Mortalidade das Empresas Paulistas de Um a Cinco Anos*. São Paulo, SEBRAE-SP.

Seely, Richard L., H.J. Iglarsh and David Edgell. 1980. "Utilizing the Delphi Technique at International Conferences: A Method for Forecasting International Tourism Conditions". *Travel Research Journal* 1: 30–35.

Seidman, Gaye. 1994. *Manufacturing Militance: Workers' Movements in Brazil and South Africa*. California, Berkeley.

SENAC. 1986. *Sondagem Nacional do Destino Profisional dos Exalunos do Senac.* Rio de Janeiro, SENAC.

Sheldon, Pauline. 1990. "Review of Tourism Expenditure Research". Pp. 130–158 in Chris Cooper (ed.) *Progress in Tourism, Recreation and Hospitality Management.* London, Belhaven.

Shioji, Etsuro. 2001. "Public Capital and Economic Growth: A Convergence Approach". *Journal of Economic Growth* 6: 205–227.

Silva, Nilton and Dean Hansen. 2001. *Econômia Regional e Outros Ensaios.* Aracaju, Universidade Federal de Sergipe.

Sinclair, Thea. 1998. "Tourism and Economic Development: A Survey". *Journal of Development Studies* 34: 1–51.

Sinclair, Thea and Mike Stabler. 1997. *Economics of Tourism.* London, Routledge.

Singer, Paul. 1973. *Économia Política da Urbanização.* São Paulo, Brasilense.

——. 1998. *Globalização e Desemprego: Diagnóstico e Alternativas.* São Paulo, Contexto.

Singer, Paul and André Ricardo de Souza. 2000. *Economia Solidária no Brasil: A Autogestão Como Resposta ao Desemprego.* São Paulo, Economia Contexto.

Smith, James. 1980. *Female Labor Supply: Theory and Estimation.* Princeton, Princeton.

Spath, Brigitte (ed.). 1993. *Small Firms and Development in Latin America: Role of Institutional Environment, Human Resources and Industrial Relations.* Geneva, International Institute for Labor Studies.

Spence, Andrew. 1975. "Job Market Signalling". *Quarterly Journal of Economics* 87: 355–374.

Stern, David et al. 1995. *School to Work: Research on Programmes in the United States.* London, Falmer.

Stiglitz, Joseph. 1969. "Effects of Income, Wealth and Capital Gains Taxation on Risk Taking". *Quarterly Journal of Economics* 83: 262–283.

——. 1988. *Economics of the Public Sector.* New York, Norton.

——. 1996. "Some Lessons From the East Asian Miracle". *World Bank Research Observer* 11: 151–177.

——. 2006. *Making Globalization Work.* New York, Norton.

Stinchcombe, Arthur. 1968. *Constructing Social Theories.* Chicago, Chicago.

Stokes, Randall and G. Anderson. 1990. "Disarticulation and Human Welfare in Less Developed Countries". *American Sociological Review* 55: 63–74.

Streeck, Wolfgang. 1992. *Social Institutions and Economic Performance: Studies of Industrial Relations in Advanced Capitalist Economies.* London, Sage.

Streeck, Wolfgang and Kozo Yamamura. 2005. *Origins of Nonliberal Capitalism: Germany and Japan in Comparison.* Ithaca, Cornell.

Sudene and Banco do Nordeste. 1986. *O Sistema FINOR: Resultados e Sugestões de Aperfeicoamento.* Fortaleza, Banco do Nordeste.

Sunkel, Osvaldo. 1993. "From Inward Looking Development to Development From Within". Pp 23–61 in Osvaldo Sunkel (ed.) *Development From Within: Toward a Neostructuralist Approach for Latin America.* Boulder, Lynne Reiner.

Surrey, Stanley. 1958. "Tax Administration in Underdeveloped Countries". *University of Miami Law Review* 12: 158–188.

Suter, Christian. 1992. *Debt Cycles in the World Economy: Foreign Loans, Financial Crises and Debt Settlements.* Boulder, Westview.

Szirmai, Adam. 2005. *Dynamics of Socio-economic Development: An Introduction.* New York, Cambridge.

Teeple, Gary. 1995. *Globalization and the Decline of Social Reform*. Toronto, Garamond.

Teles, João Agostinho. 2005. *Efeitos Globais do Prodetur/NE I: Enfoque Turistico*. Fortaleza, Banco do Nordeste.

Tendler, Judith. 1998. *Good Government in the Tropics*. Baltimore, Johns Hopkins.

Thomas, James 1992. *Informal Economic Activity*. Ann Arbor, Michigan.

Thurow, Lester. 1975. *Generating Inequality: Mechanisms of Distribution in the American Economy*. New York, Basic.

Tisdell, Clement and Roy Kartik. 1998. *Tourism and Development: Economic, Social, Political and Environmental Issues*. Commack, New York, Nova Science.

Trevizan, Antonio. 1985. *Servicos Federais de Formacão Profissional Nao Formal – Criticas e Sugestões*. Curitiba, Secretaria do Estado da Industria, e do Comercio – Departmento do Trabalho.

Urani, Andre. 1997. "Elementos Para Uma Politica de Emprego no Brasil". Pp. 21–46 in Lucia Bogus and Ana Yara Paulino (eds) *Politícas de Emprego, Politicas de População e Direitos Sociais*. São Paulo EDUC.

Uzzi, Brian. 1996. "Sources and Consequences of Embeddedness for the Economic Performance of Organizations". *American Sociological Review* 61: 674–688.

——. 1999. "Embeddedness in the Making of Financial Capital: How Social Relations Benefit Firms Seeking Financing". *American Sociological Review* 64: 481–505.

Vanhove, Norbert. 2005. *Economics of Tourism Destinations*. Amsterdam, Elsevier.

Vroman, Wayne. 1967. *Macroeconomic Effects of Social Insurance*. Ph.D. Dissertation. Department of Economics, University of Michigan.

Wade, Robert. 1990. *Governing the Market: Economic Theory and the Role of Government in East Asian Industrialization*. Princeton, Princeton.

Walker, Robert. 2003. "Payroll Taxes Stifle Economic Growth". *Chicago Sun Times* January 31. p. 36.

Wallerstein, Immanuel. 1974. *The Modern World System*. Volume 1. New York, Academic.

Weeks, John. 1986. *Population: Introduction to Concepts and Issues*. Belmont, California, Wadsworth.

Weiss, Linda. 1998. *Myth of the Powerless State*. Ithaca, Cornell.

Whalen, Charles. 2001. "Why Not a Payroll Tax Cut?" *Business Week* 3719. February 12: 28–30.

Wikipedia. Apagão Aérea de 2006. pt.wikipedia.org/wiki/crise_no_setor_aéreo_brasileiro

World Bank. 1993. *East Asian Miracle: Economic Growth and Public Policy*. New York, Oxford.

——. 2002. *Globalization, Growth and Poverty*. Washington, World Bank.

Wynne, Pires. 1973. *Historia de Sergipe*. Rio de Janeiro, Ponghetti.

Zinder, Hans. 1969. *Future of Tourism in the Eastern Caribbean*. Washington D.C., Zinder and Associates.

Index